THE
THE D
AND

MRS OLIPHANT, born Margaret Oliphant Wilson in 1828, was a Scotswoman and grew up in Midlothian, Glasgow, and Liverpool. One of the most prolific writers of her time, she published her first novel in 1849 and married her cousin, Frank Oliphant, three years later. He died in 1859, leaving her with three small children to support. Soon afterwards she began her most famous work, the *Chronicles of Carlingford* series, to which *The Doctor's Family* belongs. After 1868 she had to support her brother and his children, as well as another brother who was an alcoholic, and her reputation has suffered because she was forced to work too hard. Her best novels (she left over ninety) include *Miss Marjoribanks* (1866), *The Ladies Lindores* (1883), *A Country Gentleman and his Family* (1886), and *Kirsteen* (1890), and she wrote some outstanding short stories. She died in 1897.

MERRYN WILLIAMS is a poet and critic. Her biography, *Margaret Oliphant* (1986), is the first full account of this remarkable woman. She is the author of *Thomas Hardy and Rural England, Preface to Hardy,* and *Women in the English Novel, 1800–1900.*

THE WORLD'S CLASSICS

MARGARET OLIPHANT

The Doctor's Family

and Other Stories

Edited with an Introduction by
MERRYN WILLIAMS

Oxford   New York

OXFORD UNIVERSITY PRESS

1986

Oxford University Press, Walton Street, Oxford OX2 6DP

Oxford New York Toronto
Delhi Bombay Calcutta Madras Karachi
Kuala Lumpur Singapore Hong Kong Tokyo
Nairobi Dar es Salaam Cape Town
Melbourne Auckland

and associated companies in
Beirut Berlin Ibadan Nicosia

Oxford is a trade mark of Oxford University Press

Introduction, Note on the Text, Select Bibliography,
Chronology, and Explanatory Notes
© Merryn Williams 1986

First issued as a World's Classics paperback 1986

British Library Cataloguing in Publication Data

Oliphant, Mrs.
The doctor's family and other stories.—
(The World's classics)
I. Title II. Williams, Merryn
823'.8 [F] PR5113.A4
ISBN 0-19-281733-7

Library of Congress Cataloging in Publication Data

Oliphant, Mrs. (Margaret), 1828-1897.
The doctor's family and other stories.
(The World's classics)
Bibliography: p.
I. Title.
PR5113.D6 1986 823'.8 85-15420
ISBN 0-19-281733-7 (pbk.)

Set by Grove Graphics
Printed in Great Britain by
Hazell Watson & Viney Ltd.
Aylesbury, Bucks

CONTENTS

INTRODUCTION

MARGARET OLIPHANT was one of the great Victorian novelists. Yet for much of the twentieth century her name has been almost unknown and her work largely unavailable. Only in the last few years have things begun to change; some of her best novels and short stories are coming back into print and more and more people are discovering them, with delight and excitement. The three stories in this volume represent her first mature work.

Briefly popular in the 1860s, she saw her reputation decline thereafter because she wrote far too much. All through her adult life she had to support various hard-up relations—husband, children, brothers, cousins, nephew, and nieces—and she could only do this by turning out books for sale. She sat up far into the night, like the heroine of *The Doctor's Family*, writing articles, translations, biographies, travel books, and nearly a hundred novels, most of them second-rate. It was easy for critics, then and now, to point out that she produced a vast amount of poor work. But, as a contemporary wrote, it is not true that 'her work at its best was injured by her immense productiveness. Her best work was of a very high order of merit. The harm that she did to her literary reputation seems rather the surrounding of her best with so much which she knew to be of inferior quality.'

Very early, she got into the habit of writing at the sitting-room table while the life of the household went on around her. Born into a fairly obscure family, Scottish Presbyterians who had moved to Liverpool, she published her first novel in 1849 when she was twenty-one. The fiction market was expanding, and she soon found that publishers were willing to take as many books as she could write. But her professional success was overshadowed by domestic troubles. Her brother, Willie, kept falling into debt and had bouts of drinking; when she was a teenager, Margaret and her mother sometimes sat up all night waiting for him to come home. He was sincerely religious and found employment for a short time as a Presbyterian minister. But something went wrong and, rather than face a Church court which would have unfrocked him, he ran back to his family and was dependent on them for the rest of his life:

The days and weeks and months in which he smoked and read old novels and the papers and, most horrible of all, got to content himself with that life [his sister wrote long afterwards]. The anguish in all our hearts looking at him, not knowing what to do . . . the dreary spectacle of that content is before me, with almost as keen a sense of the misery as if it had been yesterday.

Fred Rider in *The Doctor's Family* is obviously based on Willie, although the latter had no wife or children. His brief career in the Church also had a lasting effect on Margaret's work. In *The Rector*, and in several full-length novels, she studies the psychology of the priest, the man who has taken it upon himself to guide others, but who is a vulnerable human being and may easily fail.

Willie's collapse came in 1852. Soon afterwards Margaret married her cousin, Frank Oliphant, an artist and stained-glass designer (whose work can still be seen in Ely Cathedral and Aylesbury parish church). She was always reticent about her marriage, but it was certainly not entirely happy. For the next seven years she was constantly pregnant—three babies died— and constantly writing; her earnings were needed to support the family because her husband's stained-glass business ate up money. She formed a close relationship with the editors of *Blackwood's Magazine*, which published several of her novels and articles in the 1850s. But Frank developed tuberculosis and in 1859 the Oliphants left England for Italy, where he died. Six weeks later, Margaret gave birth to another baby. She came home with her three small children and settled in Edinburgh, deeply in debt and desperate to find literary work.

For over a year, it was a very hard struggle. As she wrote in her *Autobiography*, her publishers had lost faith in her:

It was a very severe winter, 1860–61, and it was severe on me too . . . I had not been doing very well with my writing. I had sent several articles, though of what nature I don't remember, to 'Blackwood', and they had been rejected. Why, this being the case, I should have gone to them (John Blackwood and the Major were the firm at that moment) to offer them, or rather to suggest to them that they should take a novel from me for serial publication, I can't tell . . . But I was in their debt, and had very little to go on with. They shook their heads of course, and thought it would not be possible to take such a story,—both very kind and truly sorry for me, I have no doubt. I think I see their figures now against the light . . . and myself all blackness and whiteness in my widow's dress, taking leave of them as if it didn't matter, and oh! so much afraid that they would see the tears in my eyes. I went home to my little ones, running to the door to meet me . . . and that night, as soon as I had got them all to bed, I sat down and wrote a story which I think was something about a lawyer, John Brownlow [*sic*], and which formed the first of the Carlingford series,—a series pretty well forgotten now, which made a considerable stir at the time, and *almost* made me one of the popularities of literature. *Almost*, never quite, though 'Salem Chapel' really went very near it, I believe. I sat up nearly all night in a passion of composition, stirred to the very bottom of my mind. The story was successful, and my fortune, comparatively speaking, was made.

No wonder she wrote, in the second chapter of *The Executor*, 'the poor woman was half-crazed with the whirl of passion in her brain'. That must have been exactly how she felt as she worked on the story, knowing it was her last chance.

The Executor was published in *Blackwood's* in May 1861, and *The Rector* and *The Doctor's Family* later that same year. Margaret was thirty-three, and had already written over twenty novels, none of them especially good. But with these stories, as I have written elsewhere, she suddenly made the breakthrough from hack-work to literature. The publishers and readers recognized their quality and in 1862 John Blackwood agreed to let her expand them into a series, *The Chronicles of Carlingford*.

The form of this series was influenced by George Eliot's *Scenes of Clerical Life* and Trollope's novels about 'Barset'. The setting is a quiet country town; the same characters appear in different works and the clergy are prominent figures (the public appetite for novels about clerics and religious

problems was almost insatiable). *The Doctor's Family* was
followed by three full-length novels. *Salem Chapel* (1863) was
unusual because it dealt with Dissenters rather than members
of the Church of England, and was a great success. For a time
it was attributed to George Eliot, who was not pleased. *The
Perpetual Curate* (1864) completed the story of Mr Proctor,
Frank Wentworth, and the two Miss Wodehouses which had
begun in *The Rector*. The superb *Miss Marjoribanks* (1866)—
whose heroine appears briefly in *The Doctor's Family*—is one
of the few Oliphant novels to have been revived in our own
time. *Phoebe, Junior: A Last Chronicle of Carlingford* (1876)
was written much later, and is only loosely connected with the
rest. The late Q. D. Leavis has argued that they should all be
made available again 'since they can rival Trollope's
Barchester series in several respects and contain material
much more valuable as sociology and social criticism than
anything in his'.

The Carlingford stories brought their creator fame and
popularity. She was to write other, and even better, things,
but, meanwhile, the Victorians knew that a remarkable young
novelist had arrived.

If the three stories in this volume have one quality in common,
it is their anti-romantic tone. Bessie marries a prosaic man twice
her age because he is at least kind and reliable. The Rector gives
up his foolish dreams of a young bride in favour of a more
suitable marriage with a woman who shares his own disabilities;
Nettie knows that the man she marries is not prepared to make
any real sacrifices for her. Already the author was slightly
contemptuous of happy endings and felt that there were more
important questions than who married whom on the last page.

The Executor—which has not been reprinted before—is the
weakest of the three. It is sharp and amusing, and we will have a
better understanding of *The Doctor's Family* if we read it first.
But there have been too many stories, then and since, about
missing heirs and unjust wills. Margaret often fell back on this
kind of plot in later years, when she needed to write something
quickly, but she never succeeded in making it work

because, fundamentally, it bored her. If Wilkie Collins had written *The Executor*, everything would have hinged on the will and the hunt for Phoebe Thomson; in the story as it exists, they do not much matter. The real centre of interest is Bessie Christian, who has to 'carry her father on her shoulders, and drag her mother by her side wherever she goes'. She is set apart from 'those other smiling young women who were enjoying their youth', like Nettie in *The Doctor's Family*, and like the author, who had already had eighteen months' experience of being a young widow with children. Bessie herself is a rather flat character, conventionally sweet and patient, but she is extremely important for what she represents.

Margaret Oliphant had had some very hard experiences by the time she began to write the *Chronicles of Carlingford*. She had given birth to six children and buried three, got Willie out of various scrapes, undergone some painful domestic conflicts, and nursed her husband and mother through their last illnesses. (It is not surprising that death-beds are so important in *The Rector*.) Like all middle-class women at the time, she employed servants, but she still had to do a great deal of the child-minding and housework herself. She was acutely aware that however much she might have liked certain things, such as a perfect marriage or a life of pure intellectual activity, there were pressing jobs which had to be done, no matter how she felt. This awareness infuses these two small masterpieces, *The Rector* and *The Doctor's Family*.

'Now and then it feels hard, and all that,' says Nettie. 'But what did one come into the world for, I should like to know? Does anybody suppose it was just to be comfortable, and have one's own way?' In both stories, there is a distinction between those who do useful work and those who do not. At the end of *The Rector*, the central character decides that he needs a harder and more challenging life.

The story begins in a comfortable garden, separated by high walls from the 'dusty dry road'. The young author had never written anything better than the lyrical description of the fruit trees, the 'sweet summer snow', and the 'narcissus in a great dazzling sheaf upon the grass'. There are no urgent problems in such a setting; we gather that Lucy and Wentworth are in love and can't get married, but this does not disturb us very much. We move on to lively comedy in the scenes between Mr Proctor and his mother (based on a real old lady whom Margaret had known in Edinburgh). In the end, though, *The Rector* turns out to be a profoundly serious work.

The Victorians, as has been said, were fascinated by novels about religion. Readers of Trollope will remember the battles between his High and Low Churchmen, and many other, long-forgotten writers produced novels arguing the case for their own sects. The first pages of *The Rector* describe the hostility between Wentworth and the late Mr Bury because one is 'on the very topmost pinnacle of Anglicanism' and the other was Evangelical. Having been brought up a Scottish Presbyterian, Margaret viewed the bitter feuds in the Church of England with some amusement. As the story develops, she reminds the reader that, after all, there are things which matter more.

No one can find out Mr Proctor's views—'High, or Low, or Broad'—perhaps because he is not sufficiently committed to the priesthood to have any. At first he thinks all he need do is deliver a weekly sermon, 'which nobody cared much about, and which disturbed nobody', and then go back to his Greek studies. Up to the age of fifty he has been 'living out of nature' as a Fellow of an Oxford college. This is not an attack on universities or the intellectual life as such. The point was that, in the 1860s, Oxford dons did live in an unnatural way, remaining in their colleges and in most cases being forbidden to marry. They were all clergymen, but spent far more time on the classics (which Margaret did not know and, I think, faintly despised) than on pastoral work.

As a result, Mr Proctor shrinks from his 'female parishioners' just as Dr Rider, in the next story, shrinks from children. He cannot even face getting married, let alone helping people in need. After he has failed to do any good to the tubercular woman, he asks himself:

What was he doing here, among that little world of human creatures who were dying, being born, perishing, suffering, falling into misfortune and anguish, and all manner of human vicissitudes, every day? Young Wentworth knew what to say to that woman in her distress; and so might the Rector, had her distress concerned a disputed translation, or a disused idiom.

In the end, he will have to come out of the walled garden and begin to grapple with 'the thorns and briars outside'.

The author considered the same question in a later novel, *The Curate in Charge*, which also has an Oxford don among its characters. He, too, worries about being cut off from ordinary human problems, and feels that he will only be saved by marrying a woman who has had a difficult time as the mainstay of her family. In most Oliphant novels, women are a good deal stronger than men and take on jobs—usually inside the home—which would appal them. As Dr Rider tells Nettie, who is looking after his brother's children, 'it ought to be my business quite as much as it is yours':

Nettie looked at him with a certain careless scorn of the inferior creature—'Ah, yes, I daresay; but then you are only a man', said Nettie.

We have already met the young doctor who got out of marrying Bessie Christian in *The Executor*. During the few months which separated these stories, Margaret had made enormous progress. There is no nonsense about missing heirs in *The Doctor's Family*; instead we have a serious and believable story about a man's fear of responsibility, and about the perennial contrast between those who give and those who take.

She also showed a new talent for creating character, particularly in the key figure of Nettie Underwood. There is a vast difference between the meek Bessie and this formidable young woman, 'flashing dangerous sudden glances', and not above throwing a 'stinging word' at Fred. Nettie, of course, is carrying the same kind of burdens as Margaret, and the author's sympathy for her is unmistakable. But she does not become over-involved with her heroine, as Charlotte Brontë and George Eliot so often did, with disastrous results for their work.

Dr Rider comes across as equally real, imperfect, and convincing. The depressing atmosphere of his house is evoked just as skilfully as the charming scene in Mr Wodehouse's garden. He gets a hangover after an 'unlovely evening' drinking with his brother; he grows 'furious over his charred chops and sodden potatoes' (more virile than the Rector, he is obviously sick of being a bachelor). His role is unheroic, but we sympathize with him because he is young, poor, hard-working, and in a highly unpleasant situation.

The situation is, briefly, that these two young people are expected to look after a pair of older relations who seem incapable of doing anything at all for themselves, and who have three small children. Modern readers who say that they should have refused to do it forget the social context. There was no Welfare State in those days to take care of people like Fred and Susan, and if their families had not helped them they would have ended up in the workhouse or in prison. Margaret Oliphant was already supporting one brother, Willie, when she began the *Chronicles of Carlingford*, and a few years later when a second brother and his family lost their income she looked after them, too. She is never known to have refused an appeal to her generosity, yet, like Nettie, she sometimes had doubts:

Was she so entirely *right* as she had supposed? Was it best to relieve the helpless hands of Fred and Susan of their natural duties, and bear these burdens for them, and disable herself, when her time came, from the nobler natural yoke in which her full womanly influence might have told to an extent impossible to it now?

Here she is not just considering the duties of the priest (as in *The Rector*), but, more fundamentally, the duties of all human beings towards each other. The question is 'dark and perplexing', a 'doubtful complicated matter, most hard and difficult of mortal problems', and yet many people would not even bother to ask it. The author's considered opinion was that people did have a responsibility to one another, and especially to their blood relations. But she did not pretend that this was easy, or even that it had a good effect on the character. Dr Rider's servants sympathize with Fred because 'he is very good-natured, poor gentleman', and think his brother treats him harshly. Richard Chatham has much the same reaction to Nettie and Susan, and Susan herself regularly accuses her sister of having no feelings. As with Dickens's Harold Skimpole or Tolstoy's Stiva Oblonsky, the person who avoids responsibility is generally much better liked than the person who takes it on and is soured by it.

Compared to many Victorian novels, *The Doctor's Family* is an exceptionally tough-minded book. Margaret draws a distinction between the Rider children, who have a right to be cared for, and their appalling parents. But the children are not sentimentalized; they are 'intolerable little brats', 'detestable imps'. They scream and squabble and even the most likeable of them, Freddy, calmly tells Nettie that he will not require her when he is grown up. People who make sacrifices should not expect gratitude (this is a constant theme in Oliphant novels), for they will not get it.

Since the author had strong, even passionate feelings on the subject of givers and takers, we might have expected these feelings to spill over into the novel and ruin it. Yet her artistic control never falters. As she wrote a few years later of Jane Austen, 'she is not surprised or offended, much less horror-stricken or indignant, when her people show vulgar or mean traits of character, when they make it evident how selfish and self-absorbed they are'. The book is not solemn or tearful but, for most of the time, extremely funny. Consider the widowed Susan, 'carefully arranged upon the sofa, with a chair placed near for sympathizers'; we know that she has no real grief for her husband and will continue to be a dead weight on her sister but our instinct is to laugh rather than to be shocked. The same lightness of touch can be seen at the beginning of the second chapter:

Next morning Dr Rider rose mightily vexed with himself, as was to be supposed. He was half an hour late for breakfast: he had a headache, his hand shook, and his temper was 'awful'. Before he was dressed, ominous knocks came to the door; and all feverish and troubled as he was, you may imagine that the prospect of the day's work before him did not improve his feelings, and that self-reproach, direst of tormentors, did not mend the matter.

The doctor has been drinking too much; he does not particularly like himself or the life he is leading; if it goes on, he could disintegrate and become the same type of man as Fred. All this information is quietly conveyed in the language of comedy. The situation was so dreadful—Margaret apparently felt—that she could only handle it through this kind of bitter humour.

The novel is, then, a comedy of sorts, and the Victorians would have expected a happy ending. But we do not see how Nettie can ever free herself from the five people who are dependent on her. It does not seem at all likely that Fred will stop drinking, or that Susan will suddenly become competent and sensible (although a lesser novelist might well have resorted to tricks of that kind). Nor do we believe that the Dr Rider we have come to know will agree to put up with the relations who are his as much as Nettie's. As the author says, not without sympathy, 'he could not alter his nature'.

The five dependants are gradually reduced to one through a series of twists in the plot which are unexpected, but satisfying. Fred is drowned; this may seem a little too convenient. But, after all, it is not unnatural that an alcoholic should die before his time, and it leads directly into the most serious and powerful section of the novel. His wife and children are not altered by his death (although Susan will take full advantage of it), and his brother is not deeply upset. The saddest thing is that Fred cannot be mourned as a better man would have been:

Nettie had not loved that shamed and ruined man—she had done him the offices of affection, and endured and sometimes scorned him. She stood remorseful by his side in that first dread hour, which had changed Fred's shabby presence into something awful; and her generous soul burst forth in that cry of penitence which every human creature owes its brother.

Nettie—whose feelings are little understood by those around her—reminds us that Fred was not simply an obstacle to the young lovers' happiness but a human being who tragically wasted his life. At the same time there is no death-bed repentance, no suggestion that he has gone on to a better world. The mystery of his life and death is left to haunt Nettie, and the thoughtful reader.

Others may feel it is unlikely that Richard Chatham would appear from Australia at just the right time to take Susan off her sister's hands. Yet we all know that some women will find a man in the most unpromising circumstances, and, looking back, we see that it is not really so surprising. Susan is 'incapable of deep and permanent feeling', and the author has already hinted that although we find her repellent, other people, who stand in a different relation to her, may not. The moral significance of the event is that while Nettie has nerved herself to give up her own happiness for Susan's sake Susan will shake off Nettie, when it suits her, without a qualm.

By the end of the novel, then, Nettie has had to learn that she is not indispensable, and Dr Rider has had to accept Freddy (we are relieved that he is not to get off scot-free). They will settle into Carlingford society and be as happy as most people. Yet there is a hint, in the final pages, that this marriage will not be what Miss Wodehouse calls 'perfection'. After all, as Nettie says, 'an obstacle which is only removed by Richard Chatham . . . does not count for much'. The serious point which has been raised, 'Love, patience, charity . . . are but human qualities, when they have to be held against daily disgusts, irritations, and miseries,' remains true. The young couple have been lucky, but things might well have gone the other way. There is still a great gulf between the privileged and the unfortunate.

As a very young woman, Margaret Oliphant wrote books just like those of scores of minor novelists, in which all the clergymen are heroic and all the lovers devoted and faultless. By the time she wrote *The Rector* and *The Doctor's Family*, she had become a mature artist, whose work deals with recognizable human beings and explores extremely complex states of mind. She had learned a great deal from her own experience, and something, too, from the work of Jane Austen and the early George Eliot. At her best, she is fully worthy to stand beside these two great novelists, and, in the two longer stories in this volume, she is very near her best. Many more famous Victorian 'classics' are far less vivid and disturbing.

NOTE ON THE TEXT

THE text of *The Executor* is that printed in *Blackwood's Magazine* in May 1861. *The Rector* and *The Doctor's Family* first appeared, also in *Blackwood's*, later in the same year, and were published in one volume in 1863. The present edition is based on that volume, which corrected some misprints and internal inconsistencies in the original text. A few other obvious errors have been silently corrected.

SELECT BIBLIOGRAPHY

MOST Oliphant novels, including some of the best, have long been out of print. The first to be rediscovered was *Miss Marjoribanks* (Zodiac Press, 1969, with an introduction by Q. D. Leavis). Two more novels, *Hester* (Virago Modern Classics, with an introduction by Jennifer Uglow), and *Kirsteen* (Everyman Classics, with an introduction by Merryn Williams), appeared in 1984. Her famous ghost story, 'The Open Door', is in several collections, the most recent being *The Penguin Book of Ghost Stories* (ed. J. A. Cuddon, 1984).

The Autobiography and Letters of Mrs M. O. W. Oliphant, edited by her cousin, Mrs Harry Coghill, appeared in 1899, two years after her death. It is a most moving document, and essential for those who want to know more about her, but it does not pretend to tell the full story of her life, and some of the most interesting letters (as well as parts of the manuscript text) have been left out. Mrs Coghill wrote a rather sentimental commentary which depicted the novelist as a much more conventional person than she really was. It was reissued by Leicester University Press in 1974, with an introduction and notes by Q. D. Leavis.

The Equivocal Virtue: Mrs Oliphant and the Victorian Literary Market Place, by Vineta and Robert A. Colby (1966), gives a full account of her relations with her publishers, and has two chapters on her works on the supernatural and the *Chronicles of Carlingford*. The biographical part of this book is sketchy, because at that time little was known about her life apart from what is in the *Autobiography*. But in 1973 her great-niece presented the National Library of Scotland with a very large collection of her private letters and other documents, and these were of great help to me when I was writing my own account of her, *Margaret Oliphant, A Critical Biography* (1986). The NLS also owns her letters to the Blackwoods, which fill several volumes. Letters to her other publishers, Bentley and Macmillan, are in the British Museum.

A full list of her novels and contributions to *Blackwood's Magazine* is provided in the *Autobiography*.

The *Chronicles of Carlingford* are discussed in *Gains and Losses: Novels of Faith and Doubt in Victorian England*, by Robert Lee Wolff (1977), and in *Victorian Popular Fiction 1860–80*, by R. C. Terry

(1983). There is a hostile account of *Salem Chapel* in *Everywhere Spoken Against, Dissent in the Victorian Novel*, by Valentine Cunningham (1975). I have discussed her work briefly in *Women in the English Novel, 1800–1900* (1984), and in much more detail in the above-mentioned biography.

A CHRONOLOGY OF
MARGARET OLIPHANT

1828   4 April: Margaret Oliphant Wilson born at Wallyford,
       Midlothian, youngest child of Francis Wilson, clerk, and
       Margaret (née Oliphant).

1830–8 Family moves to Lasswade and then Glasgow. Margaret
       probably educated at home by her mother.

1838   Family moves to Liverpool and lives at several addresses in
       Everton over the next twelve years. Problems with alcoholic
       brother, Willie.

1843   Disruption of Church of Scotland; the Wilsons join Free
       Presbyterian congregation.

1849   First novel, *Margaret Maitland*, published. Goes to London
       to look after Willie, now a theology student. Meets first
       cousin, Francis Wilson Oliphant (Frank), an artist and
       stained-glass designer.

1850–1 Moves to Birkenhead with parents and writes several more
       novels. Willie becomes a Presbyterian minister at Etal,
       Northumberland.

1852   *Katie Stewart* serialized in *Blackwood's Magazine*. Willie
       breaks down, leaves the ministry, and becomes dependent on
       his family. Margaret marries Frank Oliphant (4 May) and
       moves to London. Parents follow and there is family friction.

1853   Daughter, Maggie, born.

1854   Second daughter, Marjorie, born. Margaret's mother dies.

1855   Publishes regular articles in *Blackwood's* and frequent
       novels. Marjorie dies. Baby boy dies at birth.

1856   Son, Cyril, born.

1857   Frank's glass-painting business loses money and he shows
       first signs of tuberculosis.

1858   Son, Stephen, born and dies. Father dies.

1859   January: Oliphants leave for continent and witness
       revolution (27 April) in Florence. 20 October: Frank dies in
       Rome aged 41. 12 December: youngest child, Francis
       Romano (Cecco) born.

1860   Margaret returns to England with three children and settles in Edinburgh. Researches biography of Edward Irving and meets Thomas and Jane Welsh Carlyle.

1861   Financial troubles. *Blackwood's* refuses her work for several months but eventually prints *The Executor* (May). Follows it with *The Rector* (September) and *The Doctor's Family* (October–January). Moves to Ealing.

1862   *Chronicles of Carlingford* series very successful; *Salem Chapel* serialized in *Blackwood's* and attributed to George Eliot.

1863   November: Returns to Rome with children to see Willie.

1864   27 January: Ten-year-old daughter Maggie dies suddenly in Rome. Margaret, in a deep depression, roams about Europe for the next eighteen months. *The Perpetual Curate* published.

1865   Writes *Miss Marjoribanks* in Paris. Returns to England and settles in Windsor (December) so that sons can attend Eton as day-boys.

1866   *Miss Marjoribanks* and *A Son of the Soil* published.

1868   Brother, Frank Wilson, loses job; she takes in his young son Frank and pays for his education. She receives a Civil List pension of £100.

1870   Frank Wilson and his small daughters, Madge and Denny, move in with her. Writing hard, especially for *Blackwood's*, to support two families; has constant financial crises and reputation damaged by over-production.

1875   Brother Frank dies; his son gets an appointment in India. Meets Leslie Stephen and Anne Thackeray in Switzerland. Cyril to Balliol College, Oxford.

1876   *The Curate in Charge* and *Phoebe, Junior, A Last Chronicle of Carlingford* are published.

1878   Cecco joins his brother at Balliol.

1879   Margaret worries about Cyril, who fails to get either a good degree or a job. Nephew, Frank Wilson, dies of fever in India.

1880   *A Beleaguered City* published. Expresses sympathy with women's suffrage movement (*Fraser's Magazine*, May).

1882   Ghost stories, 'The Open Door' and 'A Little Pilgrim', published in magazines; reputation as a 'supernatural' writer grows. Cecco takes fourth class at Oxford; neither boy finds work.

1883   _Hester_ and _The Ladies Lindores_ published.

1884   Cyril gets appointment in Ceylon but returns (July) because of health problems. Depression and deep disappointment with sons.

1885   Begins writing autobiography. Willie dies in Rome.

1886   _A Country Gentleman and his Family_ published.

1887   Cecco threatened with tuberculosis, and both sons miss job opportunities. Reputation declines. Begins autobiographical story, 'Mr Sandford' (December).

1890   March: To Jerusalem to write travel book. _Kirsteen_ published. 8 November: Cyril dies suddenly.

1892   _The Marriage of Elinor_ published. Nursing Cecco and spending most winters abroad with him.

1893   Niece, Madge, marries and moves to Dundee.

1894   1 October: Cecco dies after tremendous struggle by his mother to save him.

1896   January: Attacks Hardy's _Jude the Obscure_ in _Blackwood's_ article, 'The Anti-Marriage League', and publishes ghost story, 'The Library Window', in the same issue. April: moves to The Hermitage, Wimbledon Common, with younger niece Denny. Still no settled income and health breaking up, works hole in finger with writing.

1897   Finishes second volume of _Annals of a Publishing House: William Blackwood and his Sons_. 25 June: Dies at Wimbledon.

1899   _The Autobiography and Letters of Mrs M. O. W. Oliphant_ (ed. Mrs Harry Coghill) published posthumously.

THE EXECUTOR

CHAPTER I

'THE woman was certainly mad,' said John Brown.

It was the most extraordinary of speeches, considering the circumstances and place in which it was spoken. A parlour of very grim and homely aspect, furnished with dark mahogany and black haircloth, the blinds of the two windows solemnly drawn down, the shutters of one half-closed; two traditional decanters of wine standing reflected in the shining uncovered table; half-a-dozen people all in mourning, in various attitudes of surprise, disappointment, and displeasure; and close by one of the windows Mr Brown, the attorney, holding up to the light that extraordinary scrap of paper, which had fallen upon them all like a thunderbolt. Only half an hour ago he had attended her funeral with decorum and perfect indifference, as was natural, and had come into this parlour without the slightest idea of encountering anything which could disturb him. Fate, however, had been lying in wait for the unsuspecting man at the moment he feared it least. He had not been employed to draw out this extraordinary document, nor had he known anything about it. It was a thunderbolt enclosed in a simple envelope, very securely sealed up, and delivered to him with great solemnity by the next of kin, which carried him off his balance like a charge of artillery, and made everybody aghast around him. The sentiment and exclamation were alike natural: but the woman was not mad.

By the side of the table, very pale and profoundly discomposed, sat the next of kin; a woman, of appearance not unaccordant with that of the house, over fifty, dark-complexioned and full of wrinkles, with a certain cloud of habitual shabbiness, not to be cast aside, impairing the perfection of her new mourning. Her *new* mourning, poor soul! got on the strength of that letter containing the will,

which had been placed in her safe keeping. She was evidently
doing everything she could to command herself, and conceal
her agitation. But it was not a very easy matter. Cherished
visions of years, and hopes that this morning had seemed on the
point of settling into reality, were breaking up before her, each
with its poignant circumstances of mortification and bitterness
and dread disappointment. She looked at everybody in the room
with a kind of agonised appeal—could it really be true, might
not her ears have deceived her?—and strained her troubled gaze
upon that paper, not without an instinctive thought that it was
wrongly read, or misunderstood, or that some mysterious
change had taken place on it in the transfer from her possession
to that of Mr Brown. His amazement and dismay did not
convince the poor dismayed woman. She stretched out her hand
eagerly to get the paper to read it for herself. He might have
changed it in reading it; he might have missed something, or
added something, that altered the meaning. Anything might
have happened, rather than the reality that her confidence had
been deceived and her hopes were gone.

'Did you know of this, Mrs Christian?' said the rector, who
stood at the other end of the room with his hat in his hand.

Did she know! She could have gnashed her teeth at the
foolish question, in her excitement and exasperation. She
made a hysterical motion with her head to answer. Her
daughter, who had come to the back of her chair, and who
knew the rector must not be offended, supplied the words that
failed to her mother—'No; we thought we were to have it,'
said the poor girl, innocently. There was a little movement of
sympathy and compassion among the other persons present.
But mingled with this came a sound of a different description;
a cough, not an expression of physical weakness, but of moral
sentiment; an irritating, critical, inarticulate remark upon that
melancholy avowal. It came from the only other woman
present, the servant of the house. When the disappointed
relation heard it, she flushed into sudden rage, and made an
immediate identification of her enemy. It was not dignified,
but it was very natural. Perhaps, under the circumstances, it
was the only relief which her feelings could have had.

'But I know whose doing it was!' said poor Mrs Christian, trembling all over, her pale face reddening with passion. There was a little movement at the door as the servant-woman stepped farther into the room to take her part in the scene which interested her keenly. She was a tall woman, thin and dry, and about the same age as her accuser. There was even a certain degree of likeness between them. As Nancy's tall person and white apron became clearly visible from among the little group of gentlemen, Mrs Christian rose, inspired with all the heat and passion of her disappointment, to face her foe.

'Did *you* know of this?' said the excellent rector, with his concerned malaprop face. Nancy did not look at him. The three women stood regarding each other across the table; the others were only spectators—they were the persons concerned. The girl who had already spoken, and who was a little fair creature, as different from the belligerents as possible, stood holding her mother's hand tightly. She had her eyes on them both, with an extraordinary air of control and unconscious authority. They were both full of rage and excitement, the climax of a long smouldering quarrel; but the blue eyes that watched, kept them silent against their will. The crisis lasted only for a moment. Poor Mrs Christian, yielding to the impulse of the small fingers that closed so tightly on her hand, fell back on her chair, and attempted to recover her shattered dignity. Nancy withdrew to the door; and Mr Brown repeated the exclamation in which his dismay and trouble had first expressed itself, 'Certainly the woman must have been mad!'

'Will you have the goodness to let me see it?' said Mrs Christian, with a gasp. It is impossible to say what ideas of tearing it up, or throwing it into the smouldering fire, might have mingled with her desire; but, in the first place, she was eager to see if she could not make something different out of that paper than those astounding words she had heard read. Mr Brown was an honest man, but he was an attorney; and Mrs Christian was an honest woman, but she was next of kin. If she had known what was in that cruel paper, she might not, perhaps, have preserved it so carefully. She read it over, trembling, and not understanding the very words she muttered under her breath. Bessie read it also, over her shoulder. While they were so occupied, Mr Brown relieved his perplexed mind with a vehemence not much less tragical than that of the disappointed heir.

'I have known many absurd things in the way of wills,' said Mr Brown, 'but this is the crown of all. Who on earth ever heard of Phœbe Thomson? Who's Phœbe Thomson? Her daughter? Why, she never had any daughter in the memory of man. I should say it is somewhere like thirty years since she settled down in Carlingford—with no child, nor appearance of ever having one—an old witch with three cats, and a heart like the nether millstone. Respect? don't speak to me! why should I respect her? Here she's gone, after living a life which nobody was the better for; certainly *I* was none the better for it; why, she did not even employ me to make this precious will; and saddled me—me, of all men in the world—with a burden I wouldn't undertake for my own brother. I'll have nothing to do with it. Do you suppose I'm going to give up my own business, and all my comfort, to seek Phœbe Thomson? The idea's ridiculous! the woman was mad!'

'Hush! for we're in the house of our departed friend, and have just laid her down,' said the inappropriate rector, 'in the sure and certain hope——'

Mr Brown made, and checked himself in making, an extraordinary grimace. 'Do you suppose I'm bound to go hunting Phœbe Thomson till that day comes?' said the attorney. 'Better to be a ghost at once, when one could have surer information. I'm very sorry, Mrs Christian; I have no hand in it, I assure you. Who do you imagine this Phœbe Thomson is?'

'Sir,' said Mrs Christian, 'I decline to give you any information. If my son was here, instead of being in India, as everybody knows, I might have some one to act for me. But you may be certain I shall take advice upon it. You will hear from my solicitor, Mr Brown; I decline to give you any information on the subject.'

Mr Brown stared broadly at the speaker; his face reddened.

He watched her get up and make her way out of the room with a perplexed look, half angry, half compassionate. She went out with a little of the passionate and resentful air which deprives such disappointments of the sympathy they deserve—wrathful, vindictive, consoling herself with dreams that it was all a plot, and she could still have her rights; but a sad figure, notwithstanding her flutter of bitter rage—a sad figure to those who knew what home she was going to, and how she had lived. Her very dress, so much better than it usually was, enhanced the melancholy aspect of the poor woman's withdrawal. Her daughter followed her closely, ashamed, and not venturing to lift her eyes. They were a pathetic couple to that little group that knew all about them. Nancy threw the room-door open for them, with a revengeful satisfaction. One of the funeral attendants who still lingered outside opened the outer one. They went out of the subdued light, into the day, their hearts tingling with a hundred wounds. At least the mother's heart was pierced, and palpitating in every nerve. There was an instinctive silence while they went out, and after they were gone. Even Mr Brown's 'humph!' was a very subdued protest against the injustice which Mrs Christian had done him. Everybody stood respectful of the real calamity.

'And so, there they are just where they were!' cried the young surgeon, who was one of the party; 'and pretty sweet Bessie must still carry her father on her shoulders, and drag her mother by her side wherever she goes; it's a very hard burden for a girl of her years.'

'But it is a burden of which she might be relieved,' said Mr Brown, with a smile.

The young man coloured high and drew back a little. 'Few men have courage enough to take up such loads of their own will,' he said, with a little heat—'I have burdens of my own.'

A few words may imply a great deal in a little company, where all the interlocutors know all about each other. This, though it was simple enough, disturbed the composure of the young doctor. A minute after he muttered something about his further presence being unnecessary, and hastened away.

There were now only left the rector, the churchwarden, and Mr Brown.

'Of course you will accept her trust, Mr Brown,' said the rector.

The attorney made a great many grimaces, but said nothing. The whole matter was too startling and sudden to have left him time to think what he was to do.

'Anyhow the poor Christians are left in the lurch,' said the churchwarden; 'for, I suppose, Brown, if you don't undertake it, it'll go into Chancery. Oh! I don't pretend to know; but it's natural to suppose, of course, that it would go into Chancery, and stand empty with all the windows broken for twenty years. But couldn't they make you undertake it whether you pleased or no? I am only saying what occurs to me; of course, I'm not a lawyer—I can't know.'

'Well, never mind,' said Mr Brown; 'I cannot undertake to say just at this identical moment what I shall do. I don't like the atmosphere of this place, and there's nothing more to be done just now that I know of. We had better go.'

'But the house—and Nancy—some conclusion must be come to directly. What will you do about them?' said the rector.

'To be sure! I don't doubt there's plate and jewellery and such things about—they ought to be sealed and secured, and that sort of thing,' said the still more energetic lay functionary. 'For anything we know, she might have money in old stockings all about the house. I shouldn't be surprised at anything, after what we've heard to-day. Twenty thousand pounds! and a daughter! If any one had told me that old Mrs Thomson had either the one or the other yesterday at this time, I should have said they were crazy. Certainly, Brown, the cupboards and desks and so forth should be examined and sealed up. It is your duty to Phœbe Thomson. You must do your duty to Phœbe Thomson, or she'll get damages of you. I suppose so—*you* ought to know.'

'Confound Phœbe Thomson!' said the attorney, with great unction; 'but notwithstanding, come along, let us get out of this. As for her jewellery and her old stockings, they must take their chance. I can't stand it any longer—pah! there's no air to breathe. How did the old witch ever manage to live to eighty here?'

'You must not call her by such improper epithets. I have no doubt she was a good woman,' said the rector; 'and recollect, really, you owe a little respect to a person who was only buried to-day.'

'If she were to be buried to-morrow,' cried the irreverent attorney, making his way first out of the narrow doorway, 'I know one man who would have nothing to do with the obsequies. Why, look here! what right had that old humbug to saddle me with her duties, after neglecting them all her life; and, with that bribe implied, to lure me to undertake the job, too. Ah, the old wretch! don't let us speak of her. As for respect, I don't owe her a particle—that is a consolation. I knew something of the kind of creature she was before to-day.'

So saying, John Brown thrust his hands into his pockets, shrugged up his shoulders, and went off at a startling pace up the quiet street. It was a very quiet street in the outskirts of a very quiet little town. The back of the house which they had just left was on a line with the road—a blank wall, broken only by one long staircase-window. The front was to the garden, entering by a little side-gate, through which the indignant executor had just hurried, crunching the gravel under his rapid steps. A line of such houses, doleful and monotonous, with all the living part of them concealed in their gardens, formed one side of the street along which he passed so rapidly. The other side consisted of humbler habitations, meekly contented to look at their neighbours' back-windows. When John Brown had shot far ahead of his late companions, who followed together, greatly interested in this new subject of talk, his rapid course was interrupted for a moment. Bessie Christian came running across the street from one of the little houses. She had no bonnet on, and her black dress made her blonde complexion and light hair look clearer and fairer than ever; and when the lawyer drew up all at once to hear what she had to say, partly from compassion, partly from curiosity, it did not fail to strike him how like a child she was, approaching him thus simply with her message. 'Oh, Mr

Brown,' cried Bessie, out of breath, 'I want to speak to you. If you will ask Nancy, I am sure she can give you whatever information is to be had about—about aunt's friends. She has been with aunt all her life. I thought I would tell you in case you might think, after what mamma said—'

'I did not think anything about it,' said Mr Brown.

'That we knew something, and would not tell you; but we don't know anything,' said Bessie. 'I never heard of Phœbe Thomson before.'

Mr Brown shrugged up his shoulders higher than ever, and thrust his hands deeper into his pockets. 'Thank you,' he said, a little ungraciously. 'I should have spoken to Nancy, of course, in any case; but I'm sure its very kind of you to take the trouble—good-by.'

Bessie went back blushing and disconcerted; and the rector and the churchwarden, coming gradually up on the other side of the road, seeing her eager approach and downcast withdrawal, naturally wondered to each other what she could want with Brown, and exchanged condolences on the fact that Brown's manners were wonderfully bearish—really too bad. Brown, in the mean time, without thinking anything about his manners, hurried along to his office. He was extremely impatient of the whole concern; it vexed him unconsciously to see Bessie Christian; it even occurred to him that the sight of her and of her mother about would make his unwelcome office all the more galling to him. In addition to all the annoyance and trouble, here would be a constant suggestion that he had wronged these people. He rushed into his private sanctuary the most uncomfortable man in Carlingford. An honest, selfish, inoffensive citizen, injuring no one, if perhaps he did not help so many as he might have done—what grievous fault had he committed to bring upon him such a misfortune as this?

The will which had caused so much conversation was to this purport. It bequeathed all the property of which Mrs Thomson of Grove Street died possessed, to John Brown, attorney in Carlingford, in trust for Phœbe Thomson, the only child of the testatrix, who had not seen or heard of her for thirty years; and in case of all lawful means to find the said Phœbe proving unsuccessful, at the end of three years the property in question was bequeathed to John Brown, his heirs and administrators, absolutely and in full possession. No wonder it raised a ferment in the uncommunicative bosom of the Carlingford attorney, and kept the town in talk for more than nine days. Mrs Thomson had died possessed of twenty thousand pounds: such an event had not happened at Carlingford in the memory of man.

CHAPTER II

THE divers emotions excited by this very unexpected occurrence may be better evidenced by the manner in which the evening of that day was spent in various houses in Carlingford than by any other means.

First, in the little house of the Christians. It was a cottage on the other side of Grove Street*—a homely little box of two stories, with a morsel of garden in front, and some vegetables behind. There, on that spring afternoon, matters did not look cheerful. The little sitting-room was deserted—the fire had died out—the hearth was unswept—the room in a litter. Bessie's pupils had not come to-day. They had got holiday three days ago, in happy anticipation of being dismissed for ever; and only their young teacher's prudential remonstrances had prevented poor Mrs Christian from making a little speech to them, and telling them all that henceforward Miss Christian would have other occupations, but would always be fond of them, and glad to see her little friends in their new house. To make that speech would have delighted Mrs Christian's heart. She had managed, however, to convey the meaning of it by many a fatal hint and allusion. In this work of self-destruction the poor woman had been only too successful; for already the mothers of the little girls had begun to inquire into the terms and capabilities of other teachers, and the foundations of Bessie's little empire were shaken and tottering, though fortunately they did not know of it to-day.

Everything was very cold, dismal, and deserted in that little parlour. Faint sounds overhead were the only sounds audible in the house; sometimes a foot moving over the creaky boards: now and then a groan. Upstairs there were two rooms; one a close, curtained, fire-lighted, stifling, invalid's room. There was Bessie sitting listlessly by a table, upon which were the familiar tea-things, which conveyed no comfort to-night; and there was her paralytic father sitting helpless, sometimes shaking his head, sometimes grumbling out faint half-articulate words, sighs, and exclamations. 'Dear, dear! ah! well! that's what it has come to!' said the sick man, hushed by long habit into a sort of spectatorship, and feeling even so great a disappointment rather by way of sympathy than personal emotion. Bessie sat listless by, feeling a vague exasperation at this languid running accompaniment to her thoughts. The future had been blotted out suddenly, and at a blow, from Bessie's eyes. She could see nothing before her— nothing but this dark, monotonous, aching present moment, pervaded by the dropping sounds of that faint, half-articulate voice. Other scene was not to dawn upon her youth. It was hard for poor Bessie. She sat silent in the stifling room, with the bed and its hangings between her and the window, and the fire scorching her cheek. She could neither cry, nor scold, nor blame anybody. None of the resources of despair were possible to her. She knew it would have to go on again all the same, and that now things never would be any better. She could not run away from the prospect before her. It was not so much the continuance of poverty, of labour, of all the dreadful pinches of thrift; it was the end of possibility—the knowledge that now there was no longer anything to expect.

On the other side of the passage Bessie's own sleeping-room was inhabited by a restless fever of disappointment and despair and hope. There was Mrs Christian lying on her daughter's bed. The poor woman was half-crazed with the whirl of passion in her brain. That intolerable sense of having been duped and deceived, of actually having a hand in the overthrow of all her own hopes, aggravated her natural disappointment into frenzy. When she recollected her state of exultation that morning, her confident intentions—when they were to remove, what changes were to be in their manner of life, even what house they were to occupy—it is not wonderful if the veins swelled in her poor head, and all her pulses throbbed with the misery of the contrast. But with all this there mingled a vindictive personal feeling still more exciting. Nancy, whom she knew more of than any one else did—her close, secret, unwavering enemy; and even the innocent lawyer, whom, in her present condition of mind, she could not believe not to have known of this dreadful cheat practised upon her, or not to care for that prize which, now that it was lost, seemed to her worth everything that was precious in life. The poor creature lay goading herself into madness with thoughts of how she would be revenged upon these enemies; how she would watch, and track out, and reveal their hidden plots against her; how she would triumph over and crush them. All these half-frenzied cogitations were secretly pervaded—a still more maddening exasperation—by a consciousness of her own impotence. The evening came creeping in, growing dark around her—silence fell over the little house, where nobody moved or spoke, and where all the world, the heavens, and the earth, seemed changed since this morning; but the wonder was how that silence could contain her—all palpitating with pangs and plans, a bleeding, infuriated, wounded creature—and show no sign of the frenzy it covered. She had lain down to rest, as the saying is. How many women are there who go thus to a voluntary crucifixion and torture by lying down to rest! Mrs Christian lay with her dry eyes blazing through the darkness, no more able to sleep than she was to do all that her burning fancy described to her. She was a hot-blooded Celtic woman, of that primitive island* which has preserved her name. If she could have sought sympathy, here was nobody to bestow it. Not the heart which that poor ghost of manhood in the next room had lost out of his chilled bewildered bosom; not Bessie's steadfast, unexcited spirit. The poor soul saved herself from going wild by thinking of her boy; holding out her passionate arms to him thousands of miles away; setting him forth as the deliverer, with all the absolute folly of love and passion. He would come home and have justice done to his mother. Never fancy was more madly unreasonable; but it saved her from some of the effects of the agitation in her heart.

On the other side of the road, at the same hour, Nancy prepared her tea in the house of which she was temporary mistress. There could not be any doubt, to look at her now, that this tall, dry, withered figure, and face full of characteristic wrinkles, was like Mrs Christian. The resemblance had been noticed by many. And as old Mrs Thomson had not hesitated to avow that her faithful servant was connected with her by some distant bond of relationship, it was not difficult to imagine that these two were really related, though both denied it strenuously. Nancy had a friend with her to tea. They were in the cheerful kitchen, which had a window to the garden, and a window in the side wall of the house, by which a glimpse of the street might be obtained through the garden gate. The firelight shone pleasantly through the cheerful apartment. All the peculiar ornaments of a kitchen—the covers, the crockery, the polished sparkles of shining pewter and brass—adorned the walls. Through it all went Nancy in her new black dress and ample snowy-white apron. She carried her head high, and moved with a certain rhythmical elation. It is surely an unphilosophical conclusion that there is no real enjoyment in wickedness. Nancy had no uneasiness in her triumph. The more she realised what her victory must have cost her opponent, the more entire grew her satisfaction. Remorse might have mixed with her exultation had she had any pity in her, but she had not; and, in consequence, it was with unalloyed pleasure that she contemplated the overthrow of her adversary. Perhaps the very satisfaction of a good man in a good action is inferior to the absolute satisfaction with which, by times, a bad man is permitted to contemplate the issue of his wickedness. Nancy marched about her kitchen, preparing her tea with an enjoyment which possibly would not have attended a benevolent exercise of her powers. Possibly she could almost have painted to herself, line by line, the dark tableau of that twilight room where Mrs Christian lay, driving herself crazy with wild thoughts. She did the gloom of the picture full justice. If she could have peeped into the window and seen it with her own eyes, she would have enjoyed the sight.

'I'll make Mr Brown keep me in the house,' said Nancy, sitting down at a table piled with good things, and which looked an embodiment of kitchen luxury and comfort, 'and get me a girl. It was what missis always meant to do. I'll show it to him out of the will that I was left in trust to be made commforable. And in course of nature her things all comes to me. It's a deal easier to deal with a single gentleman than if there was a lady poking her nose about into everything. Thank my stars, upstarts such like as them Christians shall never lord it over me; and now I have more of my own way, I'll be glad to see you of an evening whenever you can commforable. Bring a bit of work, and we'll have a quiet chat. I consider myself settled for life.'

The young surgeon's house was at the other end of the town; it was close to a region of half-built streets*—for Carlingford was a prosperous town—where successive colonies were settling, where houses were damp and drainage incomplete, and a good practice to be had with pains. The house had a genteel front to the road, a lamp over the door, and a little surgery round the corner, where it gave forth the sheen of its red and blue bottles across a whole half-finished district. Mr Rider had come home tired, unaccountably tired. He had kicked off one boot, and taken a cigar from his case and forgotten to light it. He sat plunged in his easy-chair in a drear brown study—a brown study inaccessible to the solaces which generally make such states of mind endurable. His cigar went astray among the confused properties of his writing table; the book he had been reading last night lay rejected in the farthest corner of the room. He was insensible to the charms of dressing-gown and slippers. On the whole, he was in a very melancholy, sullen, not to say savage mood. He sat and gazed fiercely into the fire, chewing the cud of fancies, in which very little of the sweet seemed to mingle with the bitter. He had been the medical attendant of Mrs Thomson of Grove Street, and had assisted this afternoon at her funeral, and you might have supposed he had hastened the advent of that melancholy day, had you seen his face.

On the whole, it was a hard dilemma in which the poor young man found himself. He, too, like Nancy, kept realising the interior of that other little house in Grove Street. Both of them, by dint of that acquaintance with their neighbours which everybody has in a small community, came to a moderately correct guess at what was going on there. Young Mr Rider sat in heavy thought, sometimes bursting out into violent gestures which fortunately nobody witnessed; sometimes uttering sighs which all but blew out his lights— impatient, urgent sighs, not of melancholy but of anger and resistance—the sighs of a young man who found circumstances intolerable, and yet was obliged to confess, with sore mortification and humbling, that he could not mend them, and behoved to endure. The visions that kept gliding across his eyes drove him half as wild as poor Mrs Christian: one moment a pretty young wife, all the new house wanted to make it fully tenable; but he had scarcely brought her across the threshold when a ghastly figure in a chair was carried over it after her, upstairs into the bridal apartments, and another woman, soured and drawn awry by pressure of poverty, constitutionally shabby, vehement, and high-tempered, pervaded the new habitation. No use saying pshaw! and pah!—no use swearing bigger oaths,—no use pitching unoffending books into the corners, or breathing out those short deep breaths of desperation. This was in reality the state of affairs. Midnight did not change the aspect it had worn in the morning. Pondering all the night through would bring no light on the subject. Nothing could change those intolerable circumstances. The poor young surgeon threw his coat off in the heat and urgency of his thoughts, and pitched it from him like the books. There was no comfort or solace to be found in all that world of fancy. Only this morning sweeter dreams had filled this disordered apartment. In imagination, he had helped his Bessie to minister to the comfort of the poor old sick parents in Mrs Thomson's house. Now he knitted his brows desperately over it, but could find no outlet. Unless some good fairy sent him a patient in the middle of the night, the chances were that the morning would find him pursuing that same interminable brown study of which nothing could come.

Mr Brown's house was an old house in the middle of the town. The offices were in the lower floor, occupying one side of the building. On the other side of the wide old-fashioned hall was his dining-room. There he sat all by himself upon this agitating night. It was a large, lofty, barely-furnished room, with wainscoted walls, and curious stiff panelling, and a high mantel-shelf which he, though a tall man, could scarcely reach with his arm. It was dimly lighted, as well as barely furnished—altogether an inhuman, desert place—the poorest though the grandest of all we have yet looked into in Carlingford. Mr Brown was not sensible of its inhospitable aspect; he was used to it, and that was enough. It occurred to him as little to criticise his house as to criticise his manners. Thus they *were*, and thus they would continue; at least he had always believed so till to-night.

He sat in his easy-chair with his feet on the fender, and a little table at his elbow with his wine. As long as there was anything in his glass he sipped it by habit, without being aware of what he was doing; but when the glass was empty, though he had two or three times raised it empty to his lips, he was too much absorbed in his thoughts to replenish it. He was not by any means a handsome man; and he was five-and-forty or thereabouts, and had a habit of making portentous faces, when anyway specially engaged in thought; so that, on the whole, it was not a highly attractive or interesting figure which reclined back in the crimson chair, and stretched its slippered feet to the fire, sole inmate of the dim, spacious, vacant room. He was thinking over his new position with profound disgust and perplexity. Nevertheless it cannot be denied that the subject lured him on, and drew out into stretches of imagination far beyond his wont;—hunting all the world over after Phœbe Thomson! But, after all, that was only a preliminary step; he was required only to use reasonable means, and for three years. If she turned up, there was an end of it; if she did not turn up——Here Mr Brown sprang up hurriedly and assumed the favourite position of Englishmen in front of his fire. There, all glittering in the distance, rose up, solid and splendid, an appearance which few men could see without emotion—twenty thousand pounds! It was not life and death to him, as it was to poor Mrs Christian. It did not make all the difference between sordid want and comfortable existence; but you may well believe it did not appear before the lawyer's eyes without moving him into a considerable degree of excitement. Such a fairy apparition had never appeared before in that cold, spacious, uninhabited room. Involuntarily to himself, Mr Brown saw his house expand, his life open out, his condition change. Roseate lights dropped into the warming atmosphere which had received that vision; the fairy wand waved through the dim air before him in spite of all his sobriety. The wiles of the enchantress lured John Brown as effectually as if he had not been five-and-forty, an old bachelor, and an attorney; and after half an hour of these slowly-growing, half-conscious, half-resisted thoughts, any chance that had brought the name of the dead woman's lost daughter to his memory, would have called forth a very different 'confound Phœbe Thomson!' from that which burst from his troubled lips in the house in Grove Street. Possibly it was some such feeling which roused him up a moment after, when the great cat came softly purring to his feet and rubbed against his slippers. Mr Brown started violently, thrust puss away, flung himself back into his chair, grew very red, and murmured something about 'an ass!' ashamed to detect himself in his own vain imaginations. But that sudden waking up did not last. After he had filled his glass and emptied it—after he had stirred his fire, and made a little noise, with some vague idea of dispelling the spell he was under—the fairy returned and re-took possession under a less agreeable aspect. Suppose *he* were to be enriched, what was to become of the poor Christians? They were not very near relations, and the old woman had a right to leave her money where she liked. Still there was a human heart in John Brown's bosom. Somehow that little episode in the street returned to his recollection; Bessie running across, light and noiseless, with her message. How young the creature must be after all, to have so much to do. Poor little Bessie! she had not only lost her chance of being a great fortune, and one of the genteel young ladies of Carlingford, but she had lost her chance of the doctor, and his new house and rising practice. Shabby fellow! to leave the pretty girl he was fond of, because she was a good girl, and was everything to her old father and mother. 'I wonder will they say that's my fault too?' said John Brown to himself; and stumbled up to his feet again on the stimulus of that thought, with a kind of sheepish, not unpleasant embarrassment, and a foolish half-smile upon his face. Somehow at the moment, looking before him, as he had done so many hundred times standing on his own hearthrug, it occurred to him all at once what a bare room this was that he spent his evenings in—what an inhuman, chilly, penurious place! scarcely more homelike than that bit of open street, across which Bessie came tripping this afternoon, wanting to speak to him. Nobody wanted to speak to him here. No wonder he had a threatening of rheumatism last winter. What a cold, wretched barn of a room! He could not help wondering to himself whether the drawing-room was any better. In the new start his long-dormant imagination had taken, John Brown actually shivered in the moral coldness of his spacious, lonely apartment. In his mind he daresaid that the Christians looked a great deal more comfortable in that little box of theirs, with that poor little girl working, and teaching, and keeping all straight. What a fool that young doctor was! what if he did work a little harder to make the old people an allowance? However, it was no business of his. With a sigh of general discontent Mr Brown pulled his bell violently, and had the fire made up, and asked for his tea. His tea! he never touched it when it came, but sat pshawing and humphing at it, making himself indignant over that fool of a young doctor. And what if these poor people, sour and sore after their misfortune, should think that this too was *his* fault?

CHAPTER III

NEXT morning Mr Brown, with his hands in his pockets and his shoulders up to his ears as usual, went down at his ordinary rapid pace to old Mrs Thomson's house. Nancy had locked the house-door, which, like an innocent almost rural door as it was, opened from without. She was upstairs, very busy in a most congenial occupation—turning out the old lady's wardrobe, and investigating the old stores of lace and fur and jewellery. She knew them pretty well by heart before; but now that according to her idea, they were her own, everything naturally acquired a new value. She had laid them out in little heaps, each by itself, on the dressing-table; a faintly-glittering row of old rings and brooches, most of them entirely valueless, though Nancy was not aware of that. On the bed—the bed where two days ago that poor old pallid figure still lay in solemn ownership of the 'property' around it—Nancy had spread forth her mistress's ancient boas and vast muffs, half a century old: most of them were absolutely dropping to pieces; but as long as they held together with any sort of integrity, Nancy was not the woman to lessen the number of her possessions. The bits of lace were laid out upon the old sofa, each at full length. With these delightful accumulations all round her, Nancy was happy. She had entered, as she supposed, upon an easier and more important life. Mistress of the empty house and all its contents, she carried herself with an air of elation and independence which she had never ventured to display before. No doubt had ever crossed her mind on the subject. She had taken it for granted that the expulsion of the Christians meant only her own triumph. She had even taken credit, both to herself and other people, for greater guiltiness than she really had incurred. The will was not her doing, though Mrs Christian said so and Nancy was willing to believe as much; but she was glad to be identified as the cause of it, and glad to feel that she was the person who would enjoy the benefit. She was in this holiday state of mind, enjoying herself among her supposed treasures, when she was interrupted by the repeated and imperative demands of entrance made by Mr Brown at the locked door.

Nancy went down to open it, but not in too great a hurry. She was rather disposed to patronise the attorney. She put on her white apron, and went to the door spreading it down with a leisurely hand. To Nancy's surprise and amazement, Mr Brown plunged in without taking any notice of her. He went into the parlour, looked all round, then went up-stairs, three steps at a time, into the best parlour, uncomfortably near the scene of Nancy's operations. There was the old cabinet for which he had been looking. When he saw it he called to her to look here. Nancy, who had followed him close, came forward immediately. He was shaking the door of the cabinet to see if it was locked. It was a proceeding of which Nancy did not approve.

'I suppose this is where she kept her papers,' said Mr Brown; 'get me the keys. I want to see what's to be found among her papers touching this daughter of hers. You had better bring me *all* the keys. Make haste, for I have not any time to lose.'

'Missis never kept any papers there,' said Nancy, alarmed and a little anxious. 'There's the best china tea-set and the silver service—that's all you'll find there.'

'Bring me the keys, however,' said Mr Brown. 'Where did she keep her papers, eh? You know all about her, I suppose. Do you know anything about Phœbe Thomson, that I've got to hunt up? She was Mrs Thomson's daughter, I understand. What caused her to leave her mother? I suppose you know. What is she? How much can you tell me about her?'

'As much as anybody living,' said Nancy, too well pleased to divert him from his inquiries after the keys. 'I was but a girl when it happened; but I remember it like yesterday. She went off—missis never liked to have it mentioned,' said Nancy, coming to a dead stop.

'Go on,' cried Mr Brown; 'she can't hear you now, can she? Go on.'

'She went off with a soldier—that's the truth. They were married after; but missis never thought that mattered. He was a common man, and as plain a looking fellow as you'd see anywhere. Missis cast her off, and would have nothing to say to her. She over-persuaded me, and I let her in one night; but missis wouldn't look at her. She never came back. She was hurt in her feelin's. We never heard of her more.'

'Nor asked after her, I suppose?' said the lawyer, indignantly. 'Do you mean the old wretch never made any inquiry about her own child?'

'Meaning missis?' said Nancy. 'No—I don't know as she ever did. She said she'd disown her; and she was a woman as always kept her word.'

'Old beast!' said John Brown between his teeth; 'but, look here; if she's married, she is not Phœbe Thomson. What's her name?'

'I can't tell,' said Nancy, looking a little frightened. 'Sure, neither she is—to think of us never remarking that! But dear, dear! will that make any difference to the will?'

Mr Brown smiled grimly, but made no answer. 'Have you got anything else to tell me about her? Did she ever write to her mother? Do you know what regiment it is, or where it was at that time?' said the attorney. 'Think what you are about, and tell me clearly—what year was she married, and where were you at the time?'

Nancy grew nervous under this close questioning. She lost her self-possession and all her fancied importance. 'We were in the Isle o' Man, where the Christians come from. I was born there myself. Missis's friends was mostly there. It was by her husband's side she belonged to Carlingford. It was about a two miles out of Douglas—a kind of a farmhouse. It was the year—the year—I was fifteen,' said Nancy, faltering.

'And how old are you now?' said the inexorable questioner, who had taken out his memorandum-book.

Nancy dropped into a chair and began to sob. 'It's hard on a person bringing things back,' said Nancy,—'and to think if she should actually turn up again just as she was! As for living in the house with her, I couldn't think of such a thing. Sally

Christian, or some poor-spirited person might do it, but not me as am used to be by own mistress,' cried Nancy, with increasing agitation. 'She had the temper of — oh! she was her mother's temper. Dear, dear! to think as she might be alive, and come back to put all wrong! It was in the year 'eight*—that's the year it was.'

'Then you didn't think she would come back,' said Mr Brown.

'It's a matter o' five-and-thirty years; and not knowing even her name, nor the number of the regiment, nor nothing—as I don't,' said Nancy, cautiously; 'and never hearing nothing about her, what was a person to think? And if it's just Phœbe Thomson you're inquiring after, and don't say nothing about the marriage nor the regiment, you may seek long enough before you find her,' said Nancy, with a glance of what was intended to be private intelligence between herself and her questioner, 'and all correct to the will.'

Mr Brown put up his memorandum-book sharply in his pocket. 'Bring me the keys. Look here, bring me *all* the keys,' he said. 'What's in this other room, eh? It was her bedroom, I suppose. Hollo, what's all this?'

For all Nancy's precautions had not been able to ward off this catastrophe. He pushed into the room she had left to admit him, where all her treasures were exhibited. His quick eye glanced round in an instant, and understood it. Trembling as Nancy was with new alarms, she had still strength to make one struggle.

'Missis's things fall to me,' said Nancy, half in assertion, half in entreaty; 'that's how it always is; the servant gets the lady's wardrobe—the servant as has nursed her and done for her, when there's no daughter—that's always understood.'

'Bring me the keys,' said Mr Brown.

The keys were in the open wardrobe, a heavy bunch. John Brown seized hold of the furs on the bed and began to toss them into the wardrobe. Some of them dropped in pieces in his hands and were tossed out again. He took no notice of the lace or the trinkets, but swiftly locked every keyhole he could find in the room—drawers, boxes, cupboards, everything.

Nancy looked on with fierce exclamations. She would have her rights—she was not to be put upon. She would have the law of him. She would let everybody know how he was taking upon himself as if he was the master of the house.

'And so I am, my good woman; when will you be ready to leave it?' said Mr Brown. 'You shall have due time to get ready, and I won't refuse you the trumpery you've set your heart upon. Judging from the specimen, it won't do Phœbe Thomson much good. But not in this sort of way, you know. I must put a stop to this. Now let me hear what's the earliest day you can leave the house.'

'I'm not going to leave the house!' cried Nancy; 'I've lived here thirty years, and here I'll die. Missis's meaning was to leave me in the house, and make me commforable for life. Many's the time she's said so. Do you think you're going to order *me* about just as you please? What do you suppose she left the property like that for but to spite the Christians, and to leave a good home to me?'

'When will you be ready to leave?' repeated Mr Brown, without paying the least attention to her outcries and excitement.

'I tell you I'm not agoing to leave!' screamed Nancy. 'To leave?—*me!*—no, not for all the upstarts in Carlingford, if they was doubled and tripled. My missis meant me to stay here commforable all my days. She meant me to have a girl and make myself commforable. Many and many's the time she's said so.'

'But she did not say so in the will,' said the inexorable executor; 'and so out you must go, and that very shortly. Now don't say anything. It is no use fighting with me. You'll be well treated if you leave directly and quietly; otherwise, you shan't have anything. The other keys, please. Now mind what I say. You're quite able to make a noise and a disturbance, but you're not able to resist me. You shall have time to make your preparations and look out another home for yourself; but take care you don't compel me to use severe measures—that's enough.'

'But I won't!—not if you drag me over the stones. I won't

go. I'll speak to Mr Curtis,' cried the unfortunate Nancy.

'Pshaw!' said John Brown. Mr Curtis was the other attorney ⸳ ₁ Carlingford, the one whom probably Mrs Christian had in her mind when she threatened him with her solicitor. He laughed to himself angrily as he went downstairs. If he was to undertake this troublesome business, at least he was not going to be hampered by a parcel of furious women. When he had locked up everything and was leaving the house, Nancy threw open an upper window and threw a malediction after him. 'You'll never find her! It'll go back to them as it belongs to,' shouted Nancy. He smiled to himself again as he turned away. Was it possible that John Brown began to think it might be as well if he never did find her? The prophecy certainly was not unpleasant to him, though poor Nancy meant it otherwise. Mr Brown hurried up the monotonous side of Grove Street, we are afraid not without a little private exhilaration in the thought that Phœbe Thomson was not unlike the proverbial needle in the bundle of hay. The chances were she was dead years ago; and though he would neither lose a minute in beginning, nor leave any means unused in pursuing the search for her, it was certain he would not be inconsolable if he never heard any more of Phœbe Thomson. Doubtless he would not have acknowledged as much in words, and did not even have any express confidences with himself on the subject, lest his own mind might have been shocked by the disclosure of its involuntary sentiment. Still he took an interest in Mrs Thomson's bequest, greater than he took in the properties intrusted to him by his other clients. He could not help himself. He felt affectionately interested in that twenty thousand pounds.

But as he came up to it, John Brown remembered, with a little interest, that spot of the quiet street where Bessie, yesterday, ran across to speak to him. He could not help recalling her appearance as she approached him, though young girls were greatly out of his way. Poor Bessie! The baker's cart occupied at that moment the spot which Bessie had crossed; and one of the Carlingford ladies was leaving the door of the Christians' little house. Mr Brown, though no man was less given to colloquies with his acquaintances in the street, crossed over to speak to her. He could not help being interested in everything about that melancholy little house, nor feeling that the very sight of it was a reproach to his thoughts. Poor Bessie! there she stood yesterday in her black frock—the lightfooted, soft-voiced creature—not much more than a child beside the middle-aged old bachelor who could find it in his heart to be harsh to her. Across that very spot he passed hastily, with many compunctions in the mind which had been roused so much out of its usual ways of thinking by the events and cogitations of the last four-and-twenty hours. The lady to whom he paid such a marked token of respect was quite flattered and excited to meet him. He was the hero of the day at Carlingford. The last account of this extraordinary affair was doubtless to be had from himself.

'You've been at the Christians'. I suppose you were there for some purpose so early in the morning,' said the abrupt Mr Brown, after the necessary salutations were over.

'Yes—but I am a very early person,' said the lady. 'Oh, forgive me. I know quite well you don't care to hear what sort of a person I am; but really, Mr Brown, now that you are quite the hero of the moment yourself, do let me congratulate you. They say there is not a chance of finding this Phœbe Thomson. Some people even say she is a myth and never existed; and that it was only a device of the old lady to give her an excuse for leaving you the money. Dear me! *did* you ask me a question? I forget. I am really so interested to see *you*.'

'I like an answer when it's practicable,' said the lawyer. 'I said I supposed you were about some business at Miss Christian's house?'

'I must answer you this time, mustn't I, or you won't talk to me any longer?' said the playful interlocutor, whom John Brown could have addressed in terms other than complimentary. 'Yes, poor thing, I've been at Miss Christian's, and on a disagreeable business too, in the present circumstances. We are going to send our Mary away to a finishing-school. So I had to tell poor Bessie we shouldn't want any more music-lessons after this quarter. I was very sorry, I am sure—and there was Mrs Mayor taking her little girls away from the morning-class. When they expected to get Mrs Thomson's money they had been a little careless, I suppose; and to give three days' holiday in the middle of the quarter, without any reason for it but an old person's death, you know—a death *out* of the house—is trying to people's feelings; and Mrs Christian had given everybody to understand that *her* daughter would soon have no occasion for teaching. People don't like these sort of things; and Mrs Mayor heard of somebody else a little nearer, who is said to be very good at bringing on little children. I said all I could to induce her to change her mind; but I believe they're to leave next quarter. Poor Bessie! I am very sorry for her, I am sure.'

'And this is how you ladies comfort a good young woman when she meets with a great disappointment?' said John Brown.

'La!—a disappointment! You know that only means *one thing* to a girl,' said the lady, 'but you're always so severe. Bessie has had no *disappointment*, as people understand the word; yet there's young Dr Rider, you know, very attentive, and I do hope he'll propose directly, and set it all right for her, poor thing, for she's a dear good girl. But to hear *you* speak so—of all people—Mr Brown. Why, isn't it your fault? I declare I would hate you if I was Bessie Christian. If the doctor were to be off too, and she really had a disappointment, it would be dreadfully hard upon her, poor girl; but it's to be hoped things will turn out better than that. Good morning! but you have not told me a word about your own story—all Carlingford is full of it. People say you are the luckiest man!'

These words overtook, rather than were addressed to, him as he hurried off indignant. John Brown was not supposed to be an observant person, but somehow he saw the genteel people of Carlingford about the streets that day in a surprisingly distinct manner—saw them eager to get a little occupation for themselves anyhow—saw them coming out for their walks, and their shopping, and their visits, persuading themselves by such means that they were busy people, virtuously employed, and making use of their life. What was

Bessie doing? Mr Brown thought he would like to see her, and that he would not like to see her. It was painful to think of being anyhow connected with an arrangement which condemned to that continued labour such a young soft creature—a creature so like, and yet so unlike, those other smiling young women who were enjoying their youth. And just because it was painful Mr Brown could not take his thoughts off that subject. If Phœbe Thomson turned up he should certainly try to induce her to do something for the relations whom her mother had disappointed so cruelly. If Phœbe Thomson did not turn up—well, what then?—if she didn't? Mr Brown could not tell: it would be his duty to do something. But, in the mean time, he did nothing except shake his fist at young Rider's drag* as it whirled the doctor past to his patients, and repeat the 'shabby fellow!' of last night with an air of disgust. John Brown had become very popular just at that moment; all his friends invited him to dinner, and dropped in to hear about this story which had electrified Carlingford. And all over the town the unknown entity called Phœbe Thomson was discussed in every possible kind of hypothesis, and assumed a diffferent character in the hands of every knot of gossips. Nobody thought of Bessie Christian; but more and more as nobody thought of her, that light little figure running across the quiet street, and wanting to speak to him, impressed itself like a picture upon the retentive but not very fertile imagination of Mrs Thomson's executor. It troubled, and vexed, and irritated, and unsettled him. One little pair of willing hands—one little active cheerful soul—and all the burden of labour, and patience, and dread monotony of life that God had allotted to that pretty creature; how it could be, and nobody step in to prevent it, was a standing marvel to John Brown.

CHAPTER IV

MR BROWN was well known everywhere as a famous business man—not perhaps in that sense so familiar to modern observers, which implies the wildest flights of speculation, and such skilful arts of bookmaking as ruin themselves by their very cleverness. Mr Brown did not allow the grass to grow below his feet; his advertisements perpetually led off that list of advertisements in the *Times* which convey so many skeleton romances to a curious public. All over the country people began to entertain guesses about that Phœbe Thomson who was to hear something so much to her own advantage; and Phœbe Thomsons answered to the call through all the breadth of the three kingdoms.* Mr Brown had a detective officer in his pay for the whole year. He made journeys himself, and sent this secret agent on innumerable journeys. He discovered the regiment, a detachment of which had been stationed at the Isle of Man during the year 1808; he went to the island; he left no means untried of finding out this hypothetical person. Nearer at home, Mr Brown had made short work of Nancy, who, too deeply mortified by the failure of her hopes to remain in Carlingford, had returned to her native place with a moderate pension, her own savings, and her mistress's old clothes, not so badly satisfied on the whole, but still a defeated woman. While poor Mrs Christian, compelled by sore dint of time and trouble to give up her forlorn hope of getting justice done her, and reclaiming the wealth that had been so nearly hers from the hands of Mr Brown, was half reconciled to him by his summary dealings with her special enemy. A whole year had passed, and other things had happened at Carlingford. Everybody now did not talk of Mrs Thomson's extraordinary will, and John Brown's wonderful chance of coming into twenty thousand pounds. People had even given over noting that the young doctor had thought better of that foolish fancy of his for Bessie Christian. All the persons in this little drama had relapsed into the shade. It was a very heavy shadow so far as Grove Street was concerned. The little pupils had fallen off, collected again, fallen off once more. If the cheerful glimmer of firelight had never failed in the sick-room—if the helpless old father, sitting in that calm of infirmity and age, making comments which would have irritated his careful attendants beyond bearing if they had not been used to them, never missed anything of his usual comforts—nobody knew at what cost these comforts were bought. But there did come a crisis in which patience and courage, and the steadfast soul which had carried the young breadwinner through the drear monotony of that year, failed her at last. Her mother, who was of a different temper from Bessie, and had gone through a thousand despairs and revivals before the young creature at her side began to droop, saw that the time had come when everything was at stake; and, more reluctantly and slowly, Bessie herself came to see it. She could not set her back against the wall of that little house of theirs and meet every assailant; she could not tide it out in heroic silence, and abstinence alike from comfort and complaint. That was her natural impulse; and the victory, if slow, would have been certain: so Bessie thought at least. But want was at the door, and they could not afford to wait; something else must be attempted. Bessie must go out into the market-place and seek new masters—there was no longer work for her here.

This was how the scene was shifted in the following conclusive act.

John Brown, travelling, and fuming and aggravating himself much over the loss of his time and the distraction of his thoughts, was in London that day—a May-day, when everybody was in London. He had seen his detective, and no further intelligence had been obtained. Phœbe Thomson was as far off as ever—farther off; for now that all these efforts had been made, it was clear that either she must be dead or in some quarter of the world impervious to newspaper advertisements and detective officers. Mr Brown bore the disappointment with a very good grace. He felt contented now to slacken his efforts; he even felt as if he himself were already the possessor of old Mrs Thomson's twenty thousand pounds. As he went leisurely through the streets, he paused before one of those 'Scholastic Agency'* offices which abound in the civilised end of London. It was in the ground-floor of a great faded, sombre house, in a street near St James's Park—a place of aching interest to some people in that palpitating world of human interests. It occurred to Mr Brown to go in and see if there were any lists to be looked over. Phœbe Thomson might have a daughter who might be a governess. It was an absurd idea enough, and he knew it to be so; nevertheless he swung open the green baize door.

Inside, before the desk, stood a little figure which he knew well, still in that black dress which she had worn when she ran across Grove Street and wanted to speak to him; with a curl of the light hair, which looked so fair and full of colour on her black shawl, escaped from under her bonnet, talking softly and eagerly to the clerk. Was there no other place he could send her to? She had come up from the country, and was so very reluctant to go down without hearing of something. The man shook his head, and read over to her several entries in his book. Bessie turned round speechless towards the door. Seeing some one standing there, she lifted her eyes full upon John Brown. Troubled and yet steady, full of tears yet clear and seeing clear, shining blue like the skies, *with a great patience*, these eyes encountered the unexpected familiar face. If she felt an additional pang in seeing him, or if any grudge against the supplanter of her family trembled in Bessie's heart, it made no sign upon her face. She said 'good morning' cheerfully as she went past him, and only quickened her pace a little to get out of sight. She did not take any notice of the rapid step after her; the step which could have made up to her in two paces, but did not, restrained by an irresolute will. Probably she knew whose step it was, and interpreted rightly, to some superficial degree, the feelings of John Brown. She thought he was a good-hearted man—she thought he was sorry to know or guess the straits which Bessie thanked heaven nobody in this world did fully know—she thought, by-and-by, shy of intruding upon her, that step would drop off, and she would hear it no more. But it was not so to be.

'Miss Christian, I want to speak to you,' said John Brown.

She turned towards him directly without any pretence of surprise; and with a smile, the best she could muster, waited to hear what it was.

'We are both walking the same way,' said Mr Brown.

In spite of herself amazement woke upon Bessie's face.

'That is true: but was that all you had to say?' said Bessie, with the smiles kindling all her dimples. The dimples had only been hidden by fatigue, and hardship, and toil. They were all there.

'No, not quite. Were you looking for employment in that office? and why are you seeking employment here?' said the attorney, looking anxiously down upon her.

'Because there's a great many of us in Carlingford,' said Bessie, steadily; 'there are half as many governesses as there are children. I thought I might perhaps get on better here.'

'In London! Do you think there are fewer governesses here?' said Mr Brown, going on with his questions, and meanwhile studying very closely his little companion's face; not rudely. To be sure it was a very honest direct investigation, but there was not a thought of rudeness or disrespect either in the eyes that made it or the heart.

'I daresay it's as bad everywhere,' said Bessie, with a little sigh; 'but when one cannot get work in one place, one naturally turns to another. I had an appointment to-day to come up to see a lady; but I was not the proper person. Perhaps I shall have to stay at home after all.'

'Have you any grudge at me?' said Mr Brown.

Bessie looked up open-eyed and wondering. 'Grudge? at *you*? How could I? I daresay,' said Bessie, with a sigh and a smile, 'mamma had, a year ago; but not me. The times I have spoken to you, Mr Brown, you have always been kind to me.'

'Have I?' said the lawyer. He gave her a strange look, and stopped short, as if his utterance was somehow impeded. Kind to her! He remembered that time in Grove Street, and could have scourged himself at the recollection. Bessie had taken him entirely aback by her simple expression. He could have sobbed under that sudden touch. To see her walking beside him, cheerful, steadfast, without a complaint—a creature separated from the world, from youth and pleasure, and mere comfort even—enduring hardness, for all her soft childlike dimples and unaffected smiles—his composure was entirely overcome. He was going to do something very foolish. He gasped, and gave himself up.

'If you don't bear me a grudge, come over into the Park here, where we can hear ourselves speak. I want to speak to you,' said Mr Brown.

She turned into the Park with him quite simply, as she did everything without any pretence of wonder or embarrassment. There he walked a long time by her side in silence, she waiting for what he had to say, he at the most overwhelming loss how to say it. The next thing he said was to ask her to sit down in a shady quiet corner, where there was an unoccupied seat. She was very much fatigued. It was too bad of him to bring her out of her way.

'But it is so noisy in the street,' said Mr Brown. Then, with a pause after this unquestionable truism, 'I've been thinking about you this very long time.'

Bessie looked up quickly with great amazement; thinking of her! She was wiser when she cast her eyes down again. Mr Brown had not the smallest conception that he had explained himself without saying a syllable, but he had, notwithstanding, leaving Bessie thunderstruck, yet with a moment's time to deliberate. While he went on with his embarrassed slow expressions, fancying that he was gradually conveying to her mind what he meant, Bessie, in a dreadful silent flutter and agitation, was revolving the whole matter, and asking herself what she was to answer. She had ten full minutes for this before he came to the point, and before, according to his idea, the truth burst upon her. But it is doubtful whether that ten minutes' preparation was any advantage to Bessie. It destroyed the unconsciousness, which was her greatest charm; it made an end of her straightforwardness; worst of all, it left her silent. She gave a terrified glance up at him when it actually happened. There he stood full in the light, with all his awkwardnesses more clearly revealed than usual; six-and-forty, abrupt, almost eccentric; telling that story very plainly, without compliment or passion; would she have him? He was content that she should think it over—he was content to wait for her answer; but if it was to be no, let her say it out.

Strange to say, that word which she was exhorted to say out did not come to Bessie's lips. Perhaps because she trembled

a great deal, and really lost her self-possession, and for the
moment did not know what she was about. But even in her
agitation she did not think of saying it. Mr Brown, when he
had his say out, marched up and down the path before her,
and did not interrupt her deliberations. Another dreadful ten
minutes passed over Bessie. The more she thought it over the
more bewildered she became as to what she was to say.

'Please would you walk with me to the railway,' were the
words that came from Bessie's lips at last. She rose up
trembling and faint, and with a kind of instinct took Mr
Brown's arm. He, on his part, did not say anything to her. His
agitation melted away into a subdued silent tenderness which
did not need any expression. He took her back into the streets,
all along that tiresome way. He suffered the noise to surround
and abstract her without any interruption which would make
her conscious of his presence. It was a strange walk for both.
To have called them lovers would have been absurd—to have
supposed that here was a marriage of convenience about to be
arranged would have been more ridiculous still. What was it?
Bessie went along the street in a kind of cloud, aware of
nothing very clearly; feeling somehow that she leant upon
somebody, and that it was somebody upon whom she had a
right to lean. They reached the railway thus, without any
further explanation. Mr Brown put the trembling girl into a
carriage, and did not go with her. The Carlingford attorney
had turned into a paladin. Was it possible that his outer man itself
had smoothed out and expanded too?

'I am not going with you,' he said, grasping her hand
closely, 'I won't embarrass or distress you, Bessie; but
recollect you have not said no; and when I come to Grove
Street to-morrow, I'll hope to hear you say yes. I'll let you off,'
said John Brown, grasping the little soft hand so tight and
hard that it hurt Bessie. 'I'll let you off with liking, if you'll
give me that; at my age I don't even venture to say for myself
that I'm very much in love.'

And with that, the eyes, which had betrayed him before,
flashed in Bessie's face a contradiction of her elderly lover's
words. Yes! it astounded himself almost as much as it did

Bessie. He would still have flatly contradicted anybody who accused him of that folly; but he went away with an undeniable blush into the London streets, self-convicted. A year's observation and an hour's talk had resulted in a much less philosophical sentiment than Mr Brown was prepared for. He went back to the streets, wondering what she would like in all those wonderful shop-windows. He traced back, step for step, the road they had come together. He was not six-and-forty— six-and-twenty was the true reading. That was a May-day of his youth that had come to him, sweet if untimely; a missed May-day, perhaps all the better that it had been kept for him these many tedious years.

And though Bessie cried all the way down to Carlingford, the no she had not said did not occur to her as any remedy for her tears; and, indeed, when she remembered how she had taken Mr Brown's arm, and felt that she had committed herself by that act, the idea was rather a relief to Bessie. 'It was as bad as saying yes at once,' said she to herself, with many blushes. But thus, you perceive, it was done, and could not be altered. She must stand to the consequences of her weakness now.

It made a great noise in Carlingford, as might be supposed; it made a vast difference in the household of Mrs Christian, which was removed to the house in which she had formerly hoped to establish herself as heir-at-law. But the greatest difference of all was made in that dim, spacious, wainscoted dining-room, which did not know itself in its novel circumstances. That was where the change was most remarkably apparent; and all these years Phœbe Thomson's shadow has thrown no cloud as yet over the path of John Brown.

THE RECTOR

CHAPTER I

IT is natural to suppose that the arrival of the new Rector was a rather exciting event for Carlingford. It is a considerable town, it is true, nowadays, but then there are no alien activities to disturb the place—no manufactures, and not much trade. And there is a very respectable amount of very good society at Carlingford. To begin with, it is a pretty place—mild, sheltered, not far from town; and naturally its very reputation for good society increases the amount of that much-prized article. The advantages of the town in this respect have already put five per cent upon the house-rents; but this, of course, only refers to the *real* town, where you can go through an entire street of high garden-walls, with houses inside full of the retired exclusive comforts, the dainty economical refinement peculiar to such places; and where the good people consider their own society as a warrant of gentility less splendid, but not less assured, than the favour of Majesty itself. Naturally there are no Dissenters in Carlingford—that is to say, none above the rank of a greengrocer or milkman; and in bosoms devoted to the Church it may be well imagined that the advent of the new Rector was an event full of importance, and even of excitement.

He was highly spoken of, everybody knew; but nobody knew who had spoken highly of him, nor had been able to find out, even by inference, what were his views. The Church had been Low during the last rector's reign—profoundly Low—lost in the deepest abysses of Evangelicalism.* A determined inclination to preach to everybody had seized upon that good man's brain; he had half emptied Salem Chapel,* there could be no doubt; but, on the other hand, he had more than half filled the Chapel of St Roque, half a mile out of Carlingford, where the perpetual curate,* young, handsome, and fervid,

was on the very topmost pinnacle of Anglicanism.* St Roque's
was not more than a pleasant walk from the best quarter of
Carlingford, on the north side of the town, thank heaven!
which one could get at without the dread passage of that new
horrid suburb, to which young Mr Rider, the young doctor,
was devoting himself. But the Evangelical rector was dead,
and his reign was over, and nobody could predict what the
character of the new administration was to be. The obscurity
in which the new Rector had buried his views was the most
extraordinary thing about him. He had taken high honours at
college, and was 'highly spoken of;' but whether he was High,
or Low, or Broad, muscular or sentimental,* sermonising or
decorative, nobody in the world seemed able to tell.

'Fancy if he were just to be a Mr Bury over again! Fancy
him going to the canal, and having sermons to the bargemen,
and attending to all sorts of people except to us, whom it is
his duty to attend to!' cried one of this much-canvassed
clergyman's curious parishioners. 'Indeed I do believe he
must be one of these people. If he were in society at all,
somebody would be sure to know.'

'Lucy dear, Mr Bury christened you,' said another not less
curious but more tolerant inquirer.

'Then he did you the greatest of all services,' cried the third
member of the little group which discussed the new Rector
under Mr Wodehouse's blossomed apple-trees. 'He conferred
such a benefit upon you that he deserves all reverence at your
hand. Wonderful idea! a man confers this greatest of Christian
blessings on multitudes, and does not himself appreciate the
boon he conveys!'*

'Well, for that matter, Mr Wentworth, you know——' said
the elder lady; but she got no farther. Though she was verging
upon forty, leisurely, pious, and unmarried, that good Miss
Wodehouse was not polemical. She had 'her own opinions,'
but few people knew much about them. She was seated on a
green garden-bench which surrounded the great May-tree in
that large, warm, well-furnished garden. The high brick walls,
all clothed with fruit-trees, shut in an enclosure of which not
a morsel except this velvet grass, with its nests of daisies, was

not under the highest and most careful cultivation. It was such a scene as is only to be found in an old country town; the walls jealous of intrusion, yet thrusting tall plumes of lilac and stray branches of apple-blossom, like friendly salutations to the world without; within, the blossoms dropping over the light bright head of Lucy Wodehouse underneath the apple-trees, and impertinently flecking the Rev. Frank Wentworth's* Anglican coat. These two last were young people, with that indefinable harmony in their looks which prompts the suggestion of 'a handsome couple' to the bystander. It had not even occurred to them to be in love with each other, so far as anybody knew, yet few were the undiscerning persons who saw them together without instinctively placing the young curate of St Roque's in permanence by Lucy's side. She was twenty, pretty, blue-eyed, and full of dimples, with a broad Leghorn hat* thrown carelessly on her head, untied, with broad strings of blue ribbon falling among her fair curls—a blue which was 'repeated,' according to painter jargon, in ribbons at her throat and waist. She had great gardening gloves on, and a basket and huge pair of scissors on the grass at her feet, which grass, besides, was strewed with a profusion of all the sweetest spring blossoms—the sweet narcissus, most exquisite of flowers, lilies of the valley, white and blue hyacinths, golden ranunculus globes—worlds of sober, deep-breathing wallflower. If Lucy had been doing what her kind elder sister called her 'duty,' she would have been at this moment arranging her flowers in the drawing-room; but the times were rare when Lucy did her duty according to Miss Wodehouse's estimate; so instead of arranging those clusters of narcissus, she clubbed them together in her hands into a fragrant dazzling sheaf, and discussed the new Rector—not unaware, perhaps, in her secret heart, that the sweet morning, the sunshine and flowers, and exhilarating air, were somehow secretly enhanced by the presence of that black Anglican figure under the apple-trees.

'But I suppose,' said Lucy, with a sigh, 'we must wait till we see him; and if I must be very respectful of Mr Bury because he christened me, I am heartily glad the new Rector has no claim upon my reverence. I have been christened, I have been confirmed——'

'But, Lucy, my dear, the chances are he will marry you,' said Miss Wodehouse, calmly; 'indeed, there can be no doubt that it is only natural he should, for he *is* the Rector, you know; and though we go so often to St Roque's, Mr Wentworth will excuse me saying that he is a very young man.'

Miss Wodehouse was knitting; she did not see the sudden look of dismay and amazement which the curate of St Roque's darted down upon her, nor the violent sympathetic blush which blazed over both the young faces. How shocking that elderly quiet people should have such a faculty for suggestion! You may be sure Lucy Wodehouse and young Wentworth, had it not been 'put into their heads' in such an absurd fashion, would never, all their virtuous lives, have dreamt of anything but friendship. Deep silence ensued after this simple but startling speech. Miss Wodehouse knitted on, and took no notice; Lucy began to gather up the flowers into the basket, unable for her life to think of anything to say. For his part, Mr Wentworth gravely picked the apple-blossoms off his coat, and counted them in his hand. That sweet summer snow kept dropping, dropping, falling here and there as the wind carried it, and with a special attraction to Lucy and her blue ribbons; while behind, Miss Wodehouse sat calmly on the green bench, under the May-tree just beginning to bloom, without lifting her eyes from her knitting. Not far off, the bright English house, all beaming with open doors and windows, shone in the sunshine. With the white May peeping out among the green overhead, and the sweet narcissus in a great dazzling sheaf upon the grass, making all the air fragrant around them, can anybody fancy a sweeter domestic out-of-door scene? or else it seemed so to the perpetual curate of St Roque's.

Ah me! and if he was to be perpetual curate, and none of his great friends thought upon him, or had preferment to bestow,* how do you suppose he could ever, ever marry Lucy Wodehouse, if they were to wait a hundred years?

Just then the garden gate—the green gate in the wall—opened to the creaking murmur of Mr Wodehouse's own key.

Mr Wodehouse was a man who creaked universally. His boots were a heavy infliction upon the good-humour of his household; and like every other invariable quality of dress, the peculiarity became identified with him in every particular of his life. Everything belonging to him moved with a certain jar, except, indeed, his household, which went on noiseless wheels, thanks to Lucy and love. As he came along the garden path, the gravel started all round his unmusical foot. Miss Wodehouse alone turned round to hail her father's approach, but both the young people looked up at her instinctively, and saw her little start, the falling of her knitting-needles, the little flutter of colour which surprise brought to her maidenly, middle-aged cheek. How they both divined it I cannot tell, but it certainly was no surprise to either of them when a tall embarrassed figure, following the portly one of Mr Wodehouse, stepped suddenly from the noisy gravel to the quiet grass, and stood gravely awkward behind the father of the house.

'My dear children, here's the Rector—delighted to see him! we're all delighted to see him!' cried Mr Wodehouse. 'This is my little girl Lucy, and this is my eldest daughter. They're both as good as curates, though I say it, you know, as shouldn't. I suppose you've got something tidy* for lunch, Lucy, eh? To be sure, you ought to know—how can I tell? She might have had only cold mutton, for anything I knew—and that won't do, you know, after college fare. Hollo, Wentworth! I beg your pardon—who thought of seeing you here? I thought you had morning service,* and all that sort of thing. Delighted to make you known to the Rector so soon. Mr Proctor—Mr Wentworth of St Roque's.'

The Rector bowed. He had no time to say anything, fortunately for him; but a vague sort of colour fluttered over his face. It was his first living; and cloistered in All-Souls for fifteen years of his life, how is a man to know all at once how to accost his parishioners? especially when these curious unknown specimens of natural life happen to be female creatures, doubtless accustomed to compliment and civility. If ever any one was thankful to hear the sound of another man's voice, that person was the new Rector of Carlingford, standing in the bewildering garden-scene into which the green door had so suddenly admitted him, all but treading on the dazzling bundle of narcissus, and turning with embarrassed politeness from the perpetual curate, whose salutation was less cordial than it might have been, to those indefinite flutters of blue ribbon from which Mr Proctor's tall figure divided the ungracious young man.

'But come along to lunch. Bless me! don't let us be too ceremonious,' cried Mr Wodehouse. 'Take Lucy, my dear sir—take Lucy. Though she has her garden-gloves on, she's manager indoors for all that. Molly here is the one we coddle up and take care of. Put down your knitting, child, and don't make an old woman of yourself. To be sure, it's your own concern—you should know best; but that's my opinion. Why, Wentworth, where are you off to? 'Tisn't a fast, surely—is it, Mary?—nothing of the sort; it's Thursday*—*Thursday*, do you hear? and the Rector newly arrived. Come along.'

'I am much obliged, but I have an appointment,' began the curate, with restraint.

'Why didn't you keep it, then, before *we* came in,' cried Mr Wodehouse, 'chatting with a couple of girls like Lucy and Mary? Come along, come along—an appointment with some old woman or other, who wants to screw flannels* and things out of you—well, I suppose so! I don't know anything else you could have to say to them. Come along.'

'Thank you. I shall hope to wait on the Rector shortly,' said young Wentworth, more and more stiffly; 'but at present I am sorry it is not in my power. Good morning, Miss Wodehouse—good morning; I am happy to have had the opportunity——' and the voice of the perpetual curate died off into vague murmurs of politeness as he made his way towards the green door.

That green door! what a slight, paltry barrier—one plank and no more; but outside a dusty dry road, nothing to be seen but other high brick walls, with here and there an apple-tree or a lilac, or the half-developed flower-turrets of a chestnut looking over—nothing to be seen but a mean little coster-

monger's cart, with a hapless donkey, and, down in the direction of St Roque's, the long road winding, still drier and
dustier. Ah me! was it paradise inside? or was it only a merely
mortal lawn dropped over with apple-blossoms, blue ribbons,
and other vanities? Who could tell? The perpetual curate
wended sulky on his way. I fear the old woman would have
made neither flannel nor tea and sugar out of him in that
inhuman frame of mind.

'Dreadful young prig that young Wentworth,' said Mr
Wodehouse, 'but comes of a great family, you know, and gets
greatly taken notice of—to be sure he does, child. I suppose
it's for his family's sake: I can't see into people's hearts. It may
be higher motives, to be sure, and all that. He's gone off in
a huff about something; never mind, luncheon comes up all
the same. Now, let's address ourselves to the business of life.'

For when Mr Wodehouse took knife and fork in hand a
singular result followed. He was silent—at least he talked no
longer: the mystery of carving, of eating, of drinking—all the
serious business of the table—engrossed the good man. He had
nothing more to say for the moment; and then a dread unbroken
silence fell upon the little company. The Rector coloured,
faltered, cleared his throat—he had not an idea how to get into
conversation with such unknown entities. He looked hard at
Lucy, with a bold intention of addressing her; but, having the
bad fortune to meet her eye, shrank back, and withdrew the
venture. Then the good man inclined his profile towards Miss
Wodehouse. His eyes wandered wildly round the room in search
of a suggestion; but, alas! it was a mere dining-room, very
comfortable, but not imaginative. In this dreadful dilemma he
was infinitely relieved by the sound of somebody's voice.

'I trust you will like Carlingford, Mr Proctor,' said Miss
Wodehouse, mildly.

'Yes—oh yes; I trust so,' answered the confused but grateful
man; 'that is, it will depend very much, of course, on the kind
of people I find here.'

'Well, we are a little vain. To tell the truth, indeed, we
rather pride ourselves a little on the good society in
Carlingford,' said his gentle and charitable interlocutor.

'Ah, yes—ladies?' said the Rector: 'hum—that was not what I was thinking of.'

'But, oh, Mr Proctor,' cried Lucy, with a sudden access of fun, 'you don't mean to say that you dislike ladies' society, I hope?'

The Rector gave an uneasy half-frightened glance at her. The creature was dangerous even to a Fellow of All-Souls.

'I may say I know very little about them,' said the bewildered clergyman. As soon as he had said the words he thought they sounded rude; but how could he help it?—the truth of his speech was indisputable.

'Come here, and we'll initiate you—come here as often as you can spare us a little of your time,' cried Mr Wodehouse, who had come to a pause in his operations. 'You couldn't have a better chance. They're head people in Carlingford, though I say it. There's Mary, she's a learned woman; take you up in a false quantity,* sir, a deal sooner than I should. And Lucy, she's in another line altogether; but there's quantities of people swear by her. What's the matter, children, eh? I suppose so—people tell me so. If people tell me so all day long, I'm entitled to believe it, I presume?'

Lucy answered this by a burst of laughter, not loud but cordial, which rang sweet and strange upon the Rector's ears. Miss Wodehouse, on the contrary, looked a little ashamed, blushed a pretty pink old-maidenly blush, and mildly remonstrated with papa. The whole scene was astonishing to the stranger. He had been living out of nature so long that he wondered within himself whether it was common to retain the habits and words of childhood to such an age as that which good Miss Wodehouse put no disguise upon, or if sisters with twenty years of difference between them were usual in ordinary households. He looked at them with looks which to Miss Wodehouse appeared disapproving, but which in reality meant only surprise and discomfort. He was exceedingly glad when lunch was over, and he was at liberty to take his leave. With very different feelings from those of young Wentworth the Rector crossed the boundary of that green door. When he saw it closed behind him he drew a long breath of relief, and looked up and down the dusty road, and through those lines of garden walls, where the loads of blossom burst over everywhere, with a sensation of having escaped and got at liberty. After a momentary pause and gaze round him in enjoyment of that liberty, the Rector gave a start and went on again rapidly. A dismayed, discomfited, helpless sensation came over him. These parishioners!—these female parishioners! From out of another of those green doors had just emerged a brilliant group of ladies, the rustle of whose dress and murmur of whose voices he could hear in the genteel half-rural silence. The Rector bolted: he never slackened pace nor drew breath till he was safe in the vacant library of the Rectory, among old Mr Bury's book-shelves. It seemed the only safe place in Carlingford to the languishing transplanted Fellow of All-Souls.

CHAPTER II

A MONTH later, Mr Proctor had got fairly settled in his new rectory, with a complete modest establishment* becoming his means—for Carlingford was a tolerable living. And in the newly-furnished sober drawing-room sat a very old lady, lively but infirm, who was the Rector's mother.* Nobody knew that this old woman kept the Fellow of All-Souls still a boy at heart, nor that the reserved and inappropriate man forgot his awkwardness in his mother's presence. He was not only a very affectionate son, but a dutiful good child to her. It had been his pet scheme for years to bring her from her Devonshire cottage, and make her mistress of his house. That had been the chief attraction, indeed, which drew him to Carlingford; for had he consulted his own tastes, and kept to his college, who would insure him that at seventy-five his old mother might not glide away out of life without that last gleam of sunshine long intended for her by her grateful son?

This scene, accordingly, was almost the only one which reconciled him to the extraordinary change in his life. There she sat, the lively old lady; very deaf, as you could almost divine by that vivid inquiring twinkle in her eyes; feeble too, for she had a silver-headed cane beside her chair, and even with that assistance seldom moved across the room when she could help it. Feeble in body, but alert in mind, ready to read anything, to hear anything, to deliver her opinions freely; resting in her big chair in the complete repose of age, gratified with her son's attentions, and overjoyed in his company; interested about everything, and as ready to enter into all the domestic concerns of the new people as if she had lived all her life among them. The Rector sighed and smiled as he listened to his mother's questions, and did his best, at the top of his voice, to enlighten her. His mother was, let us say, a hundred years or so younger than the Rector. If she had been his bride, and at the blithe commencement of life, she could not have shown more inclination to know all about Carlingford. Mr Proctor was middle-aged, and preoccupied by right of his years; but his mother had long ago got over that stage of life. She was at that point when some energetic natures, having got to the bottom of the hill, seem to make a fresh start and reascend. Five years ago, old Mrs Proctor had completed the human term; now she had recommenced her life.

But, to tell the very truth, the Rector would very fain, had that been possible, have confined her inquiries to books and public affairs. For to make confidential disclosures, either concerning one's self or other people, in a tone of voice perfectly audible in the kitchen, is somewhat trying. He had become acquainted with those dread parishioners of his during this interval. Already they had worn him to death with dinner-parties—dinner-parties very pleasant and friendly, when one got used to them; but to a stranger frightful reproductions of each other, with the same dishes, the same dresses, the same stories, in which the Rector communicated gravely with his next neighbour, and eluded as long as he could those concluding moments in the drawing-room, which were worst of all. It cannot be said that his parishioners made much progress in their knowledge of the Rector. What his 'views' were, nobody could divine any more than they could before his arrival. He made no innovations whatever; but he did not pursue Mr Bury's Evangelical ways,* and never preached a sermon or a word more than was absolutely necessary. When zealous Churchmen discussed the progress of Dissent, the Rector scarcely looked interested; and nobody could move him to express an opinion concerning all that lovely upholstery with which Mr Wentworth had decorated St Roque's. People asked in vain, what was he? He was neither High nor Low, enlightened nor narrow-minded; he was a Fellow of All-Souls.

'But now tell me, my dear,' said old Mrs Proctor, 'who's Mr Wodehouse?'

With despairing calmness, the Rector approached his voice to her ear. 'He's a churchwarden!' cried the unfortunate man, in a shrill whisper.

'He's what?—you forget I don't hear very well. I'm a great deal deafer, Morley, my dear, than I was the last time you were in Devonshire. What did you say Mr Wodehouse was?'

'He's an ass!' exclaimed the baited Rector.

Mrs Proctor nodded her head with a great many little satisfied assenting nods.

'Exactly my own opinion, my dear. What I like in your manner of expressing yourself, Morley, is its conciseness,' said the laughing old lady. 'Just so—exactly what I imagined; but being an ass, you know, doesn't account for him coming here so often. What is he besides, my dear?'

The Rector made spasmodic gestures towards the door, to the great amusement of his lively mother; and then produced, with much confusion and after a long search, his pocketbook, on a leaf of paper in which he wrote—loudly, in big characters—'He's a churchwarden—they'll hear in the kitchen.'

'He's a churchwarden! And what if they do hear in the kitchen?' cried the old lady, greatly amused; 'it isn't a sin. Well, now, let me hear: has he a family, Morley?'

Again Mr Proctor showed a little discomposure. After a troubled look at the door, and pause, as if he meditated a remonstrance, he changed his mind, and answered, 'Two daughters!' shouting sepulchrally into his mother's ear.

'Oh so!' cried the old lady—'*two daughters*—so, so—that explains it all at once. I know now why he comes to the

Rectory so often. And, I declare, I never thought of it before. Why, you're always there!—so, so—and he's got *two daughters*, has he? To be sure; now I understand it all.'

The Rector looked helpless and puzzled. It was difficult to take the initiative and ask why—but the poor man looked so perplexed and ignorant, and so clearly unaware what the solution was, that the old lady burst into shrill, gay laughter as she looked at him.

'I don't believe you know anything about it,' she said. 'Are they old or young? are they pretty or ugly? Tell me all about them, Morley.'

Now Mr Proctor had not the excuse of having forgotten the appearance of the two Miss Wodehouses: on the contrary, though not an imaginative man, he could have fancied he saw them both before him—Lucy lost in noiseless laughter, and her good elder sister deprecating and gentle as usual. We will not even undertake to say that a gleam of something blue did not flash across the mind of the good man, who did not know what ribbons were. He was so much bewildered that Mrs Proctor repeated her question, and, as she did so, tapped him pretty smartly on the arm to recall his wandering thoughts.

'One's one thing,' at last shouted the confused man, 'and t'other's another!' An oracular deliverance which surely must have been entirely unintelligible in the kitchen, where we will not deny that an utterance so incomprehensible awoke a laudable curiosity.

'My dear, you're lucid!' cried the old lady. 'I hope you don't preach like that. T'other's another!—is she so? and I suppose that's the one you're wanted to marry—eh? For shame, Morley, not to tell your mother!'

The Rector jumped to his feet, thunderstruck. Wanted to marry!—the idea was too overwhelming and dreadful—his mind could not receive it. The air of alarm which immediately diffused itself all over him—his unfeigned horror at the suggestion—captivated his mother. She was amused, but she was pleased at the same time. Just making her cheery outset on this second lifetime, you can't suppose she would have been glad to hear that her son was going to jilt her, and appoint another queen in her stead.

'Sit down and tell me about them,' said Mrs Proctor; 'my dear, you're wonderfully afraid of the servants hearing. They don't know who we're speaking of. Aha! and so you didn't know what they meant—didn't you? I don't say you shouldn't marry, my dear—quite the reverse. A man *ought* to marry, one time or another. Only it's rather soon to lay their plans. I don't doubt there's a great many unmarried ladies in your church, Morley. There always is in a country place.'

To this the alarmed Rector answered only by a groan—a groan so expressive that his quick-witted mother heard it with her eyes.

'They will come to call on me,' said Mrs Proctor, with fun dancing in her bright old eyes. 'I'll tell you all about them, and you needn't be afraid of the servants. Trust to me, my dear— I'll find them out. And now, if you wish to take a walk, or go out visiting, don't let me detain you, Morley. I shouldn't wonder but there's something in the papers I would like to see—or I even might close my eyes for a few minutes: the afternoon is always a drowsy time with me. When I was in Devonshire, you know, no one minded what I did. You had better refresh yourself with a nice walk, my dear boy.'

The Rector got up well pleased. The alacrity with which he left the room, however, did not correspond with the horror-stricken and helpless expression of his face, when, after walking very smartly all round the Rectory garden, he paused with his hand on the gate, doubtful whether to retreat into his study, or boldly to face that world which was plotting against him. The question was a profoundly serious one to Mr Proctor. He did not feel by any means sure that he was a free agent, or could assert the ordinary rights of an Englishman, in this most unexpected dilemma. How could he tell how much or how little was necessary to prove that a man had 'committed himself?' For anything he could tell, somebody might be calculating upon him as her lover, and settling his future life for him. The Rector was not vain—he did not think himself an Adonis; he did not understand anything about the matter, which indeed was beneath the consideration of a Fellow of All-Souls. But have not women been incomprehensible since ever there was in this world a pen with sufficient command of words to call them so? And is it not certain that, whether it may be to their advantage or disadvantage, every soul of them is plotting to marry somebody? Mr Proctor recalled in dim but frightful reminiscences stories which had dropped upon his ear at various times of his life. Never was there a man, however ugly, disagreeable, or penniless, but he could tell of a narrow escape he had, some time or other. The Rector recollected and trembled. No woman was ever so dismayed by the persecutions of a lover, as was this helpless middle-aged gentleman under the conviction that Lucy Wodehouse meant to marry him. The remembrance of the curate of St Roque's gave him no comfort: her sweet youth, so totally unlike his sober age, did not strike him as unfavourable to her pursuit of him. Who could fathom the motives of a woman? His mother was wise, and knew the world, and understood what such creatures meant. No doubt it was entirely the case—a dreadful certainty—and what was he to do?

At the bottom of all this fright and perplexity must it be owned that the Rector had a guilty consciousness within himself, that if Lucy drove the matter to extremities, he was not so sure of his own powers of resistance as he ought to be? She might marry him before he knew what he was about; and in such a case the Rector could not have taken his oath at his own private confessional that he would have been so deeply miserable as the circumstances might infer. No wonder he was alarmed at the position in which he found himself; nobody could predict how it might end.

When Mr Proctor saw his mother again at dinner, she was evidently full of some subject which would not bear talking of before the servants. The old lady looked at her son's troubled apprehensive face with smiles and nods and gay hints, which he was much too preoccupied to understand, and which only increased his bewilderment. When the good man was left alone over his glass of wine, he drank it slowly, in funereal silence, with profoundly serious looks; and what between eagerness to understand what the old lady meant, and reluctance to show the extent of his curiosity, had a very heavy half-hour of it in that grave solitary dining-room. He roused himself with an effort from this dismal state into which he was falling. He recalled with a sigh the classic board of All-Souls. Woe for the day when he was seduced to forsake that dear retirement! Really, to suffer himself to fall into a condition so melancholy, was far from being right. He must rouse himself—he must find some other society than parishioners; and with a glimpse of a series of snug little dinner-parties, undisturbed by the presence of women, Mr Proctor rose and hurried after his mother, to hear what new thing she might have to say.

Nor was he disappointed. The old lady was snugly posted, ready for a conference. She made lively gestures to hasten him when he appeared at the door, and could scarcely delay the utterance of her news till he had taken his seat beside her. She had taken off her spectacles, and laid aside her paper, and cleared off her work into her work-basket. All was ready for the talk in which she delighted.

'My dear, they've been here,' said old Mrs Proctor, rubbing her hands—'both together, and as kind as could be—exactly as I expected. An old woman gets double the attention when she's got an unmarried son. I've always observed that; though in Devonshire, what with your fellowship and seeing you so seldom, nobody took much notice. Yes, they've been here; and I like them a great deal better than I expected, Morley, my dear.'

The Rector, not knowing what else to say, shouted 'Indeed, mother!' into the old lady's ear.

'Quite so,' continued that lively observer—'nice young women—not at all like their father, which is a great consolation. That elder one is a very sensible person, I am sure. She would make a nice wife for somebody, especially for a clergyman. She is not in her first youth, but neither are some other people. A very nice creature indeed, I am quite sure.'

During all this speech the Rector's countenance had been falling, falling. If he was helpless before, the utter woe of his expression now was a spectacle to behold. The danger of being married by proxy was appalling certainly, yet was not entirely without alleviations; but Miss Wodehouse! who ever thought of Miss Wodehouse? To see the last remains of colour fade out of his cheek, and his very lip fall with disappointment, was deeply edifying to his lively old mother. She perceived it all, but made no sign.

'And the other is a pretty creature—certainly pretty: shouldn't you say she was pretty, Morley?' said his heartless mother.

Mr Proctor hesitated, hemmed—felt himself growing red—tried to intimate his sentiments by a nod of assent; but that would not do, for the old lady had presented her ear to him, and was blind to all his gestures.

'I don't know much about it, mother,' he made answer at last.

'*Much* about it! it's to be hoped not. I never supposed you did; but you don't mean to say you don't think her pretty?' said Mrs Proctor—'but, I don't doubt in the least, a sad flirt. Her sister is a very superior person, my dear.'

The Rector's face lengthened at every word—a vision of these two Miss Wodehouses rose upon him every moment clearer and more distinct as his mother spoke. Considering how ignorant he was of all such female paraphernalia, it is extraordinary how correct his recollection was of all the details of their habitual dress and appearance. With a certain dreadful consciousness of the justice of what his mother said, he saw in imagination the mild elder sister in her comely old-maidenhood. Nobody could doubt her good qualities, and could it be questioned that for a man of fifty, if he was to do anything so foolish, a woman not quite forty was a thousand times more eligible than a creature in blue ribbons? Still the unfortunate Rector did not seem to see it: his face grew longer and longer—he made no answer whatever to his mother's address; while she, with a spice of natural female malice against the common enemy triumphing for the moment over the mother's admiration of her son, sat wickedly enjoying his distress, and aggravating it. His dismay and perplexity amused this wicked old woman beyond measure.

'I have no doubt that younger girl takes a pleasure in deluding her admirers,' said Mrs Proctor; 'she's a wicked little flirt, and likes nothing better than to see her power. I know very well how such people do; but, my dear,' continued this false old lady, scarcely able to restrain her laughter, 'if I were you, I would be very civil to Miss Wodehouse. You may depend upon it, Morley, that's a very superior person. She is not very young, to be sure, but you are not very young yourself. She would make a nice wife—not too foolish, you know, nor fanciful. Ah! I like Miss Wodehouse, my dear.'

The Rector stumbled up to his feet hastily, and pointed to a table at a little distance, on which some books were lying. Then he went and brought them to her table. 'I've brought you some new books,' he shouted into her ear. It was the only way his clumsy ingenuity could fall upon for bringing this most distasteful conversation to an end.

The old lady's eyes were dancing with fun and a little mischief, but, notwithstanding, she could not be so false to her nature as to show no interest in the books. She turned them over with lively remarks and comment. 'But for all that, Morley, I would not have you forget Miss Wodehouse,' she said, when her early bedtime came. 'Give it a thought now and then, and consider the whole matter. It is not a thing to be done rashly; but still you know you are settled now, and you ought to be thinking of settling for life.'

With this parting shaft she left him. The troubled Rector, instead of sitting up to his beloved studies, went early to bed that night, and was pursued by nightmares through his unquiet slumbers. Settling for life! Alas! there floated before him vain visions of that halcyon world he had left—that sacred soil at All-Souls, where there were no parishioners to break the sweet repose. How different was this discomposing real world!

CHAPTER III

MATTERS went on quietly for some time without any catastrophe occurring to the Rector. He had shut himself up from all society, and declined the invitations of the parishioners for ten long days at least; but finding that the kind people were only kinder than ever when they understood he was 'indisposed,' poor Mr Proctor resumed his ordinary life, confiding timidly in some extra precautions which his own ingenuity had invented. He was shyer than ever of addressing the ladies in those parties he was obliged to attend. He was especially embarrassed and uncomfortable in the presence of the two Miss Wodehouses, who, unfortunately, were very popular in Carlingford, and whom he could not help meeting everywhere. Notwithstanding this embarrassment, it is curious how well he knew how they looked, and what they were doing, and all about them. Though he could not for his life have told what these things were called, he knew Miss Wodehouse's dove-coloured* dress and her French grey, and all those gleams of blue which set off Lucy's fair curls, and floated about her pretty person under various pretences, had a distinct though inarticulate place in the good man's confused remembrance. But neither Lucy nor Miss Wodehouse had brought matters to extremity. He even ventured to go to their house occasionally without any harm coming of it, and lingered in that blooming fragrant garden, where the blossoms had given place to fruit, and ruddy apples hung heavy on the branches which had once scattered their petals, rosy-white, on Frank Wentworth's Anglican coat. Yet Mr Proctor was not lulled into incaution by this seeming calm. Other people besides his mother had intimated to him that there were expectations current of his 'settling in life.' He lived not in false security, but wise trembling, never knowing what hour the thunderbolt might fall upon his head.

It happened one day, while still in this condition of mind, that the Rector was passing through Grove Street on his way

home. He was walking on the humbler side of the street, where
there is a row of cottages with little gardens in front of them—
cheap houses, which are contented to be haughtily overlooked
by the staircase windows and blank walls of their richer
neighbours on the other side of the road. The Rector thought,
but could not be sure, that he had seen two figures like those of
the Miss Wodehouses going into one of these houses, and was
making a little haste to escape meeting those enemies of his
peace. But as he went hastily on, he heard sobs and screams—
sounds which a man who hid a good heart under a shy exterior
could not willingly pass by. He made a troubled pause before
the door from which these outcries proceeded, and while he
stood thus irresolute whether to pass on or to stop and inquire
the cause, some one came rushing out and took hold of his arm.
'Please, sir, she's dying—oh, please, sir, she thought a deal o'
you. Please, will you come in and speak to her?' cried the little
servant-girl who had pounced upon him so. The Rector stared
at her in amazement. He had not his prayer-book—he was not
prepared; he had no idea of being called upon in such an
emergency. In the mean time the commotion rather increased in
the house, and he could hear in the distance a voice adjuring
some one to go for the clergyman. The Rector stood uncertain
and perplexed, perhaps in a more serious personal difficulty
than had ever happened to him all his life before. For what did
he know about deathbeds? or what had he to say to any one on
that dread verge? He grew pale with real vexation and distress.

'Have they gone for a doctor? that would be more to the
purpose,' he said, unconsciously, aloud.

'Please, sir, it's no good,' said the little maid-servant. 'Please,
the doctor's been, but he's no good—and she's unhappy in her
mind, though she's quite resigned to go: and oh, please, if you
would say a word to her, it might do her a deal of good.'

Thus adjured, the Rector had no choice. He went gloomily
into the house and up the stairs after his little guide. Why did
not they send for the minister of Salem Chapel close by? or
for Mr Wentworth, who was accustomed to that sort of thing?
Why did they resort to him in such an emergency? He would
have made his appearance before the highest magnates of the

land—before the Queen herself—before the bench of bishops
or the Privy Council—with less trepidation than he entered
that poor little room.

The sufferer lay breathing heavily in the poor apartment.
She did not look very ill to Mr Proctor's inexperienced eyes.
Her colour was bright, and her face full of eagerness. Near the
door stood Miss Wodehouse, looking compassionate but
helpless, casting wistful glances at the bed, but standing back
in a corner as confused and embarrassed as the Rector himself.
Lucy was standing by the pillow of the sick woman with a
watchful readiness visible to the most unskilled eye—ready to
raise her, to change her position, to attend to her wants almost
before they were expressed. The contrast was wonderful.* She
had thrown off her bonnet and shawl, and appeared, not like
a stranger, but somehow in her natural place, despite the
sweet youthful beauty of her looks, and the gay girlish dress
with its floating ribbons. These singular adjuncts notwithstanding, no homely nurse in a cotton gown could have looked
more alert or serviceable, or more natural to the position, than
Lucy did. The poor Rector, taking the seat which the little
maid placed for him directly in the centre of the room, looked
at the nurse and the patient with a gasp of perplexity and
embarrassment. A deathbed, alas! was an unknown region to
him.

'Oh, sir, I'm obliged to you for coming—oh, sir, I'm grateful
to you,' cried the poor woman in the bed. 'I've been ill, off
and on, for years, but never took thought to it as I ought. I've
put off and put off, waiting for a better time—and now, God
help me, it's perhaps too late. Oh, sir, tell me, when a person's
ill and dying is it too late?'

Before the Rector could even imagine what he could answer,
the sick woman took up the broken thread of her own words,
and continued—

'I don't feel no trust as I ought to—I don't feel no
confidence,' she said, in anxious confession. 'Oh, sir, do you
think it matters if one feels it?—don't you think things might
be right all the same though we *were* uneasy in our minds? My
thinking can't change it one way or another. Ask the good

gentleman to speak to me, Miss Lucy, dear—he'll mind what *you* say.'

A look from Lucy quickened the Rector's speech, but increased his embarrassments. 'It—it isn't her doctor she has no confidence in?' he said, eagerly.

The poor woman gave a little cry. 'The doctor—the doctor! what can he do to a poor dying creature? Oh; Lord bless you, it's none of them things I'm thinking of; it's my soul—my soul!'

'But my poor good woman,' said Mr Proctor, 'though it is very good and praiseworthy of you to be anxious about your soul, let us hope that there is no such—no such *haste* as you seem to suppose.'

The patient opened her eyes wide, and stared, with the anxious look of disease, in his face.

'I mean,' said the good man, faltering under that gaze, 'that I see no reason for your making yourself so very anxious. Let us hope it is not so bad as that. You are very ill, but not *so* ill—I suppose.'

Here the Rector was interrupted by a groan from the patient, and by a troubled, disapproving, disappointed look from Lucy Wodehouse. This brought him to a sudden standstill. He gazed for a moment helplessly at the poor woman in the bed. If he had known anything in the world which would have given her consolation, he was ready to have made any exertion for it; but he knew nothing to say—no medicine for a mind diseased was in his repositories. He was deeply distressed to see the disappointment which followed his words, but his distress only made him more silent, more helpless, more inefficient than before.

After an interval which was disturbed only by the groans of the patient and the uneasy fidgeting of good Miss Wodehouse in her corner, the Rector again broke silence. The sick woman had turned to the wall, and closed her eyes in dismay and disappointment—evidently she had ceased to expect anything from him.

'If there is anything I can do,' said poor Mr Proctor, 'I am afraid I have spoken hastily. I meant to try to calm her mind a little; if I can be of any use?'

'Ah, maybe I'm hasty,' said the dying woman, turning round again with a sudden effort—'but, oh, to speak to me of having time when I've one foot in the grave already!'

'Not so bad as that—not so bad as that,' said the Rector, soothingly.

'But I tell you it is as bad as that,' she cried, with the brief blaze of anger common to great weakness. 'I'm not a child to be persuaded different from what I know. If you'd tell me—if you'd say a prayer—ah, Miss Lucy, it's coming on again.'

In a moment Lucy had raised the poor creature in her arms, and in default of the pillows which were not at hand, had risen herself into their place, and supported the gasping woman against her own breast. It was a paroxysm dreadful to behold, in which every labouring breath seemed the last. The Rector sat like one struck dumb, looking on at that mortal struggle. Miss Wodehouse approached nervously from behind, and went up to the bedside, faltering forth questions as to what she could do. Lucy only waved her hand, as her own light figure swayed and changed, always seeking the easiest attitude for the sufferer. As the elder sister drew back, the Rector and she glanced at each other with wistful mutual looks of sympathy. Both were equally well-disposed, equally helpless and embarrassed. How to be of any use in that dreadful agony of nature was denied to both. They stood looking on, awed and self-reproaching. Such scenes have doubtless happened in sick-rooms before now.

When the fit was over, a hasty step came up the stair, and Mr Wentworth entered the room. He explained in a whisper that he had not been at home when the messenger came, but had followed whenever he heard of the message. Seeing the Rector, he hesitated, and drew back with some surprise, and, even (for he was far from perfect) in that chamber, a little flush of offence. The Rector rose abruptly, waving his hand, and went to join Miss Wodehouse in her corner. There the two elderly spectators looked on silent at ministrations of which both were incapable; one watching with wondering yet affectionate envy how Lucy laid down the weakened but relieved patient upon her pillows; and one beholding with a surprise he could not conceal, how a young man, not half his own age, went softly, with all the confidence yet awe of nature, into those mysteries which he dared not touch upon. The two young creatures by the deathbed acknowledged that their patient was dying; the woman stood by her watchful and affectionate—the man held up before her that cross, not of wood or metal, but of truth and everlasting verity, which is the only hope of man. The spectators looked on, and did not interrupt—looked on, awed and wondering—unaware of how it was, but watching as if it were a miracle wrought before their eyes. Perhaps all the years of his life had not taught the Rector so much as did that half-hour in an unknown poor bed-chamber, where, honest and humble, he stood aside, and, kneeling down, responded to his young brother's prayer. His young brother—young enough to have been his son—not half nor a quarter part so learned as he; but a world further on in that profession which they shared—the art of winning souls.

When those prayers were over, the Rector, without a word to anybody, stole quietly away. When he got into the street, however, he found himself closely followed by Miss Wodehouse, of whom he was not at this moment afraid. That good creature was crying softly under her veil. She was eager to make up to him, to open out her full heart; and indeed the Rector, like herself, in that wonderful sensation of surprised and unenvying discomfiture, was glad at that moment of sympathy too.

'Oh, Mr Proctor, isn't it wonderful?' sighed good Miss Wodehouse.

The Rector did not speak, but he answered by a very emphatic nod of his head.

'It did not use to be so when you and I were young,' said his companion in failure. 'I sometimes take a little comfort from that; but no doubt, if it had been in me, it would have shown itself somehow. Ah, I fear, I fear, I was not well brought up; but, to be sure, that dear child has not been brought up at all, if one may say so. Her poor mother died when she was born. And oh, I'm afraid I never was kind to Lucy's mother, Mr Proctor. You know she was only a year or

two older than I was; and to think of that child, that baby!
What a world she is, and always was, before me, that might
have been her mother, Mr Proctor!' said Miss Wodehouse,
with a little sob.

'But things were different in our young days,' said
the Rector, repeating her sentiment, without inquiring
whether it were true or not, and finding a certain vague
consolation in it.

'Ah, that is true,' said Miss Wodehouse—'that is true; what
a blessing things are so changed; and these blessed young
creatures,' she added softly, with tears falling out of her gentle
old eyes—'these blessed young creatures are near the
Fountainhead.'

With this speech Miss Wodehouse held out her hand to the
Rector, and they parted with a warm mutual grasp. The
Rector went straight home—straight to his study, where he
shut himself in, and was not to be disturbed; that night was
one long to be remembered in the good man's history. For the
first time in his life he set himself to inquire what was his
supposed business in this world. His treatise on the Greek
verb, and his new edition of Sophocles, were highly creditable
to the Fellow of All-Souls; but how about the Rector of
Carlingford? What was he doing here, among that little world
of human creatures who were dying, being born, perishing,
suffering, falling into misfortune and anguish, and all manner
of human vicissitudes, every day? Young Wentworth knew
what to say to that woman in her distress; and so might the
Rector, had her distress concerned a disputed translation, or
a disused idiom. The good man was startled in his composure
and calm. To-day he had visibly failed in a duty which even
in All-Souls was certainly known to be one of the duties of a
Christian priest. Was he a Christian priest, or what was he?
He was troubled to the very depths of his soul. To hold an
office the duties of which he could not perform, was clearly
impossible. The only question, and that a hard one, was,
whether he could learn to discharge those duties, or whether
he must cease to be Rector of Carlingford. He laboured over
this problem in his solitude, and could find no answer.

'Things were different when we were young,' was the only thought that was any comfort to him, and that was poor consolation.

For one thing, it is hard upon the most magnanimous of men to confess that he has undertaken an office for which he has not found himself capable. Magnanimity was perhaps too lofty a word to apply to the Rector; but he was honest to the bottom of his soul. As soon as he became aware of what was included in the duties of his office, he must perform them, or quit his post. But how to perform them? Can one *learn* to convey consolation to the dying, to teach the ignorant, to comfort the sorrowful? Are these matters to be acquired by study, like Greek verbs or intricate measures? The Rector's heart said No. The Rector's imagination unfolded before him, in all its halcyon blessedness, that ancient paradise of All-Souls, where no such confounding demands ever disturbed his beatitude. The good man groaned within himself over the mortification, the labour, the sorrow, which this living was bringing upon him. 'If I had but let it pass to Morgan, who wanted to marry,'* he said with self-reproach; and then suddenly bethought himself of his own most innocent filial romance, and the pleasure his mother had taken in her new house and new beginning of life. At that touch the tide flowed back again. Could he dismiss her now to another solitary cottage in Devonshire, her old home there being all dispersed and broken up, while the house she had hoped to die in cast her out from its long-hoped-for shelter? The Rector was quite overwhelmed by this new aggravation. If by any effort of his own, any sacrifice to himself, he could preserve this bright new home to his mother, would he shrink from that labour of love?

Nobody, however, knew anything about those conflicting thoughts which rent his sober bosom. He preached next Sunday as usual, letting no trace of the distressed, wistful anxiety to do his duty which now possessed him gleam into his sermon. He looked down upon a crowd of unsympathetic, uninterested faces, when he delivered that smooth little sermon, which nobody cared much about, and which disturbed

nobody. The only eyes which in the smallest degree com-
prehended him were those of good Miss Wodehouse, who
had been the witness and the participator of his humiliation.
Lucy was not there. Doubtless Lucy was at St Roque's, where
the sermons of the perpetual curate differed much from those
of the Rector of Carlingford. Ah me! the rectorship, with all
its responsibilities, was a serious business; and what was to
become of it yet, Mr Proctor could not see. He was not a hasty
man—he determined to wait and see what events might make
of it; to consider it ripely—to take full counsel with himself.
Every time he came out of his mother's presence, he came
affected and full of anxiety to preserve to her that home which
pleased her so much. She was the strong point in favour of
Carlingford; and it was no small tribute to the good man's
filial affection, that for her chiefly he kept his neck under the
yoke of a service to which he knew himself unequal, and
sighing, turned his back upon his beloved cloisters. If there
had been no other sick-beds immediately in Carlingford, Mrs
Proctor would have won the day.

CHAPTER IV

SUCH a blessed exemption, however, was not to be hoped
for. When the Rector was solemnly sent for from his very
study to visit a poor man who was not expected to live many
days, he put his prayer-book under his arm, and went off
doggedly, feeling that now was the crisis. He went through it
in as exemplary a manner as could have been desired, but it
was dreadful work to the Rector. If nobody else suspected
him, he suspected himself. He had no spontaneous word of
encouragement or consolation to offer; he went through
it as his duty with a horrible abstractness. That night he
went home disgusted beyond all possible power of self-
reconciliation. He could not continue this. Good evangelical
Mr Bury, who went before him, and by nature loved preaching, had accustomed the people to much of such visitations.
It was murder to the Fellow of All-Souls.

That night Mr Proctor wrote a long letter to his dear cheery old mother, disclosing all his heart to her. It was written with a pathos of which the good man was wholly unconscious, and finished by asking her advice and her prayers. He sent it up to her next morning on her breakfast tray, which he always furnished with his own hands, and went out to occupy himself in paying visits till it should be time to see her, and ascertain her opinion. At Mr Wodehouse's there was nobody at home but Lucy, who was very friendly, and took no notice of that sad encounter which had changed his views so entirely. The Rector found, on inquiry, that the woman was dead, but not until Mr Wentworth had administered to her fully the consolations of the Church. Lucy did not look superior, or say anything in admiration of Mr Wentworth, but the Rector's conscience supplied all that was wanting. If good Miss Wodehouse had been there with her charitable looks, and her disefficiency so like his own, it would have been a consolation to the good man. He would have turned joyfully from Lucy and her blue ribbons to that distressed dove-coloured woman, so greatly had recent events changed him. But the truth was, he cared nothing for either of them nowadays. He was delivered from those whimsical distressing fears. Something more serious had obliterated those lighter apprehensions. He had no leisure now to think that somebody had planned to marry him; all his thoughts were fixed on matters so much more important that this was entirely forgotten.

Mrs Proctor was seated as usual in the place she loved, with her newspapers, her books, her work-basket, and silver-headed cane at the side of her chair. The old lady, like her son, looked serious. She beckoned him to quicken his steps when she saw him appear at the drawing-room door, and pointed to the chair placed beside her, all ready for this solemn conference. He came in with a troubled face, scarcely venturing to look at her, afraid to see the disappointment which he had brought upon his dearest friend. The old lady divined why it was he did not lift his eyes. She took his hand and addressed him with all her characteristic vivacity.

'Morley, what is this you mean, my dear? When did I ever

give my son reason to distrust me? Do you think I would suffer you to continue in a position painful to yourself for my sake? How dare you think such a thing of me, Morley? Don't say so; you didn't mean it? I can see it in your eyes.'

The Rector shook his head, and dropped into the chair placed ready for him. He might have had a great deal to say for himself could she have heard him. But as it was, he could not shout all his reasons and apologies into her deaf ear.

'As for the change to me,' said the old lady, instinctively seizing upon the heart of the difficulty, 'that's nothing—simply nothing. I've not had time to get attached to Carlingford. I've no associations with the place. Of course I shall be very glad to go back to all my old friends. Put that out of the question, Morley.'

But the Rector only shook his head once more. The more she made light of it, the more he perceived all the painful circumstances involved. Could his mother go back to Devonshire and tell all her old ladies that her son had made a failure in Carlingford? He grieved within himself at the thought. His brethren at All-Souls might understand *him;* but what could console the brave old woman for all the condolence and commiseration to which she would be subject? 'It goes to my heart, mother,' he cried in her ear.

'Well, Morley, I am very sorry you find it so,' said the old lady; 'very sorry you can't see your way to all your duties. They tell me the late rector was very Low Church, and visited about like a Dissenter, so it is not much wonder you, with your different habits, find yourself a good deal put out; but, my dear, don't you think it's only at first? Don't you think after a while the people would get into your ways, and you into theirs? Miss Wodehouse was here this morning, and was telling me a good deal about the late rector. It's to be expected you should find the difference; but by-and-by, to be sure, you might get used to it, and the people would not expect so much.'

'Did she tell you where we met the other day?' asked the Rector, with a brevity rendered necessary by Mrs Proctor's infirmity.

'She told me—she's a dear confused good soul,' said the old lady—'about the difference between Lucy and herself, and how the young creature was twenty times handier than she, and something about young Mr Wentworth of St Roque's. Really, by all I hear, that must be a very presuming young man,' cried Mrs Proctor, with a lively air of offence. 'His interference among your parishioners, Morley, is really more than I should be inclined to bear.'

Once more the good Rector shook his head. He had not thought of that aspect of the subject. He was indeed so free from vanity or self-importance, that his only feeling in regard to the sudden appearance of the perpetual curate was respect and surprise. He would not be convinced otherwise even now. 'He can do his duty, mother,' he answered, sadly.

'Stuff and nonsense!' cried the old lady, 'Do you mean to tell me a boy like that can do his duty better than my son could do it, if he put his mind to it? And if it is your duty, Morley, dear,' continued his mother, melting a little, and in a coaxing persuasive tone, 'of course I know you *will* do it, however hard it may be.'

'That's just the difficulty,' cried the Rector, venturing on a longer speech than usual, and roused to a point at which he had no fear of the listeners in the kitchen; 'such duties require other training than mine has been. I can't!—do you hear me, mother?—I must not hold a false position; that's impossible.'

'You shan't hold a false position,' cried the old lady; 'that's the only thing that *is* impossible—but, Morley, let us consider, dear. You are a clergyman, you know; you ought to understand all that's required of you a great deal better than these people do. My dear, your poor father and I trained you up to be a clergyman,' said Mrs Proctor, rather pathetically, 'and not to be a Fellow of All-Souls.'

The Rector groaned. Had it not been advancement, progress, unhoped-for good fortune, that made him a member of that learned corporation? He shook his head. Nothing could change the fact now. After fifteen years' experience of that Elysium, he could not put on the cassock and surplice with all his youthful fervour. He had settled into his life-habits long ago. With the quick perception which made up for her deficiency, his mother read his face, and saw the cause was hopeless; yet with female courage and pertinacity made one effort more.

'And with an excellent hard-working curate,' said the old lady—'a curate whom, of course, we'd do our duty by, Morley, and who could take a great deal of the responsibility off your hands; for Mr Leigh, though a nice young man, is not, I know, the man *you* would have chosen for such a post; and still more, my dear son—we were talking of it in jest not long ago, but it is perfect earnest, and a most important matter—with a good wife, Morley; a wife who would enter into all the parish work, and give you useful hints, and conduct herself as a clergyman's wife should—with such a wife——'

'Lucy Wodehouse!' cried the Rector, starting to his feet, and forgetting all his proprieties; 'I tell you the thing is impossible. I'll go back to All-Souls.'

He sat down again doggedly, having said it. His mother sat looking at him in silence, with tears in her lively old eyes. She was saying within herself that she had seen his father take such a 'turn,' and that it was no use arguing with them under such circumstances. She watched him as women often do watch men, waiting till the creature should come to itself again and might be spoken to. The incomprehensibleness of women is an old theory, but what is that to the curious wondering observation with which wives, mothers, and sisters watch the other unreasoning animal in those moments when he has snatched the reins out of their hands, and is not to be spoken to! What he will make of it in those unassisted moments, afflicts the compassionate female understanding. It is best to let him come to, and feel his own helplessness. Such was Mrs Proctor's conclusion, as, vexed, distressed, and helpless, she leant back in her chair, and wiped a few tears of disappointment and vexation out of her bright old eyes.

The Rector saw this movement, and it once more excited him to speech. 'But you shall have a house in Oxford, mother,' he cried—'you shan't go back to Devonshire—where

I can see you every day, and you can hear all that is going on. Bravo! that will be a thousand times better than Carlingford.'

It was now Mrs Proctor's turn to jump up, startled, and put her hand on his mouth and point to the door. The Rector did not care for the door; he had disclosed his sentiments, he had taken his resolution, and now the sooner all was over the better for the emancipated man.

Thus concluded the brief incumbency of the Reverend Morley Proctor. He returned to Oxford before his year of grace was over, and found everybody very glad to see him; and he left Carlingford with universal good wishes. The living fell to Morgan, who wanted to be married, and whose turn was much more to be a working clergyman than a classical commentator. Old Mrs Proctor got a pretty house under shelter of the trees of St Giles's, and half the undergraduates fell in love with the old lady in the freshness of her second lifetime. Carlingford passed away like a dream from the lively old mother's memory, and how could any reminiscences of that uncongenial locality disturb the recovered beatitude of the Fellow of All-Souls?

Yet all was not so satisfactory as it appeared. Mr Proctor paid for his temporary absence. All-Souls was not the Elysium it had been before that brief disastrous voyage into the world. The good man felt the stings of failure; he felt the mild jokes of his brethren in those Elysian fields. He could not help conjuring up to himself visions of Morgan with his new wife in that pretty rectory. Life, after all, did not consist of books, nor were Greek verbs essential to happiness. The strong emotion into which his own failure had roused him; the wondering silence in which he stood looking at the ministrations of Lucy Wodehouse and the young curate; the tearful sympathetic woman as helpless as himself, who had stood beside him in that sick-chamber, came back upon his recollection strangely, amidst the repose, not so blessed as heretofore, of All-Souls. The good man had found out that secret of discontent which most men find out a great deal earlier than he. Something better, though it might be sadder, harder, more calamitous, was in this world. Was there ever human creature yet that had not something in him more congenial to the thorns and briars outside to be conquered, than to that mild paradise for which our primeval mother* disqualified all her children? When he went back to his dear cloisters, good Mr Proctor felt that sting: a longing for the work he had rejected stirred in him—a wistful recollection of the sympathy he had not sought.

And if in future years any traveller, if travellers still fall upon adventures, should light upon a remote parsonage in which an elderly embarrassed Rector, with a mild wife in dove-coloured dresses, toils painfully after his duty, more and more giving his heart to it, more and more finding difficult expression for the unused faculty, let him be sure that it is the late Rector of Carlingford, self-expelled out of the uneasy paradise, setting forth untimely, yet not too late, into the laborious world.

THE DOCTOR'S FAMILY

CHAPTER I

YOUNG Dr Rider lived in the new quarter of Carlingford: had he aimed at a reputation in society, he could not possibly have done a more foolish thing; but such was not his leading motive. The young man, being but young, aimed at a practice. He was not particular in the mean time as to the streets in which his patients dwelt. A new house, gazing with all its windows over a brick-field, was as interesting to the young surgeon as if it had been one of those exclusive houses in Grange Lane, where the aristocracy of Carlingford lived retired within their garden walls. His own establishment, though sufficiently comfortable, was of a kind utterly to shock the feelings of the refined community. A corner house, with a surgery round the corner, throwing the gleam of its red lamp over all that chaotic district of half-formed streets and full-developed brick-fields, with its night-bell prominent, and young Rider's name on a staring brass plate, with mysterious initials after it. M.R.C.S.* the unhappy young man had been seduced to put after his name upon that brass plate, though he was really Dr Rider, a physician, if not an experienced one. Friends had advised him that in such districts people were afraid of physicians, associating only with dread adumbrations of a guinea a visit that miscomprehended name; so, with a pang, the young surgeon had put his degree in his pocket, and put up with the inferior distinction. Of course, Dr Marjoribanks had all the patronage of Grange Lane.* The great people were infatuated about that snuffy old Scotchman—a man behind his day, who had rusted and grown old among the soft diseases of Carlingford, where sharp practice was so seldom necessary; and no opening appeared for young Rider except in the new district, in the snug corner house, with the surgery and the red lamp, and M.R.C.S. on a brass plate on his door.

If you can imagine that the young man bowed his spirit to this without a struggle, you do the poor young fellow injustice. He had been hard enough put to it at divers periods of his life. Ambition had not been possible for him either in one shape or another. Some people said he had a vulgar mind when he subsided into that house; other people declared him a shabby fellow when he found out, after the hardest night's thought he ever went through in his life, that he durst not ask Bessie Christian to marry him. You don't suppose that he did not know in his secret heart, and feel tingling through every vein, those words which nobody ever said to his face? But he could not help it. He could only make an indignant gulp of his resentment and shame, which were shame and resentment at himself for wanting the courage to dare everything, as well as at other people for finding him out, and go on with his work as he best could. He was not a hero nor a martyr; men made of that stuff have large compensations. He was an ordinary individual, with no sublimity in him, and no compensation to speak of for his sufferings—no consciousness of lofty right-doing, or of a course of action superior to the world.

Perhaps you would prefer to go up-stairs and see for your-self what was the skeleton in Edward Rider's cupboard, rather than have it described to you. His drag came to the door an hour ago, and he went off with Care sitting behind him, and a certain angry pang aching in his heart, which perhaps Bessie Christian's wedding-veil, seen far off in church yesterday, might have something to do with. His looks were rather black as he twitched the reins out of his little groom's hands, and went off at a startling pace, which was almost the only consolation the young fellow had. Now that he is certainly gone, and the coast clear, we may go up-stairs. It is true he all but kicked the curate down for taking a similar liberty, but we who are less visible may venture while he is away.

This skeleton is not in a cupboard. It is in an up-stairs room, comfortable enough, but heated, close, unwholesome—a place from which, even when the window is open, the fresh air seems shut out. There is no fresh air nor current of life in this stifling place. There is a fire, though it is not cold—a sofa near

the fire—a sickening heavy smell of abiding tobacco—not light
whiffs of smoke, such as accompany a man's labours, but a
dead pall of idle heavy vapour; and in the midst of all a man
stretched lazily on the sofa, with his pipe laid on the table
beside him, and a book in his soft, boneless, nerveless hands.
A large man, interpenetrated with smoke and idleness and a
certain dreary sodden dissipation, heated yet unexcited, reading a novel he has read half-a-dozen times before. He turns his
bemused eyes to the door when his invisible visitors enter. He
fancies he hears some one coming, but will not take the
trouble to rise and see who is there—so, instead of that
exertion, he takes up his pipe, knocks the ashes out of it upon
his book, fills it with coarse tobacco, and stretches his long
arm over the shoulder of the sofa for a light. His feet are in
slippers, his person clothed in a greasy old coat, his linen
soiled and untidy. That is the skeleton in young Rider's
house.*

The servants, you may be sure, knew all about this
unwelcome visitor. They went with bottles and jugs secretly
to bring him what he wanted; they went to the circulating
library for him; they let him in when he had been out in the
twilight all shabby and slovenly. They would not be human
if they did not talk about him. They say he is very good-
natured, poor gentleman—always has a pleasant word—is
nobody's enemy but his own; and to see how 'the doctor do
look at him, and he his own brother as was brought up with
him,' is dreadful, to be sure.

All this young Rider takes silently, never saying a word
about it to any human creature. He seems to know by intuition what all these people say of him, as he drives about
furiously in his drag from patient to patient; and wherever he
goes, as plain, nay, far more distinctly than the actual prospect
before him, he sees that sofa, that dusty slow-burning fire—
that pipe, with the little heap of ashes knocked out of it upon
the table—that wasted ruined life chafing him to desperation
with its dismal content. It is very true that it would have been
sadly imprudent of the young man to go to the little house in
Grove Street a year ago, and tell Bessie Christian he was very

fond of her, and that somehow for her love he would manage
to provide for those old people whom that cheerful little
woman toiled to maintain. It was a thing not to be done in any
way you could contemplate it; and with a heartache the poor
young doctor had turned his horse's head away from Grove
Street, and left Bessie to toil on in her poverty. Bessie had
escaped all that nowadays; but who could have forewarned the
poor doctor that his elder brother, once the hope of the
family—that clever Fred, whom all the others had been
postponed to—he who with his evil reputation had driven
poor Edward out of his first practice, and sent him to begin
life a second time at Carlingford—was to drop listlessly in
again, and lay a harder burden than a harmless old father-in-
law upon the young man's hands—a burden which no grateful
Bessie shared and sweetened? No wonder black Care sat at the
young doctor's back as he drove at that dangerous pace
through the new, encumbered streets. He might have broken
his neck over those heaps of brick and mortar, and it is
doubtful whether he would have greatly cared.

When Dr Rider went home that night, the first sight he saw
when he pulled up at his own door was his brother's large
indolent shabby figure prowling up the street. In the temper
he was then in, this was not likely to soothe him. It was not
a much-frequented street, but the young doctor knew instinctively that his visitor had been away in the heart of the town
at the bookseller's shops buying cheap novels, and ordering
them magnificently to be sent to Dr Rider's; and could guess
the curious questions and large answers which had followed.
He sprang to the ground with a painful suppressed
indignation, intensified by many mingled feelings, and waited
the arrival of the maudlin wanderer. Ah me! one might have
had some consolation in the burden freely undertaken for
love's sake, and by love's self shared and lightened: but this
load of disgrace and ruin which nobody could take part of—
which it was misery so much as to think that anybody knew
of—the doctor's fraternal sentiments, blunted by absence and
injury, were not strong enough to bear that weight.

'So, Fred, you have been out,' said Dr Rider moodily, as he

stood aside on his own threshold to let his brother pass in—not with the courtesy of a host, but the precaution of a jailer, to see him safe before he himself entered and closed the door.

'Yes, you can't expect a man to sit in the house for ever,' said the prodigal, stumbling in to his brother's favourite sitting-room, where everything was tidy and comfortable for the brief leisure of the hard-working man. The man who did no work threw himself heavily into the doctor's easy-chair, and rolled his bemused eyes round upon his brother's household gods. Those book-shelves with a bust at either corner, those red curtains drawn across the window, those prints on the walls—all once so pleasant to the doctor's eyes—took a certain air of squalor and wretchedness to-night which sickened him to look at. The lamp flared wildly with an untrimmed wick, or at least Dr Rider thought so; and threw a hideous profile of the intruder upon the wall behind him. The hearth was cold, with that chill, of sentiment rather than reality, naturally belonging to a summer night. Instead of a familiar place where rest and tranquillity awaited him, that room, the only vision of home which the poor young fellow possessed, hardened into four walls, and so many chairs and tables, in the doctor's troubled eyes.

But it bore a different aspect in the eyes of his maudlin brother. Looking round with those bewildered orbs, all this appeared luxury to the wanderer. Mentally he appraised the prints over the mantelshelf, and reckoned how much of *his* luxuries might be purchased out of them. That was all so much money wasted by the Crœsus* before him. What a mint of money the fellow must be making! and grudged a little comfort to his brother, his elder brother, the cleverest of the family! The dull exasperation of selfishness woke in the mind of the self-ruined man!

'You're snug enough here,' he exclaimed, 'though you shut me in up-stairs to burrow out of sight. By Jove! as if I were not good enough to face your Carlingford patients. I've had a better practice in my day than ever you'll see, my fine fellow, with you beggarly M.R.C.S. And you'd have me shut myself up in my garret into the bargain! You're ashamed of me, forsooth! You can go spending money on that rubbish there, and can't pay a tailor's bill for your elder brother; and as for introducing me in this wretched hole of a place, and letting me pick up a little money for myself—I, a man with twice the experience in the profession that you have——'

'Fred, stop that,' cried the doctor—'I've had about enough. Look here—I can't deny you shelter and what you call necessaries, because you're my brother; but I won't submit to be ruined a second time by any man. If I am ever to do any good in this world—and whether I do any good or not,' he added fiercely, 'I'll not have my good name tarnished and my work interfered with *again*. I don't care two straws for my life. It's hard enough—as hard as a treadmill, and never a drop of consolation in the cup; though I might have had that if I had been anything but a fool. But look here, I do care for my practice—I won't have you put your confounded spoke in my wheel again. Keep on in your own way; smoke and drink and dream if you will; but I'll stand no interference with my work—and that I tell you once for all.'

This speech was uttered with great vehemence, the speaker walking up and down the room all the while. The bitterness of ingratitude and malice had entered into the young man's soul. All the wrongs which the clever elder brother, to whose claims everybody else was subordinated, had done to his family, rose upon the recollection of the younger; all the still bitterer sting of that injury which had been personal to himself; all the burden and peril of this present undesired visit, the discontent, the threats, the evident power of doing evil, woke the temper and spirit of the young doctor. It was not Fred's fault that his brother had made that mistake in life which he repented so bitterly. Bessie Christian's bridal veil, and white ribbons; her joyful face untouched with any pensive reminiscences; and the dead dulness of that house, into which foot of woman never entered, were not of Fred's doing; but passion is not reasonable. The doctor gave Fred credit unconsciously for the whole. He walked up and down the room with a whole world of passionate mortified feeling—vexation, almost despair, throbbing within him. He seemed to have made a vast sacrifice for the sake of this brother who scorned him to his face.

'You're hot,' said the disreputable figure in Dr Rider's easy-chair, 'much hotter than there's any occasion for. Do I envy you your beggarly patients, do you suppose? But, Ned, you never were cut out for the profession—a good shopkeeping business would have been a deal better for you. Hang it! you haven't the notions of a gentleman. You think bread and water is all you're bound to furnish your brother when he's under a cloud. As for society, I never see a soul—not even yourself, though you're no great company. Look here—I am not unreasonable; order in some supper—there's a good fellow—and let's have a comfortable evening together. You're not the man you used to be, Ned. You used to be a fellow of spirit; somebody's jilted you, or something—I don't want to pry into your secrets; but let's have a little comfort for once in a way, and you shall have the whole business about the old colony, and how I came to leave it—the truth, and nothing but the truth.'

It was some time before the victim yielded; at last, half to escape the painful ferment of his own thoughts, and half with a natural yearning for some sympathy and companionship, however uncongenial, he fell out of his heat and passion into a more complacent mood. He sat down, watching with a gulp of hardly-restrained disgust that lolling figure in the chair, every gesture of which was the more distasteful for being so familiar, and recalling a hundred preliminary scenes all tending towards this total wreck and shame. Then his mind softened with fraternal instincts—strange interlacement of loathing and affection. He was tired, hungry, chilled to his heart. The spell of material comfort, even in such company, came upon the young man. They supped together, not much to the advantage of Dr Rider's head, stomach or temper, on the following morning. The elder told his story of inevitable failure, and strange unexplainable fatality. The younger dropped forth expressions of disappointment and trouble which partly eased his own mind. Thus they spent together the unlovely evening; and perhaps a few such nights would have done as much harm to the young doctor's practice as had he introduced his disreputable brother without more ado into the particular little world of Carlingford.

CHAPTER II

NEXT morning Dr Rider rose mightily vexed with himself, as was to be supposed. He was half an hour late for breakfast: he had a headache, his hand shook, and his temper was 'awful.' Before he was dressed, ominous knocks came to the door; and all feverish and troubled as he was, you may imagine that the prospect of the day's work before him did not improve his feelings, and that self-reproach, direst of tormentors, did not mend the matter. Two ladies were waiting for him, he was told when he went down-stairs—not to say sundry notes and messages in the ordinary way of business—two ladies who had brought two boxes with them, and asked leave to put them in the hall till they could see Dr Rider. The sight of this luggage in his little hall startled the doctor. Patients do not generally carry such things about with them. What did it mean? What could two ladies want with him? The young man felt his face burn with painful anticipations, a little shame, and much impatience. Probably the sister who adored Fred, and never could learn to believe that he was not unfortunate and a victim. This would be a climax to the occupation of his house.

As the poor doctor gloomily approached the door of the room in which he had spent last evening, he heard a little rustle and commotion not quite consistent with his expectations—a hum of voices and soft stir such as youthful womankind only makes. Then a voice entirely strange to him uttered an exclamation. Involuntarily he started and changed his aspect. He did not know the voice, but it was young, sweet, peculiar. The cloud lightened a little upon the doctor's face. Notwithstanding Bessie Christian, he was still young enough to feel a little flutter of curiosity when he heard such a voice sounding out of his room. Hark! what did she say? It was a profoundly prosaic speech.

'What an intolerable smell of smoke! I shouldn't wonder a bit—indeed, I rather think he must be, or he wouldn't live in a place like this—if he were exactly such another as Fred.'

'Poor Fred!' said a plaintive voice, 'if we only can learn where he is. Hush, there is a footstep! Ah, it is not my poor fellow's footstep! Nettie, hark!'

'No, indeed! twenty thousand times sharper, and more like a man,' said the other, in hurried breathless accents. 'Hark! here he is.'

The entire bewilderment, the amaze, apprehension, confusion with which Dr Rider entered the room from which this scrap of conversation reached him, is indescribable. A dreadful sense that something was about to happen seized the young man's mind with an indescribable curiosity. He paused an instant to recover himself, and then went boldly and silently into the room which had become mysterious through its new inmates. They both turned round upon him as he entered. Two young women: one who had been sitting at the table, looking faded, plaintive, and anxious, rose up suddenly, and, clasping her hands, as if in entreaty, fixed two bright but sunken eyes upon his face. The other, a younger, lighter figure, all action and haste, interposed between him and her companion. She put up one hand in warning to the petitioner behind her, and one to call the attention of the bewildered stranger before. Evidently the one thing which alarmed this young lady was that somebody would speak before her, and the conduct of the *situation* be taken out of her hands. She was little, very slight, very pretty, but her prettiness was peculiar. The young doctor, accustomed to the fair Saxon version of beauty given by Bessie Christian, did not at the first glance believe that the wonderful little person before him possessed any; for she was not only slender, but *thin*, dark, eager, impetuous, with blazing black eyes and red lips, and nothing else notable about her. So he thought, gazing fascinated, yet not altogether attracted—scarcely sure that he was not repelled —unable, however, to withdraw his eyes from that hurried, eager little figure. Nothing in the least like her had ever yet appeared before Dr Rider's eyes.

'We want to inquire about your brother,' said the little stranger; 'we know this was to be his address, and we want to know whether he is living here. His letters were to be sent to your care; but my sister has not heard from him now for a year.'

'Never mind that!—never mind telling that, Nettie,' cried the other behind her. 'Oh, sir! only tell me where my poor Fred is?'

'So she began to fear he was ill,' resumed the younger of the two, undauntedly; 'though Susan will do nothing but praise him, he has behaved to her very shamefully. Do you happen to know, sir, where he is?'

'Did you say Fred—my brother Fred?' cried the poor young doctor in utter dismay; 'and may I ask who it is that expresses so much interest in him?'

There was a momentary pause; the two women exchanged looks. 'I told you so,' cried the eager little spokeswoman. 'He never has let his friends know; he was afraid of that. I told you how it was. This,' she continued, with a little tragic air, stretching out her arm to her sister, and facing the doctor— 'this is Mrs Frederick Rider, or rather Mrs Rider, I should say, as he is the eldest of the family! Now will you please to tell us where he is?'

The doctor made no immediate answer. He gazed past the speaker to the faded woman behind, and exclaimed, with a kind of groan, 'Fred's wife!'

'Yes, Fred's wife,' cried the poor creature, rushing forward to him; 'and oh! where is he? I've come thousands of miles to hear. Is he ill? has anything happened to him? Where is Fred?'

'Susan, you are not able to manage this; leave it to me,' said her sister, drawing her back peremptorily. 'Dr Rider, please to answer us. We know you well enough, though you don't seem ever to have heard of us. It was you that my brother-in-law gave up his business to before he came out to the colony. Oh, we know all about it! To keep him separate from his wife cannot do you any benefit, Dr Edward. Yes, I know your name, and all about it; and I don't mean indeed to suffer my sister to be injured and kept from her husband. I have come all this way with her to take care of her. I mean to stay with her to take care of her. I have not parted with my money, though she gave all hers away; and I mean to see her have her rights.'

'Oh, Nettie, Nettie, how you talk!' cried the unfortunate wife. 'You keep him from answering me. All this time I cannot hear—where is Fred?'

'Be seated, please,' said the doctor, with dreadful civility, 'and compose yourselves. Fred is well enough; as well as he ever is. I don't know,' added poor Rider, with irrestrainable bitterness, 'whether he is quite presentable to ladies; but I presume, madam, if you're his wife, you're acquainted with his habits. Excuse me for being quite unprepared for such a visit. I have not much leisure for anything out of my profession. I can scarcely spare these minutes, that is the truth; but if you will favour me with a few particulars, I will have the news conveyed to my brother. I—I beg your pardon. When a man finds he has new relations he never dreamed of, it naturally embarrasses him at the moment. May I ask if you ladies have come from Australia alone?'

'Oh, not alone; the children are at the hotel. Nettie said it was no use coming unless we all came,' said his new sister-in-law, with a half-sob.

'The children!' Dr Rider's gasp of dismay was silent, and made no sound. He stood staring blankly at those wonderful invaders of his bachelor house, marvelling what was to be done with them in the first place. Was he to bring Fred down all slovenly and half-awakened? was he to leave them in possession of his private sanctuary? The precious morning moments were passing while he pondered, and his little groom fidgeted outside with a message for the doctor. While he stood irresolute, the indefatigable Nettie once more darted forward.

'Give me Fred's address, please,' said this managing woman. 'I'll see him, and prepare him for meeting Susan. He can say what he pleases to me; *I* don't mind it in the very least; but Susan of course must be taken care of. Now, look here, Dr Edward; Susan is your sister-in-law, and I am her sister. We don't want to occupy your time. I can manage everything;

but it is quite necessary in the first place that you should confide in me.'

'Confide!' cried the bewildered man. 'Fred is not under my authority. He is here in my house much against my will. He is in bed, and not fit to be awakened; and I am obliged to tell you simply, ladies,' said the unfortunate doctor, 'that my house has no accommodation for a family. If you will go back to the hotel where you left the children'—and here the speaker gave another gasp of horror—'I'll have him roused and sent to you. It is the only thing I can do.'

'Susan can go,' said the prompt Nettie; 'I'll stay here until Fred is ready, and take him to see them. It is necessary he should be prepared, you know. Don't talk nonsense, Susan—I shall stay here, and Dr Rider, of course, will call a cab for you.'

'But Nettie, Nettie dear, it isn't proper. I can't leave you all by yourself in a strange house,' remonstrated her sister.

'Don't talk such stuff; I am perfectly well able to take care of myself; I am not a London young lady,' said the courageous Nettie. 'It is perfectly unnecessary to say another word to me—I know my duty—I shall stay here.'

With which speech she seated herself resolutely in that same easy-chair which Fred had lolled in last night, took off her bonnet, for hats were not in these days, and shed off from her face, with two tiny hands, exquisite in shape if a little brown in colour, the great braids of dark brown silky hair which encumbered her little head. The gesture mollified Dr Rider in the most unaccountable way in spite of himself. The intolerable idea of leaving these two in his house became less intolerable, he could not tell how. And the little groom outside fairly knocked at the door in that softening moment with a message which could be delayed no longer. The doctor put his head out to receive the call, and looked in again perplexed and uncertain. Nettie had quite established herself in the easy-chair. She sat there looking with her bright eyes into the vacant air before her, in a pretty attitude of determination and readiness, beating her little foot on the carpet. Something whimsical, odd, and embarrassing about her position made it all the more piquant to the troubled eyes which, in spite of all their worldly wisdom, were still the eyes of a young man. He could not tell in the world what to say to her. To order that creature out of his house was simply impossible; to remain there was equally so; to leave them in possession of the field—what could the unfortunate young doctor do? One thing was certain, the impatient patient could no longer be neglected; and after a few minutes longer of bewildered uncertainty Dr Rider went off in the wildest confusion of mind, leaving his brother's unknown family triumphant in his invaded house.

To describe the feelings with which the unfortunate doctor went fasting about his day's work—the manner in which that scene returned to him after every visit he made—the continual succession in which wrath, dismay, alarm, bitter disgust with the falsehood of the brother who, no further gone than last night, had pretended to confide in him, but never breathed a syllable of this biggest unconcealable secret, swept through the mind of the victim; all culminating, however, in the softening of that moment, in the tiny figure, indomitable elf or fairy, shedding back with dainty fingers those soft abundant locks—would be impossible. The young man got through his work somehow, in a maze of confusion and excitement—angry excitement, indignant confusion, determination to yield nothing further, but to defend himself and his house once for all from the inroads of what he angrily pronounced in his own mind 'another man's family'—yet, withal, of curiosity and interest which gave zest greater than usual to the idea of going home. When he was able at last to turn his horse's head towards his own dwelling, it was with feelings very different from the usual unexpecting blank of sullen displeasure. What he should find there, was a curious, exciting, alarming question; perhaps an entire nursery with Nettie in charge; perhaps a recusant husband with Nettie mounting guard over him; perhaps a thrilling scene of family explanation and reconciliation. The day had been a specially long and hard one. He had been obliged to snatch a hurried lunch at one of his patient's houses, and to postpone his hard-earned dinner to the most fashionable of hours. It was indeed quite evening, almost twilight, when he made his way home at last. As he neared the scene of action, the tired man condoled with himself over the untimely excitement that awaited him. He said to himself with pathetic self-pity that it was hard indeed for a man who had earned a little repose to go in upon all the troubles of another man's family. He had denied himself—he had not undertaken upon his own shoulders that pleasing burden; and now what was he to be saddled with?—the burden without the consolation—the responsibility without the companionship. All this Dr Rider represented to himself very pathetically as he wended his homeward way. Yet it is astonishing, notwithstanding, with what alacrity he hastened upon that path, and how much the curiosity, the excitement, the dramatic stir and commotion made in his monotonous life by this entirely new unexpected incident, occupied his mind. With expectation highly roused, he drew up once more before his own house. It was surprising to him to see how exactly it looked like itself. The blinds half drawn down in the genteelest calm as they always were—no faces peeping at the windows—no marks of an arrival on the pavement, or in the composed countenance of Mary, who stood holding the door open for him. He went in with a little thrill of curiosity; the house was very quiet—dead-quiet in comparison with the commotion of his thoughts; so was the sitting-room where he had left Nettie resolutely planted in the easy-chair; there was nobody there now; the boxes were out of the hall, not a sound was to be heard in the house. He turned rather blankly on Mary, who was going away quite composedly, as if there was nothing which she wanted to tell or he to hear.

'Where is my brother and the ladies?' said the amazed doctor.

'They all went off to the 'otel, sir, as soon as Mr Rider came down-stairs,' said Mary, complacently. 'I assured Miss as it was the best thing she could do, sir, for that I was 'most sure you'd never have the children here,—as to be sure there wasn't no room neither,' said the doctor's factotum. 'As soon as Mr Frederick came down, she called a cab, did Miss, and took 'em both away.'

'Oh! so they're gone, are they?' said the doctor.

'Hours and hours ago,' answered Mary; 'dinner 'll be up in two minutes. But I wouldn't say much for the potatoes, sir. When a gentleman's irreg'lar, it's hard laws on the poor servants—nothink will keep, going on for two hours, and not take no harm; but all's quiet and comfortable in your room.'

And with this assurance, which she evidently thought a very grateful one, Mary went off to get the doctor's dinner. He walked to the end of the room, and then back again, with solemnity—then threw himself into that easy-chair. 'Blessed riddance!' said the doctor; but somehow he looked glum, wonderfully glum. There was no accounting for those blank looks of his; he who had been condoling with himself over the exciting scene he expected, so uncomfortable a conclusion to a long day's labour, how was it he did not look relieved when that scene was spared him? To tell the truth, when one has been expecting something to happen, of whatever description, and has been preparing one's courage, one's temper, one's fortitude, in anticipatory rehearsals—when one has placed one's self in the attitude of a martyr, and prepared to meet with fiery trials—it is mortifying, to say the least, when one finds all the necessities of the case disappear, and the mildest calm replace that tragical anticipation: the quiet falls blank upon the excited fancy. Of course Dr Rider was relieved; but it was with something mightily like disappointment that he leant back in his chair and knitted his brows at the opposite wall. Not for the world would he have acknowledged himself to be disappointed; but the calm was wonderfully monotonous after all those expectations. He was never so bored and sick of a night by himself. He tried to read, but reading did not occupy his mind. He grew furious over his charred chops and sodden potatoes. As for the tea Mary brought, he would have gladly pitched it at her by way of diversifying that blank evening with an incident. The contrast between what he had looked for, and what he had, was wonderful. How delicious this stillness should have been, this consciousness of having his house to himself, and nobody to interrupt his brief repose! But somehow it appears that human nature takes best with not having its wishes granted. It is indescribable how Dr Rider yawned—how dull he found his newspaper—how few books worth reading there were in the house—how slow the minutes ran on. If somebody had chosen to be ill that night, of all nights the best for such a purpose, the doctor would not have objected to such an interruption. Failing that, he went to bed early, dreadfully tired of his own society. Such were the wonderful results of that invasion so much dreaded, and that retreat so much hoped for. Perhaps his own society had never in his life been so distasteful to him before.

CHAPTER III

NEXT day Dr Rider audibly congratulated himself at breakfast upon having once more his house to himself—audibly, as if it were really necessary to give utterance to the thought before he could quite feel its force. A week before, if Fred had departed, however summarily, there can be no doubt that his brother's feelings of relief and comfort would have been unfeigned; now, however, he began to think the matter over, and to justify to himself his extraordinary sense of disappointment. As he poured out his own coffee with a sober face, his eye rested upon that easy-chair, which had been brought into such prominence in the history of the last two days. He kept looking at it as he sipped that gloomy coffee. Fred had faded from the great chair; his big image threw no shadow upon it. There sat a little fairy queen, tiny as Titania,* but dark as an elf of the East, putting up those two shapely tiny hands, brown and beautiful, to push aside the flood of hair, which certainly would have veiled her little figure all over, the doctor thought, had it been let down. Wonderful little sprite! She, no doubt, had dragged her plaintive sister over the seas—she it was that had forced her way into Edward Rider's house; taken her position in it, ousted the doctor; and she doubtless it was who swept the husband and wife out of it again, leaving no trace behind. Waking up from a little trance of musing upon this too interesting subject, Dr Rider suddenly raised himself into an erect position, body and mind, with an involuntary movement, as if to shake off the yoke of the enchantress. He reminded himself instinctively of his brother's falsehood and ingratitude. After throwing himself a most distasteful burden on Edward's charity for five long dreary months, the bugbear of the doctor's dreams, and heavy ever-recurring climax of his uncomfortable thoughts, here had Fred departed without a word of explanation or thanks, or even without saying good-bye. The doctor thought himself quite justified in being angry. He began to feel that the suspicious uneasiness which possessed him was equally natural and inevitable. Such a thankless, heartless departure was enough to put any man out. To imagine that Fred could be capable of it, naturally went to his brother's heart.

That day there was still no word of the party who had disappeared so mysteriously out of the doctor's house. Dr Rider went to his hard day's work vaguely expectant, feeling sure he must hear of them somehow, and more interested in hearing of them than was to be expected from his former low ebb of fraternal affection. When he returned and found still no letter, no message, the blank disappointment of the former night closed still more blankly upon him. When one is all by one's self, and has nothing at best but an easy-chair to go home to, and goes home expecting a letter, or a message, or a visitor who has not arrived, and has no chance of arriving, the revulsion of feeling is not agreeable. It did not improve the doctor's temper in the first place. The chill loneliness of that trim room, with its drawn curtains and tidy pretence of being comfortable, exasperated him beyond bearing. He felt shut up in it, and yet would not leave it. Somebody certainly might come even to-night. Fred himself perhaps, if he could escape from the rigid guardianship he was under; or was that miraculous Australian Nettie a little witch, who had spirited the whole party in a nutshell over the seas? Never was man delivered from a burden with a worse grace than was Dr Rider; and the matter had not mended in these twenty-four hours.

Next morning, however, this fever of fraternal suspense was

assuaged. A three-cornered note, addressed in an odd feminine hand, very thin, small, and rapid, came among Dr Rider's letters. He signalled it out by instinct, and opened it with an impatience wonderful to behold.

'SIR,—We are all at the Blue Boar until we can get lodgings, which I hope to be to-day. I am utterly ashamed of Fred for not having let you know, and indeed of myself for trusting to him. I should not wonder but we may have been under a mistake about him and you. If you could call about one, I should most likely be in to see you, and perhaps you could give me your advice about the lodgings. Neither of *them* have the least judgment in such matters. I am sorry to trouble you; but being a stranger, perhaps you will excuse me. I understand you are only at home in the evening, and that is just the time I can't come out, as I have the whole of them to look to, which is the reason I ask you to call on me. Begging you will pardon me, I remain,

'NETTIE UNDERWOOD.'

'She remains Nettie Underwood,' said the doctor unawares. He laughed to himself at that conclusion. Then an odd gleam came across his face. It was probably the first time he had laughed in a natural fashion for some months back, and the unusual exertion made his cheeks tingle. His temper was improved that morning. He went off to his patients almost in a good humour. When he passed the great house where Bessie Christian now reigned, he recalled her image with a positive effort. Astonishing what an effect of distance had floated over the apparition of that bride. Was it a year since he saw her and gnashed his teeth at the thought of his own folly, or was it only last Sunday? The doctor could not tell. He put Nettie's note in his pocket-book, and was at the hotel door punctually at one o'clock. It was in the principal street of Carlingford, George Street, where all the best shops, and indeed some of the best houses, were. From the corner window of the hotel you could see down into the bowery seclusion of Grange Lane, and Mr Wodehouse's famous apple-trees holding tempting clusters over the high wall. The prospect was very different from that which extended before Dr Rider's window. Instinctively he marvelled within himself whether, if Dr Marjoribanks were to die—people cannot live for ever even in Carlingford—whether it might not be a disadvantage to a man to live so far out of the world. No doubt it was a temptation of the Evil One. Happily the young man did not take sufficient time to answer himself, but walked forward briskly through the mazy old passages of the old inn, to a room from which sundry noises issued. Dr Rider walked in with the natural confidence of a man who has an appointment. The room was in undisturbed possession of three children—three children making noise enough for six—all very small, very precocious, with staring round eyes and the most complete independence of speech and manners. The doctor confronted the little rabble thunderstruck; they were his brother's children, unrecognisable little savages as they were. One little fellow, in a linen pinafore, was mounted on the arm of a sofa, spurring vigorously; another was pursuing his sister about the room, trying to catch her feet with the tongs, and filling the air with repeated loud snaps of disappointment. They intermitted their occupations to stare at him. 'Look here—here's a man,' said the youngest, meditatively, beholding his dismayed uncle with a philosophic eye. 'Can't some one go and tell Nettie?' said the little girl, gazing also with calm equanimity. 'If he wants Nettie he'll have to wait,' said the elder boy. A pause followed; the unhappy doctor stood transfixed by the steady stare of their three pair of eyes. Suddenly the little girl burst out of the room, and ran screaming along the passage. 'Mamma, mamma, here's a man come,' cried the wonderful colonial child. A few minutes afterwards their mother appeared, languid and faded as before. Perhaps she had been even prettier than Nettie in her bright days, if any days had ever been bright for Fred Rider's wife. She was fairer, larger, smoother than her sister; but these advantages had lapsed in a general fade, which transformed her colour into washy pinkness, made her figure stoop, and her footsteps drag. She came remonstrating all the way in feeble accents. It was not for her, certainly, that the doctor had taken the trouble to come to the Blue Boar.

'Please to sit down,' said Mrs Fred, and stood leaning on the table, looking at her brother-in-law with a calm curiosity, not unlike that of her children. 'Nettie and my husband have gone out together; but now that we are all so happy and united,' she continued, with a sort of feeble spitefulness, 'I am sure it is quite a pity to trouble you. You could not take us in, you know. You said that very plain, Mr Edward.'

'It was perfectly true, madam,' said the doctor. 'I have not ventured on the step my brother has taken, and have naturally no accommodation for a family. But I am not here for my own pleasure. Your sister, I presume it is, wrote to me. I was requested to call here to-day.'

'Oh, yes; Nettie is very self-willed—very; though, of course, we could not get on without her. She attacked Fred like a wild-cat for not writing you: but I daresay, if the truth were known, you did not expect to hear from my husband,' said the wife, recovering her voice, and fixing a vindictive gaze upon her visitor, who felt himself betrayed.

'I came by Miss Underwood's instructions and at her request,' said the unfortunate man. 'We need not enter into any question between Fred and myself.'

'Ah, yes, that is very safe and wise for you,' laughed Fred's wife.

The doctor was deeply exasperated, as was only natural: he eyed the feeble helpless creature for a moment angrily, provoked to answer her; but his gaze became one of wonder and dismay ere he withdrew it. Surely of all incomprehensible entities, the most amazing is a fool—a creature insensate, unreasoning, whom neither argument nor fact can make any impression upon. Appalled and impressed, the doctor's gaze left that pretty faded face to turn upon the children. Dreadful imps! If Fred had only taken to evil ways after he became possessed of such a family, his brother could have forgiven him. While these thoughts passed through Dr Rider's mind, however, deliverance approached. He heard Nettie's voice in the passage, long before she reached the door. Not that it was loud like the voices of this dreadful household; but the tone was sufficiently peculiar to be recognised anywhere. With a most penetrating clearness, it came through the long passages, words inaudible, only the sound of a voice, rapid, breathless, decided—with the distant sound of Fred's long, shambling, uncertain footstep coming in as the strange accompaniment. Then they entered the room—the one tiny, bright, dauntless, an intrepid, undiscourageable little soul; the other with his heavy large limbs, his bemused face, his air of hopeless failure, idleness, content. Edward Rider gazed involuntarily from one to another of this two. He saw the sprite place herself between the husband and wife, a vain little Quixote, balancing these extremes of helplessness and ruin. He could not help looking at her with a certain unconscious admiration and amazement, as he might have looked at a forlorn hope. Thousands of miles away from her friends, wherever and whatever they might be, with Fred and his wife and children on her hands, a household of incapables—what was that little creature to do?

'Good morning, Dr Edward,' said Nettie. 'I thought I should have been back sooner; but Fred is so slow, I cannot manage to get him along at all. We have found some lodgings a little way out of Carlingford, near that chapel, you know, or church, or something, that stands a little off the road; where it's open, and there's morning service, and such a handsome young clergyman. Who is he? We went into the chapel, and it's so fine, you would not believe it. Well, just a hundred yards from there is the house. Four rooms, exactly what I wanted, with a garden for the children to play in—quite quiet, and fresh and pleasant. Tell me who the people are—their name is Smith. If they're respectable, I'll go back and take it. I can afford the rent.'

'Near St Roque's? They belong to the church there. I daresay they are all right,' said the doctor, 'but it is a long way off, and inconvenient, and——'

'That is just why I want it,' said Nettie. 'We never were used to conveniences, and none of us want to be much in the town, so far as I know. It is the very thing. Why has not lunch

come up?—what do these people mean, Susan, by not
attending to their orders? Ring the bell, Freddy—ring loud;
and after lunch, as your drag is at the door, Dr Edward, you'll
drive me down to this place again, that I may secure it, won't
you? I want to have a talk with you besides.—Lunch, please,
immediately. I ordered it to be ready at one—now it is half-
past. We can't have our time wasted this way.—Dr Edward,
please, you'll stay.'

The doctor gazed with ever-increasing amazement at the
little speaker. Nobody else had spoken a word. Fred had nodded to him sullenly. Fred's wife had sunk back on the sofa—
everybody seemed to recognise Nettie as supreme. He hesitated, it must be confessed, to put his grievances so entirely
aside as to sit down in perfect amity with Fred and his
household; but to refuse to drive Nettie to St Roque's was
impossible. The blood rushed to the doctor's face at the
thought. What the world of Carlingford would say to see his
well-known vehicle proceeding down Grange Lane, through
Dr Marjoribanks's territories, under such circumstances, was
a question he did not choose to consider; neither did he enter
too minutely into the special moment at which his next patient
might be expecting him. The young man was under the spell,
and did not struggle against it. He yielded to the invitation,
which was a command. He drew near the table at which
Nettie, without hesitation, took the presiding place. A dull
amount of conversation, often interrupted by that lively little
woman, rose in the uncongenial party. Nettie cut up the meat
for those staring imps of children—did them all up in snowy
napkins—kept them silent and in order. She regulated what
Susan was to have, and which things were best for Fred. She
appealed to Dr Edward perpetually, taking him into her
confidence in a way which could not fail to be flattering to that
young man, and actually reduced to the calmness of an
ordinary friendly party this circle so full of smouldering elements of commotion. Through all she was so dainty, so pretty,
her rapid fingers so shapely, her eager talk so sweet-toned, that
it was beyond the power of mortal man to remain uninterested. It was a development of womankind unknown to Dr

Rider. Bessie Christian had exhausted the race for him until now; but Nettie was a thousand times more piquant than Bessie Christian. He gazed and wondered, and moralised secretly in his own mind, what was to become of the girl?—what could she do?

'You have left some of your things at my house, Fred,' said the doctor, making an attempt to approach his sullen brother, who evidently expected no overtures of friendship.

'Yes. Mrs Rider, you see, arrived unexpectedly,' said Fred, with confusion—'in fact, I knew nothing about it, or—or I should have told you—Nettie——'

'Nettie thought it best to come off at once, without writing,' explained Fred's wife.

'What was the use of writing?' cried that little person. 'You had written to Fred for six months without ever getting an answer. You made everybody unhappy round you with your fears and troubles about him. I knew perfectly he was quite well and enjoying himself; but, of course, Susan would not be convinced. So what was there for it but bringing her away? What else could I do, Dr Edward? And to leave the children would have been preposterous. In the first place, I should have been miserable about them; and so, as soon as she found Fred was all right, would Susan: and something would certainly have happened—scarlet fever or something—and at the end of all I should have had to go out again to fetch them. So the shortest way was to bring them at once. Don't you think so? And to see us all here so comfortable, I am sure is enough to repay any one for the trouble. Fred, don't drink any more beer.'

Nettie put out her tiny hand as she spoke to arrest the bottle. Fred stared at her with a dull red flush on his face; but he gave in, in the most inexplicable way; it seemed a matter of course to yield to Nettie. The doctor's amazement began to be mingled with amusement. To see how she managed them all was worth the sacrifice of a little time—unconsciously he became more fraternal in his thoughts. He spoke to foolish faded Mrs Fred with a total forgiveness and forgetfulness of her spiteful speech. He hoped she would like Carlingford; he said something to the children. But it was not easy to talk in presence of that amazing family party, the existence of which he had not dreamed of a few days ago. To see his brother at the head of such a group had, in spite of himself, a wonderful effect upon Dr Rider. Their children, of course, must be supported somehow. Who was to do it? Was their father, grown incapable and useless in the middle of his days, to be forced into the current of life again? Was it a vague faith in Providence which had brought the helpless household here; or was it a more distinct, if not so elevated, confidence in Nettie? The doctor's heart sank once more within him as he looked round the table. Three helpless by nature—two equally helpless who ought in nature to have been the support of the whole—nothing but one bright ready little spirit between them all and destitution; and what could Nettie do to stave that wolf from the door? Once more Dr Rider's countenance fell. If the household broke down in its attempt at independence, who had they to turn to but himself?—such a prospect was not comfortable. When a man works himself to death for his own family, he takes the pleasure with the pain; but when another's family threatens to fall upon his hands, the prospect is naturally appalling—and even if Fred could do anything, what was Fred's life, undermined by evil habit, to depend upon? Silence once more fell over the little company—silence from all but Nettie and the children, who referred to her naturally instead of to their mother. Fred was sullen, and his wife took her cue from him. Edward was uneasy and dismayed. Family parties suddenly assembled without due warning are seldom greatly successful; and even Nettie could not make immediate reconciliation and fraternal kindness out of this.

CHAPTER IV

'TAKE me down this long pretty road. There must be delicious houses inside the walls. Look here; drive slowly, and let us have a peep in at this open door,' said Nettie. 'How sweet and cosy! and who is that pretty young lady coming out? I saw her in the chapel this morning. Oh,' added Nettie, with a little sharpness, 'she knows *you*—tell me who she is.'

'That is Miss Lucy Wodehouse—one of our Carlingford beauties,' said Dr Rider.

'Do you know her very well?' asked the inquisitive Nettie. 'How she stares—why does she stare, do you suppose? Is there anything absurd about my dress? Look here—don't they wear bonnets just like this in England?'

'So far as I am able to judge,' said the doctor, looking at the tiny head overladen with hair, from which the bonnet had fallen half off.

'I suppose she is surprised to see me here. Drive on faster, Dr Edward, I want to talk to you. I see Fred has been telling us a parcel of stories. It would be cruel to tell Susan, you know, for she believes in him; but you may quite trust me. Is your brother good for anything, Dr Edward, do you suppose?'

'Not very much now, I fear,' said the doctor.

'Not very much *now*. I suppose he never was good for much,' said the indignant Nettie; 'but he was said to be very clever when he first came out to the colony. I can't tell why Susan married him. She is very self-willed, though you would fancy her so submissive. She is one of those people, you know, who fall ill when they are crossed, and threaten to die, so that one daren't cross her. Now, then, what is to be done with them? He will not go back to the colony, and I don't care to do it myself. Must I keep them here?'

'Miss Underwood——' began the perplexed doctor.

'It would save trouble to call me Nettie—everybody does,' said his strange companion; 'besides, you are my brother in a kind of a way, and the only person I can consult with; for, of course, it would not do to tell one's difficulties to strangers. Fred may not be very much to depend upon, you know, but still he is Fred.'

'Yes,' said the doctor, with a little self-reproach, 'still he is Fred; but pardon me, the name suggests long aggravations. You can't tell how often I have had to put up with affronts and injuries because it was Fred. I shouldn't like to grieve you—'

'Never mind about grieving me;—*I* am not in love with him;—let me hear all about it!' said Nettie.

Dr Rider paused a little; seeing the abyss upon the brink of which this brave little girl was standing, he had not the heart to aggravate her by telling the failures of the past. Better to soften the inevitable discovery if possible. But his hesitation was quite apparent to Nettie. With considerable impatience she turned round upon him.

'If you think I don't know what I am doing, but have gone into this business like a fool, you are quite mistaken, Dr Edward,' she said, a little sharply. 'I see how it is as well as anybody can do. I knew how it was when I left the colony. Don't be alarmed about me. Do you think I am to be turned against my own flesh and blood by finding out their follies; or to grumble at the place God put me in?—Nothing of the sort! I know the kind of situation perfectly—but one *may* make the best of it, you know: and for that reason tell me everything, please.'

'But, Miss Underwood, consider,' cried the doctor, in consternation. 'You are taking responsibilities upon yourself which nobody could lay upon you; you! young—tender' (the doctor paused for a word, afraid to be too complimentary)— 'delicate! Why, the whole burden of this family will come upon you. There is not one able to help himself in the whole bundle! I am shocked!—I am alarmed!—I don't know what to say to you—'

'Don't say anything, please,' said Nettie. 'I know what I am about. Do you call this a street or a lane, or what do you call it? Oh, such nice houses! shouldn't I like to be able to afford to have one of them, and nurses, and governesses, and everything proper for the children! I should like to dress them so nicely, and give them such a good education. I don't know anything particular to speak of, myself—I shall never be able to teach them when they grow older. If Fred, now, was only to be trusted, and would go and work like a man and make something for the children, I daresay I could keep up the house;—but if he won't do anything, you know, it will take us every farthing just to live. Look here, Dr Edward: I have two hundred a-year;—Susan had the same, you know, but Fred got all the money when they were married, and muddled it away. Now, how much can one do in Carlingford with three children upon two hundred a-year?'

'Fred will be the meanest blackguard in existence,' cried the doctor, 'if he takes his living from you.'

'He took his living from *you*, it appears,' said Nettie, coolly, 'and did not thank you much. We must make the best of him. We can't help ourselves. Now, there is the pretty church, and there is our little house. Come in with me and answer for me, Dr Edward. You can say I am your sister-in-law, you know, and then, perhaps, we can get into possession at once; for,' said Nettie, suddenly turning round upon the doctor with her brilliant eyes shining out quaintly under the little brow all puckered into curves of foresight, 'it is so sadly expensive living where we are now.'

To look at the creature thus flashing those shining eyes, not without a smile lurking in their depths, upon him—to see the triumphant, undaunted, undoubting youthfulness which never dreamt of failure—to note that pretty anxiety, the look which might have become a bride in her first troubles 'playing at housekeeping,' and think how desperate was the position she had assumed, how dreary the burden she had taken upon her—was almost too much for the doctor's self-control. He did not know whether to admire the little heroine as half-divine, or to turn from her as half-crazy. Probably, had the strange little spirit possessed a different frame, the latter was the sentiment which would have influenced the unimaginative mind of Edward Rider. But there was no resisting that little brown Titania, with her little head overladen with its beautiful hair, her red, delicate mouth closing firm and sweet above that little decided chin, her eyes which seemed to concentrate the light. She seemed only a featherweight when the bewildered doctor helped her to alight—an undoubted sprite and creature of romance. But to hear her arrranging about all the domestic necessities within, and disclosing her future plans for the children, and all the order of that life of which she took the charge so unhesitatingly, bewildered the mistress of the house as much as it did the wondering doctor. The two together stood gazing at her as she moved about the room, pouring forth floods of eager talk. Her words were almost as rapid as her step,—her foot, light as it was, almost as decided and firm as her resolutions. She was a wonder to behold as she pushed about the furniture, and considered how it could be brightened up and made more comfortable. Gazing at her with his silent lips apart, Dr Rider sighed at the word. Comfortable! Was she to give her mind to making Fred and his children comfortable—such a creature as this? Involuntarily it occurred to Edward that, under such ministrations, sundry changes might come over the aspect of that prim apartment in which he had seen her first; the room with the bookcase and the red curtains, and the prints over the mantelpiece—a very tidy, comfortable room before any bewitching imp came to haunt it, and whisper suspicions of its imperfection—the doctor's own retirement, where he had chewed the cud of sweet and bitter fancies often enough, without much thought of his surroundings. But Nettie now had taken possession of the prosaic place, and, all unconscious of that spiritual occupation, was as busy and as excited about Mrs Smith's lodgings at St Roque's Cottage as if it were an ideal home she was preparing, and the life to be lived in it was the brightest and most hopeful in the world.

When Dr Rider reached home that night, and took his lonely meal in his lonely room, certain bitter thoughts of unequal fortune occupied the young man's mind. Let a fellow be but useless, thankless, and heartless enough, and people spring up on all sides to do his work for him, said the doctor to himself, with a bitterness as natural as it was untrue. The more worthless a fellow is, the more all the women connected with him cling to him and make excuses for him, said Edward Rider in his indignant heart. Mother and sister in the past— wife and Nettie now—to think how Fred had secured for himself such perpetual ministrations, by neglecting all the duties of life! No wonder an indignant pang transfixed the lonely bosom of the virtuous doctor, solitary and unconsoled as he was. *His* laborious days knew no such solace. And as he fretted and pondered, no visions of Bessie Christian perplexed his thoughts. He had forgotten that young woman. All his mind was fully occupied chafing at the sacrifice of Nettie. He was not sorry, he was angry, to think of her odd position, and the duties she had taken upon herself. What had she to do with those wretched children, and that faded spiteful mother? Edward Rider was supremely disgusted. He said to himself, with the highest moral indignation, that such a girl ought not to be permitted to tie herself to such a fate.

CHAPTER V

ST ROQUE'S COTTAGE was considered rather a triumph of local architecture. A Carlingford artist had built it 'after' the Church, which was one of Gilbert Scott's churches,* and perfect in its way, so that its Gothic qualities were unquestionable. The only thing wanting was size, which was certainly an unfortunate defect, and made this adaptation of ecclesiastical architecture to domestic purposes a very doubtful experiment. However, in bright sunshine, when the abundance of light neutralised the want of window, all was well, and there was still abundance of sunshine in Carlingford in October, three months after the entrance of Fred Rider and his family into Mrs Smith's little rooms. It was a bright autumn day, still mild, though with a crispness in the air, the late season showing more in the destitution of the flower-borders than in any more sensible sign. It was a pretty spot enough for a roadside. St Roque's stood on the edge of a little common, over which, at the other margin, you could see some white cottages, natural to the soil, in a little hamlet-cluster, dropped along the edge of the grey-green unequal grass; while between the church and the cottage ran the merest shadow of a brook, just enough to give place and nutriment to three willow-trees which had been the feature of the scene before St Roque's was, and which now greatly helped the composition of the little landscape, and harmonised the new building with the old soil. St Roque's Cottage, by special intervention of Mr Wentworth, the perpetual curate, had dropped no intervening wall between its garden and those trees; but, not without many fears, had contented itself with a wooden paling on the side nearest the willows. Consequently, the slope of grass at that side, which Mrs Smith was too prudent to plant with anything that could be abstracted, was a pretty slope with the irregular willow shadows swept over it, thin, but still presenting a pale obstruction to the flood of sunshine on this special afternoon. There a little group was collected, in full enjoyment of the warmth and the light. Mrs Rider, still faded, but no longer travel-worn, sat farther up in the garden, on the green bench, which had been softened with cushions for her use, leisurely working at some piece of needlework, in lonely possession of the chrysanthemums and Michaelmas daisies round her; while on the grass, dropped over with yellow flecks of willow leaves, lightly loosened by every passing touch of wind, sat Nettie, all brown and bright, working with the most rapid fingers at a child's frock, and 'minding' with a corner of her eye, the possessor of the same, the tiny Freddy, an imp of mischief, uncontrollable by other hand or look than hers. A little lower down, poking into the invisible brook through the paling, was the eldest boy, silent from sheer delight in the unexpected pleasure of coating himself with mud without remark from Nettie. This unprecedented escape arose from the fact that Nettie had a visitor, a lady who had bent down beside her in a half-kneeling attitude, and was contemplating her with a mingled amaze and pity which intensified the prevailing expression of kindness in the mildest face in the world. It was Miss Wodehouse, in her soft dove-coloured dress and large soft checked shawl. Her mild eyes were fixed upon that brilliant brown creature, all buoyant and sparkling with youth. These wonderful young people perplexed Miss Wodehouse; here was another incomprehensible specimen—most incomprehensible perhaps of all that had ever crossed her mild elderly horizon with bewildering unintelligible light.

'My dear,' said Miss Wodehouse, 'things used to be very

different when I was young. When we were girls we thought about our own pleasures—and—and vanities of all kinds,' said the good woman, with a little sigh; 'and, indeed, I can't think it is natural still to see you devoting yourself like this to your sister's family. It is wonderful; but dear, dear me! it isn't natural, Nettie, such self-devotion.'

'I do wish you wouldn't speak!' said Nettie, with a sudden start—'self-devotion! stuff! I am only doing what must be done. Freddy can't go on wearing one frock for ever, can he—does it stand to reason? Would you have me sit idle and see the child's petticoats drop to pieces? I am a colonial girl—I don't know what people do in England. Where I was brought up we were used to be busy about whatever lay nearest to our hand.'

'It isn't Freddy's frock,' said Miss Wodehouse, with a little solemnity. 'You know very well what I mean. And suppose you were to marry—what would happen supposing you were to marry, Nettie?'

'It is quite time enough to think of that when there is any likelihood of it happening,' said Nettie, with a little toss of her head. 'It is only idle people who have time to think of falling in love and such nonsense. When one is very busy it never comes into one's head. Why, you have never married, Miss Wodehouse; and when I know that I have everything I possibly could desire, why should I?'

Miss Wodehouse bent her troubled sweet old face over the handle of her parasol, and did not say anything for a few minutes. 'It is all very well as long as you are young,' she said, with a wistful look; 'and somehow you young creatures are so much handier than we used to be. Our little Lucy, you know, that I can remember quite a baby—I am twice as old as she is,' cried Miss Wodehouse, 'and she is twice as much use in the world as I. Well, it is all very strange. But, dear, you know, *this* isn't natural all the same.'

'It is dreadful to say so—it is dreadful to think so!' cried Nettie. 'I know what you mean—not Freddy's frock, to be sure, but only one's whole life and heart. Should one desert the only people belonging to one in the world because one happens to have a little income and they have none? If one's friends are not very sensible, is that a reason why one should go and leave them? Is it right to make one's escape directly whenever one feels one is wanted? or what do you mean, Miss Wodehouse?' said the vehement girl. 'That is what it comes to, you know. Do you imagine I had any choice about coming over to England when Susan was breaking her heart about her husband? could one let one's sister die, do you suppose? And now that they are all together, what choice have I? They can't do much for each other—there is actually nobody but me to take care of them all. You may say it is not natural, or it is not right, or anything you please, but what else can one do? That is the practical question,' said Nettie, triumphantly. 'If you will answer that, then I shall know what to say to you.'

Miss Wodehouse gazed at her with a certain mild exasperation, shook her head, wrung her hands, but could find nothing to answer.

'I thought so,' said Nettie, with a little outburst of jubilee; 'that is how it always happens to abstract people. Put the practical question before them, and they have not a word to say to you. Freddy, cut the grass with the scissors, don't cut my trimmings; they are for your own frock, you little savage. If I were to say it was my duty and all that sort of stuff, you would understand me, Miss Wodehouse; but one only says it is one's duty when one has something disagreeable to do; and I am not doing anything disagreeable,' added the little heroine, flashing those eyes which had confused Edward Rider—those brilliant, resolute, obstinate eyes, always with the smile of youth, incredulous of evil, lurking in them, upon her bewildered adviser. 'I am living as I like to live.'

There was a pause—at least there was a pause in the argument, but not in Nettie's talk, which ran on in an eager stream, addressed to Freddy, Johnnie, things in general. Miss Wodehouse pondered over the handle of her parasol. She had absolutely nothing to say; but, thoroughly unconvinced and exasperated at Nettie's logic, could not yet retire from the field.

'It is all very well to talk just now,' said the gentle woman at last, retiring upon that potent feminine argument; 'but, Nettie, think! If you were to marry——'

Miss Wodehouse paused, appalled by the image she herself had conjured up.

'Marrying is really a dreadful business, anyhow,' she added, with a sigh; 'so few people, you know, can, when they might. There is poor Mr Wentworth, who brought me here first; unless he gets preferment, poor fellow——. And there is Dr Rider. Things are very much changed from what they used to be in my young days.'

'Is Dr Rider in the same dilemma? I suppose, of course, you mean Dr Edward,' cried Nettie, with a little flash of mischievous curiosity. 'Why? He has nobody but himself. I should like to know why he can't marry—that is, if anybody would have him—when he pleases. Tell me; you know he is my brother-in-law.'

Miss Wodehouse had been thinking of Bessie Christian. She paused, partly for Dr Rider's sake, partly because it was quite contrary to decorum, to suppose that Bessie, now Mrs Brown, might possibly a year ago have married somebody else. She faltered a little in her answer. 'A professional man never marries till he has a position,' said Miss Wodehouse, abstractedly. Nettie lifted upon her, eyes that danced with mischief and glee.

'A profession is as bad as a family, then,' said the little Australian. 'I shall remember that next time you speak to me on this subject. I am glad to think Dr Edward, with all his prudence, is disabled too.'

When Nettie had made this unguarded speech, she blushed; and suddenly, in a threatening and defiant manner, raised her eyes again to Miss Wodehouse's face. Why? Miss Wodehouse did not understand the look, nor put any significance into the words. She rose up from the grass, and said it was time for her to go. She went away, pondering in her own mind those singular new experiences of hers. She had never been called upon to do anything particular all her gentle life. Another fashion of woman might have found a call to action in the management of her father's house, or the education of her motherless young sister. But Miss Wodehouse had contented herself with loving Lucy—had suffered her to grow up very much as she would, without interference—had never taken a decided part in her life. When anything had to be done, to tell the truth, she was very inexpert—unready—deeply embarrassed with the unusual necessity. Nettie's case, so wonderfully different from anything she could have conceived, lay on her mind and oppressed her as she went home to Grange Lane.

As for Nettie herself, she took her work and her children indoors after a while, and tried on the new frock, and scolded and rehabilitated the muddy hero of the brook. Then, with those light fairy motions of hers, she spread the homely table for tea, called in Susan, sought Fred in his room up-stairs with a stinging word which penetrated even his callous mind, and made him for the moment ashamed of himself. Nettie bit her red lip till it grew white and bloodless as she turned from Fred's door. It was not hard to work for the children—to support and domineer over Susan; but it was hard for such an alert uncompromising little soul to tolerate that useless hulk—that heavy encumbrance of a man, for whom hope and life were dead. She bit her lip as she discharged her sharp stinging arrow at him through the half-opened door, and then went down singing, to take her place at the table which her own hands had spread—which her own purse supplied with bread. Nobody there showed the least consciousness of that latter fact; nobody fancied it was anything but natural to rely upon Nettie. The strange household demeaned itself exactly as if things were going on in the most regular and ordinary course. No wonder that spectators outside looked on with a wonder that could scarcely find expression, and half exasperated, half admiring, watched the astonishing life of the colonial girl.

Nobody watched it with half the amount of exasperation which concentrated in the bosom of Dr Rider. He gazed and noted and observed everything with a secret rage, indignation, and incredulity impossible to describe. He could not believe it even when it went on before his very eyes. Doctor though he was, and scientific, to a certain extent, Edward Rider would have believed in witchcraft—in some philtre or potion acting upon her mind rather than in Nettie's voluntary folly. Was it folly? was it heroism? was it simple necessity, as she herself called it? Nobody could answer that question. The matter was as incomprehensible to Miss Wodehouse as to Dr Rider, but not of such engrossing interest. Bessie Christian, after all, grew tame in the Saxon composure of her beauty before this brown, sparkling, self-willed, imperious creature. To see her among her self-imposed domestic duties filled the doctor with a smouldering wrath against all surrounding her, which any momentary spark might set aflame.

CHAPTER VI

AFFAIRS went on in Carlingford with the usual commonplace pertinacity of human affairs. Notable events happened but seldom in anybody's life, and matters rolled back into their ordinary routine, or found a new routine for themselves after the ordinary course of humanity. After the extraordinary advent of Nettie and her strange household—after the setting-out of that wonderful little establishment, with all the amazed expectation it excited—it was strange to see how everything settled down, and how calmly the framework of common life took in that exceptional and half-miraculous picture. Lookers-on prophesied that it never could last—that in the very nature of things some sudden crisis or collapse must ensue, and the vain experiment prove a failure; but quiet nature and steady time prevailed over these moralists and their prophecies. The winter went on calmly day by day, and Nettie and her dependents became legitimate portions of Carlingford society. People ceased to wonder by degrees. Gradually the eyes of Carlingford grew accustomed to that dainty tiny figure sweeping along, by mere impulse of cheerful will and ceaseless activity, the three open-eyed, staring children, the faded mother. Sometimes, indeed, Nettie, too clear of the necessity of her own exertions, and too simply bent upon her business, to feel any sentimental shame of her relations, was seen quickening the sluggish steps of Fred himself, who shuffled along by her side in a certain flush of self-disgust, never perceptible upon him under any other circumstances. Even Fred was dully moved by her vicinity. When he saw other people look at them, his bemused intellect was still alive enough to comprehend that people were aware of his dismal dependence upon that fairy creature, whom it was a shame to think of as the support not only of his deserted children, but of his own base comforts and idleness. But the spur, though it pricked, did not goad him into any action. When he got home, he took refuge in his room up-stairs, in the hazy atmosphere drugged with the heavy fumes of his pipe, and stretched his slovenly limbs on his sofa, and buried his confused faculties in his old novel. So he lived day by day, circumscribed in the most dangerous of his indulgences by Nettie's unhesitating strictures and rules, which nobody dared break, but unlimited in his indolence, his novel, and his pipe. That stifling fire, that close room, the ashes of the pipe on the table, the listless shabby figure on the sofa, were the most dismal part of the interior at St Roque's Cottage, so far as it appeared to the external eye. But it is doubtful whether Mrs Fred, spiteful and useless, with her poor health, her selfish love, her utter unreason, dawdling over trifling matters which she never completed; or the three children, entirely unrespectful of father or mother, growing up amid that wonderful subversion of the ordinary rules of nature, with some loyalty to Nettie, but no reverence in them, were not as appalling companions to live with. Nettie, however, did not consider the matter as a spectator might. She did not enter into it at all as a matter to be criticised; they simply belonged to her as they were. She knew their faults without loving them less, or feeling it possible that faults could make any difference to those bonds of nature. Fred, indeed, did afflict her lively impatient spirit;—she had tried to quicken him into life at first—she gave him up with a certain frank scorn now, and accepted her position. Thus he was to be all his life long this big cumberer of the ground. Nettie, valorous and simple, made up her mind to it. He was Fred—that was all that could be said on the subject; and, being Fred, belonged to her, and had to be cared for like the rest.

It all grew into a matter of routine as that winter glided along; outside and in, everybody came to take it for granted. Miss Wodehouse, who, with a yearning admiration of a creature so totally unlike herself, came often to visit Nettie, ceased to expostulate, almost ceased to wonder. Mr Wentworth no longer opened his fine eyes in amazement when that household was named. Mrs Smith, their landlady, calmly brought her bills to Nettie, and forgot that it was not the most natural thing in the world that she should be paid by Miss Underwood. The only persistent sceptic was the doctor. Edward Rider could not, would not, believe it. He who had so chafed under Fred's society, felt it beyond the bounds of human possibility that Nettie could endure him. He watched with an eagerness which he found it difficult to account for, to see the first symptoms of disgust which must ere long mark the failure of this bold but foolish venture. It occupied his mind a great deal more than was good for his own comfort; perhaps more than was best for his patients. Though he had few people to visit in that quarter of the town, his drag was seen to pass St Roque's Cottage most days in the week; and when urgent messages came for Dr Rider in the evening, his little groom always wended his way out through the special district of Dr Marjoribanks to find his master, if the doctor was not at home. Not that all this devotion assisted him much either in increase of friendship with his relations, or in verification of his auguries. The disgust of the young doctor, when he saw his brother's slovenly figure in his own chair, was nothing to his disgust now, when he saw that same form, so out of accordance with the neat little sitting-room which Nettie's presence made dainty and refined in its homeliness, lounging in Nettie's way. He could not bring himself to speak with ordinary patience to Fred; and Fred, obtuse as he was, perceived his brother's disgust and contempt, and resented it sullenly; and betrayed his resentment to the foolish wife, who sulked and said spiteful things to Edward. It was not a pleasant family group. As for Nettie, she was much too fully occupied to give her society or conversation to Dr Rider. She came and went while he was there, busy about a thousand things, always alert, decided, uncompromising—not disinclined to snub either Fred or Susan when opportunity offered, totally unconscious even of that delicacy with which a high fantastical heroine of romance would have found it necessary to treat her dependants. It was this unconsciousness, above all, that irritated the doctor. If she had shown any feeling, he said to himself—if she had even been grandly aware of sacrificing herself and doing her duty—there would have been some consolation in it. But Nettie obstinately refused to be said to do her duty. She was doing her own will with an imperious distinctness and energy—having her own way—displaying no special virtue, but a determined wilfulness. Dr Rider was half disgusted with Nettie, to see how little disgust she showed of her companions. He was disappointed in her: he concluded to himself that she did not show that fine perception which he was disposed to expect from so dainty a little sprite. Yet, notwithstanding all these disappointed expectations, it is astonishing how he haunted that room where the society was so unattractive, and bore Mrs Fred's spiteful speeches, and suffered his eyes and his temper to be vexed beyond endurance by the dismal sight of his brother. The children, too, worried their unfortunate uncle beyond description. He did not dislike children: as a general rule, mothers in the other end of Carlingford, indeed, declared the doctor to be wonderfully tender and indulgent to his little patients: but those creatures, with their round staring eyes, the calm remarks they made upon their father's slovenly indolence and their mother's imbecility—their precocious sharp-sightedness and insubordination, moved Dr Rider with a sharp prevailing inclination, intensifying by times almost into action, to whip them all round, and banish the intolerable brats out of sight. Such was his unpaternal way of contemplating the rising hopes of his house. How Nettie could bear it all, was an unceasing marvel to the doctor. Yet, in spite of these disagreeables, he went to St Roque's all the same.

One of these winter evenings the doctor wended his way to

St Roque's Cottage in a worse frame of mind than usual. It was a clear frosty night, very pleasant to be out in, though sharp and chill; such a night as brightens young eyes, and exhilarates young hearts, when all is well with them. Young Rider could hear his own footsteps echoing along the hard frost-bound road, and could not but wonder in himself as he drew near the group of buildings which broke the solitude of the way, whether Nettie too might hear it, and *perhaps* recognise the familiar step. The shadow of St Roque's fell cold over him as he passed. Just from that spot the light in the parlour window of the cottage became perceptible to the wayfarer. A shadow crossed the blind as he came in sight—Nettie unquestionably. It occurred to Dr Rider to remember with very sharp distinctness at that moment, how Nettie's little shadow had dropped across the sunshine that first morning when he saw her in his own room. He quickened his step unawares— perhaps to-night Nettie might be more accessible than usual, less shut in and surrounded by her family. He pictured to himself, as he went past the willows, which rustled faintly with their long bare branches in the night air, that perhaps, as he was later than usual, Fred might have retired to his den up-stairs; and Susan might have gone to bear Fred company— who knows? and the children might be in bed, the dreadful little imps. And for once a half hour's talk with the strange little head of the house might comfort the young doctor's fatigued mind and troubled heart.

For he was sadly fatigued and worn out. What with incessant occupation and distracted thoughts, this year had been a very exhausting one for the doctor. He had fagged on through the whole summer and autumn without any relaxation. He had chafed over Fred's presence for half of the year, and had been occupied for the other half with matters still more absorbing and exciting. Even now his mind was in a perpetual ferment, and no comforting spirit spoke quietness to his soul—no stout heart strengthened his—no lively intelligence animated his own to worthy doings. He was very cross and fretful, and knew himself to be so that particular evening— worried and in want of rest. What a chance, if perhaps he

found Nettie, whose very provocations were somehow more
interesting than other people's most agreeable and tranquil-
lising efforts, all alone and at leisure! He went on with some
palpitations of hope. As soon as he had entered the cottage,
however, he found out the delusion he was under. The
children were the first fact that presented itself to his senses;
an uproar that pervaded the house, a novel tumult waking all
the echoes; glimpses of flying figures pursuing each other with
brushes and mops, and other impromptu weapons; one astride
upon the banisters of the stairs, sliding down from top to
bottom; another clinging now and then, in the pauses of the
conflict, to the top of one of the doors, by which it swung back
and forward. Terrible infants! there they all were in a complete saturnalia, the door of the parlour half open all the time,
and no sound of Nettie's restraining voice. Only poor Mrs
Smith standing helpless, in successions of fright and exasperation, sometimes alarmed for life and limb, sometimes ready to
give the little wretches over to all the penalties of poetic
justice. The poor woman brightened a little when she perceived the sympathetic horror on the doctor's face.

'How's this?' exclaimed young Rider, with a sigh of dismay.
Alas! however it was, no quiet imaginary conference, no
soothing glimpse of Nettie, was practicable to-night. He grew
sulky and ferocious under the thought. He seized the imp that
hung on the door, and set it down summarily with a certain
moral violence, unable to refrain from an admonitory shake,
which startled its sudden scream into a quavering echo of
alarm. 'Do you want to break your neck, sir?' cried the wrathful uncle. Dr Rider, however, had to spring aside almost
before the words were uttered to escape the encounter of a
hearth-brush levelled at him by his sweet little niece. 'How is
this, Mrs Smith?' cried the startled visitor, with indignation,
raising his voice sufficiently to be quite audible through the
half-open door.

'Bless you, sir, Miss is gone out to tea—don't say nothink—I
don't begrudge the poor young lady a bit of a holiday,' whis-
pered the frightened landlady under her breath; 'but I can't
never give in to it again. Their mamma never takes a bit of

notice exceptin' when they're found fault with. Lord! to think how blind some folks is when it's their own. But the poor dear young lady, she's gone out for a little pleasure—only to Miss Wodehouse's, doctor,' added Mrs Smith, looking up with a sudden start to catch the stormy expression on the doctor's face.

He made no reply to the troubled landlady. He pushed the children aside, and made a stride into the parlour. To be sure, if Nettie was not here, what a charming opportunity to make himself disagreeable, and give the other two a piece of his mind! Edward Rider was anything but perfect. He decided on that expedient with an angry satisfaction. Since he could not have Nettie, he would at least have this relief to his feelings, which was next best.

The room was full of smoke, which came in heavy puffs from Fred's pipe. He himself lay stretched on the little sofa; Nettie's sofa—Nettie's room—the place sacred in the doctor's heart to that bright little figure, the one redeeming presence in this dismal household. Mrs Fred sat dawdling opposite her husband over some wretched fancy-work. Eyes less prejudiced than those of Edward Rider might have imagined this a scene of coarse but not unpleasant domestic comfort. To him it was a disgusting picture of self-indulgence and selfish miserable enjoyment, almost vice. The very tobacco which polluted the atmosphere of her room was bought with Nettie's money. Pah! the doctor came in with a silent pale concentration of fury and disgust, scarcely able to compel himself to utter ordinary words of civility. His presence disturbed the pair in their stolen pleasure. Fred involuntarily put aside his pipe, and Mrs Fred made a little movement to remove from the table the glass from which her husband had been drinking; but both recollected themselves after a moment. The wife set down the glass with a little spiteful toss of her head; the husband, with that heated sullen flush upon his face, relighted his half-extinguished pipe, and put up again on the sofa the slovenly slippered feet which at Edward's first appearance he had withdrawn from it. A sullen 'How d'ye do?' was all the salutation that passed between them. *They* felt themselves found out; the visitor felt with rage and indignation that he had found them out. Defiant shame and resentment, spiteful passion and folly, on one side, encountered the gaze of a spectator outside whose opinion could not be mistaken, a known critic and possible spy. Little comfort could come from this strange reunion. They sat in uneasy silence for a few minutes, mutually ready to fly at each other. Mrs Fred, in her double capacity as a woman and a fool, was naturally the first to speak.

'Nettie's gone out to tea,' said that good wife. 'I daresay, Mr Edward, we should not have had the pleasure of seeing you here had you known that only Fred and I were at home. It is very seldom we have an evening to ourselves. It was too great a pleasure, I suppose, not to be disturbed.'

'Susan, hold your confounded tongue,' said the ungrateful Fred.

'I am sorry to disturb Mrs Rider,' said Edward, with deadly civility. 'I was not aware, indeed, of the domestic enjoyment I was likely to interrupt. But if you don't want your boys to break their necks, some one ought certainly to interfere outside there.'

'That is exactly what I expected,' said Mrs Fred. 'My poor children can't have a little amusement, poor things, but somebody must interfere with it; and my poor Fred—perhaps you have some fault to find with him, Mr Edward? Oh, I can see it in your looks! so please take your advantage, now that there's nobody to be afraid of. I can tell you have ever so many pleasant things just on your lips to say.'

'I wish you'd mind your own business, Susan,' said her husband, who was not a fool. 'Look after these imps there, and let me and Edward alone. Nettie's gone out, you understand. She's a wonderful creature, to be sure, but it's a blessed relief to get rid of her for a little. A man can't breathe under her sharp eyes,' said Fred, half apologetic, half defiant, as he breathed out a puff of smoke.

Edward Rider stared at his brother, speechless with rage and indignation. He could have rushed upon that listless figure, and startled the life half out of the nerveless slovenly

frame. The state of mingled resentment, disappointment, and
disgust he was in, made every particular of this aggravating
scene tell more emphatically. To see that heavy vapour
obscuring those walls which breathed of Nettie—to think of
this one little centre of her life, which always hitherto had
borne in some degree the impress of her womanly image, so
polluted and vulgarised, overpowered the young man's patience. Yet perhaps he of all men in the world had least right
to interfere.

'How is it possible,' burst forth the doctor all at once, 'that
you can live upon that creature, Fred? If you have the heart
of a mouse in that big body of yours—if you are not altogether
lost and degraded, how can you do it? And, by Jove, when all
is done, to go and fill the only room she has—the only place
you have left her—with this disgusting smoke and noise as
soon as her back is turned! Good heaven! it sickens one to
think of it. A fellow like you, as strong as any hodman,* to
let such a creature sacrifice herself to keep him in bread; and
the only bit of a little place she can sit down in when she
comes home—it's too much, you know—it's more than she
ought to bear.'

'And who are you, to meddle with us and our arrangements?' cried Mrs Fred. 'My husband is in his own house.
You would not take us into your house, Mr Edward—'

'Hold your confounded tongue, I tell you,' said Fred, slowly
gathering himself off the sofa. 'You're a pretty fellow to speak,
you are—that wouldn't lend a fellow a shilling to keep him
from ruin. You had better remember where you are—in—in—
as Susan says—my own house.'

What outbreak of contempt might have come from the doctor's lips was fortunately lost at that moment, since a louder
outcry than usual from outside, the screams of the children,
and wailings of the landlady, at length roused the mother to
the length of going to the door. When she was gone the two
brothers eyed each other threateningly. Fred, not without a
certain intolerable sensation of shame, rose to knock his pipe
upon the mantel-shelf among Nettie's pretty girlish ornaments. Somehow these aggravations of insult to her image

drove Edward Rider desperate. He laid his hand on Fred's shoulder and shook him violently.

'Wake up! can't you wake up and see what you're about?' cried the doctor; 'can't you show a little respect for her, at least? Look here, Fred Rider. I knew you could do anything shabby or mean, if it suited you. I knew you would consent to hang a burden on anybody that would take such a weight upon them; but, by Jove, I did not think you had the heart to insult her, after all. A man can't stand by and see that. Clear off your pipe and your brandy before she comes, or, as sure as I am made of flesh and blood, and not cast-iron——'

The doctor's threats were interrupted by the entrance of a woeful procession. Into the presence of the two brothers, eyeing each other with such lowering faces, Mrs Smith and her husband entered, carrying between them, with solemn looks, the unconscious Freddy, while his mother followed screaming, and his little brother and sister staring open-mouthed. It was some relief to the doctor's feelings, in the excitement of the moment, to rush to the window and throw it open, admitting a gust of chill December air, penetrating enough to search to the bones of the fireside loiterer. Fred was father enough to turn with anxiety to the child. But his trembling nervous fingers and bemused eyes could make nothing of the 'case' thus so suddenly brought before him. He turned fiercely and vacantly upon his wife and demanded why everything was suffered to go to ruin when Nettie was away. Mrs Fred, screaming and terrified, began to recriminate. The pallid figure of the child on the table gave a certain air of squalid tragedy to the scene, to the sordid miseries of which the night air, coming in with a rush, chilling the group in their indoor dresses, and flickering the flame of the candles, added one other point of dismal accumulation. The child had dropped from his swing on the door, and was stunned with the fall. Both father and mother thought him dead in the excitement of the moment; but the accustomed and cooler eyes of the doctor perceived the true state of affairs. Edward Rider forgot his disgust and rage as he devoted himself to the little patient—not that he loved the child more, but that the habits

of his profession were strong upon him. When he had succeeded in restoring the little fellow to consciousness, the doctor
threw a professional glance of inquiry round him to see who
could be trusted. Then, with a contemptuous shrug of his
shoulders and impatient exclamation, turned back to the table.
Fred, shivering and helpless, stood by the fire, uttering confused directions, and rubbing miserably his own flabby hands;
his wife, crying, scolding, and incapable, stood at the end of
the table, offering no assistance, but wondering when ever
Nettie would come back. Dr Rider took the patient in his arms,
and, beckoning Mrs Smith to go before him, carried the child
up-stairs. There the good mistress of the cottage listened to all
his directions, and promised devoutly to obey him—to keep
the room quiet, if she could—to tell everything he had said to
Miss Nettie. He did not enter the desecrated parlour again
when he came down-stairs. What was the use? He was glad to
go out and escape the chance of a fraternal struggle. He went
out into the cold night air all thrilling with excitement and
agitation. It was not wonderful that a scene so strange should
rouse many impatient thoughts in the young man's mind; but
the most intolerable of these had the most trifling origin. That
Fred should have smoked his pipe in Nettie's sitting-room,
when she was out of the way, was not, after all, considering
Fred's character, a very wonderful circumstance, but it exasperated his brother to a greater extent than much more important matters. That aggravation entirely overpowered Edward
Rider's self-control. It seemed the culmination of all the
wrong and silent insolent injury inflicted upon Nettie. He saw
the stain of these ashes on the little mantel-shelf, the rolling
cloud of smoke in the room, and indignation burned yet
higher and higher in his breast.

When the current of his thoughts was suddenly checked and
stimulated by the sound of voices on the road. Voices, one of
which was Nettie's, one the lofty clerical accents of the Rev
Frank Wentworth. The two were walking arm-in-arm in very
confidential colloquy, as the startled and jealous doctor imagined. What were these two figures doing together upon the
road? why did Nettie lean on the arm of that handsome young

clerical coxcomb? It did not occur to Dr Rider that the night was extremely dark, and that Nettie had been at Miss Wodehouse's, where the curate of St Roque's was a perpetual visitor. With a mortified and jealous pang, totally unreasonable and totally irresistible, Edward Rider, only a moment before so fantastically extreme in Nettie's defence—in the defence of Nettie's very 'image' from all vulgar contact and desecration—strode past Nettie now without word or sign of recognition. She did not see him, as he observed with a throbbing heart; she was talking to young Mr Wentworth with all the haste and eagerness which Dr Rider had found so captivating. She never suspected who it was that brushed past her with breathless, exasperated impatience in the darkness. They went on past him, talking, laughing lightly, under the veil of night, quite indifferent as to who heard them, though the doctor did not think of that. He, unreasonably affronted, galled, and mortified, turned his back upon that house, which at this present disappointed moment did not contain one single thing or person which he could dwell on with pleasure; and, a hundred times more discontented, fatigued, and worn out—full of disgust with things in general, and himself and his own fate in particular—than he had been when he set out from the other end of Carlingford, went sulkily, and at a terrific pace, past the long garden-walls of Grange Lane, and all Dr Marjoribanks's genteel patients. When he had reached home, he found a message waiting him from an urgent invalid, whose 'case' kept the unhappy doctor up and busy for half the night. Such was the manner in which Edward Rider got through the evening—the one wonderful exceptional evening when Nettie went out to tea.

CHAPTER VII

WITH the dawn of the morning, however, and the few hours' hurried rest which Edward Rider was able to snatch after his labours, other sentiments arose in his mind. It was quite necessary to see how the unlucky child was at St Roque's

Cottage, and perhaps what Nettie thought of all that had occurred during her absence. The doctor bethought himself, too, that there might be very natural explanations of the curate's escort. How else, to be sure, could she have got home on a dark winter night through that lonely road? Perhaps, if he himself had been less impatient and ill-tempered, it might have fallen to his lot to supersede Mr Wentworth. On the whole, Dr Rider decided that it was necessary to make one of his earliest calls this morning at St Roque's.

It was a foggy frosty day, brightened with a red sun, which threw wintry ruddy rays across the mist. Dr Rider drew up somewhat nervously at the little Gothic porch. He was taken up-stairs to the bedroom where little Freddy lay moaning and feverish. A distant hum came from the other children in the parlour, the door of which, however, was fast closed this morning; and Nettie herself sat by the child's bedside—Nettie, all alert and vigorous, in the little room, which, homely as its aspect was, displayed even to the doctor's uninitiated glance a fastidious nicety of arrangement which made it harmonious with that little figure. Nettie was singing childish songs to solace the little invalid's retirement—the 'fox that jumped up on a moonlight night,' the 'frog that would a-wooing go'— classic ditties of which the nursery never tires. The doctor, who was not aware that music was one of Nettie's accomplishments, stopped on the stairs to listen. And indeed she had not a great deal of voice, and still less science, Nettie's life having been too entirely occupied to leave much room for such studies. Yet somehow her song touched the doctor's heart. He forgave her entirely that walk with the curate. He went in softly, less impatient than usual with her crazy Quixotism. A child—a sick child especially—was a bearable adjunct to the picture. A woman could be forgiven for such necessary ministrations—actually, to tell the truth, could be forgiven most follies she might happen to do, when one could have her to one's self, without the intervention of such dreary accessories as Susan and Fred.

'Thank you very much for your care of this child last night, Dr Edward,' said the prompt Nettie, laying down the large piece of very plain needlework in her hand. 'I always said, though you don't make a fuss about the children, that you were quite to be relied on if anything should happen. He is feverish, but he is not ill; and so long as I tell him stories and keep beside him, Freddy is the best child in the world.'

'More people than Freddy might be willing to be ill under such conditions,' said the doctor, complimentary, but rueful. He felt his patient's pulse, and prescribed for him with a softened voice. He lingered and looked round the room, which was very bare, yet somehow was not like any of the rooms in *his* house. How was it?—there were no ornaments about, excepting that tiny little figure with the little head overladen with such a wealth of beautiful hair. The doctor sighed. In this little sacred spot, where she was so clearly at her post—or at least at a post which no other was at hand to take—he could not even resent Nettie's self-sacrifice. He gave in to her here, with a sigh.

'Since you think he is not ill to speak of, will you drive me and the other children into Carlingford, Dr Edward?' said the courageous Nettie. 'It will be a pleasure for them, you know, and I shall be able to do my business without losing so much time; besides, I want to talk to you; I can see you will in your eyes. Go down, please, and talk to Mr Smith, who has got a headache or something, and wants to see you. You need not trouble yourself seeing Susan, who is cross, of course. I don't wonder at her being cross; it must be very shocking, you know, to feel one's self of no use, whatever happens. Thank you; I shall be ready in a minute, as soon as you have done talking to Mr Smith.'

The doctor went down obediently, and in an unusual flutter of pleasure, to see the master of the cottage—totally indifferent to the ailments of the virtuous Smith, and thinking only of Nettie and that drive to Carlingford, where, indeed, he should not have gone, had he considered the merely abstract matters of business and duty, which led him entirely in a different direction. He was somewhat rudely recalled to himself when he went down-stairs. Smith had no headache, but only wanted to speak to the doctor about his lodgers, whose 'ways' were sadly discomposing to himself and his wife.

'You saw how it was yourself last night, sir,' said the troubled landlady. 'Them hangings—you know the smoke goes through and through them. After leaving all the windows open this frosty morning, and a draught enough to give you your death, the place smells like I don't know what. If it wasn't for Miss I wouldn't put up with it for a day: and the gentleman's own room, doctor; if you was just to go in and see it—just put your head in and say good morning—you'd believe me.'

'I know all about it,' said the doctor; 'but Miss Underwood, Mrs Smith—?'

'There's where it is, sir,' said the landlady. 'I can't find it in my heart to say a word to Miss. To see how she do manage them all, to be sure! but for all that, doctor, it stands to reason as one can't spoil one's lodgings for a family as may be gone to-morrow—not except it's considered in the rent. It's more natural-like to speak to a gentleman like you as knows the world, than to a young lady as one hasn't a word to say against—the handiest, liveliest, managingest! Ah, doctor, she'd make a deal different a wife from her sister, that young lady would! though it isn't my part to say nothink, considering all things, and that you're relations, like; but Smith and me are both o' one mind about it, Dr Rider—unless it's considered in the rent, or the gentleman drops smoking, or——

'I hear Miss Underwood coming down-stairs,' cried young Rider. 'Next time I come we'll arrange it all. But not a word to *her*, remember—not a syllable; and go up-stairs and look after that poor child, there's a good soul—she trusts you while she is gone, and so do I. There, there! another time. I'll take the responsibility of satisfying you, Mrs Smith,' said the doctor, in a prodigious hurry, ready to promise anything in this incautious moment, and bolting out of their little dark back-room, which the local architect's mullions had converted into a kind of condemned cell. Nettie stood at the door, all ready for her expedition to Carlingford, with her two children, open-eyed and calmly inquisitive, but no longer noisy.

Mrs Fred was standing sulky at the parlour door. The doctor took off his hat to her as he helped Nettie into the front seat of the drag, but took care not to approach nearer. The children were packed in behind, under charge of the little groom, and, with an exhilarating sensation of lawlessness in the present pleasure, Dr Rider turned his back upon his duty and the patient who expected him a mile on the other side of St Roque's, and drove, not too rapidly, into Carlingford.

'Mrs Smith was talking to you of us,' said Nettie, flashing her penetrating eyes upon the confused doctor. 'I know she was—I could see it in her face this morning, and in yours when you came out of the room. Dreadful little dungeon, is it not? I wonder what the man meant, to build such a place. Do they want to turn us out, Dr Edward, or do they want more rent? I am not surprised, I am sure, after last night. Was it not odious of Fred to go and smoke in the parlour, the only place we can have tidy? But it is no use speaking to him, you know; nor to Susan either, for that matter. Married people do stand up for each other so when you say a word, however they may fight between themselves. But is it more rent they want, Dr Edward? for I can't afford more rent.'

'It is an abominable shame—you oughtn't to afford anything. It is too dreadful to think of!' cried the angry doctor, involuntarily touching his horse with his whip in the energy of the moment, though he was indeed in no hurry to reach Carlingford.

'Hush,' said Nettie, lifting her tiny hand as though to put it to his incautious mouth, which, indeed, the doctor would not have objected to. 'We shall quarrel on that subject if you say anything more, so it is better to stop at once. Nobody has a right to interfere with me; this is my business, and no one else has anything to do with it.'

'You mistake,' cried the doctor, startled out of all his prudences; 'it ought to be my business quite as much as it is yours.'

Nettie looked at him with a certain careless scorn of the inferior creature—'Ah, yes, I daresay; but then you are only a man,' said Nettie; and the girl elevated that pretty drooping head, and flashed a whole torrent of brilliant reflections over the sombre figure beside her. He felt himself glow under the sudden radiance of the look. To fancy this wilful imperious creature a meek self-sacrificing heroine, was equally absurd and impossible. Was there any virtue at all in that dauntless enterprise of hers? or was it simple determination to have her own way?

'But not to quarrel,' said Nettie; 'for indeed you are the only person in the world I can say a word to about the way things are going on,' she added, with a certain momentary softening of voice and twinkling of her eyelid, as if some moisture had gathered there. 'I think Fred is in a bad way. I think he is muddling his brains with that dreadful life he leads. To think of a man that could do hundreds of things living like that! A woman, you know, can only do a thing or two here and there. If it were not wicked to say so, one would think almost that Providence forgot sometimes, and put the wrong spirit into a body that did not belong to it. Don't you think so? When I look at Fred I declare sometimes I could take hold of him and give him a good shake, and ask him what he means; and then it all seems so useless the very idea of expecting him to feel anything. I want to know what you said to him last night.'

'Not much—not half so much as I meant to have said. To see him polluting your room!' cried the doctor, with a flush growing on his face, and breaking off abruptly, not quite able to conclude the sentence. Nettie gave him a shy upward glance, and grew suddenly crimson too.

'Did you mind?' said Nettie, with a momentary timidity, against the unexpected charm of which the unhappy doctor fell defenceless; then holding out her tiny hand to him with shy frankness, 'Thank you for caring so much for me,' said the dauntless little girl, resolute not to perceive anything which could not be fully spoken out.

'Caring *so* much! I must speak to you; we can't go on like this, Nettie,' cried the doctor, holding fast the little unfaltering hand.

'Oh, here is the place I am going to. Please don't; people

might not understand,—though we *are* brother and sister in a kind of a way,' said the little Australian. 'Please, Dr Edward, we must get out here.'

For a moment Edward Rider hesitated with a wild intention of urging his horse forward and carrying her off anywhere, out of Carlingford, out of duty and practice and responsibility, and all those galling restraints of life which the noonday light and everyday sounds about brought in with so entire a discord to break up this momentary hallucination. For half a minute only the doctor lingered on the borders of that fairyland where time and duty are not, but only one ineffable moment always passing, never past. Then with a long sigh, the breath of which dispersed a whole gleaming world of visionary delights, he got down doggedly on the commonplace pavement. Ah, what a descent it was! the moment his foot touched these vulgar flags,* he was once more the hard-worked doctor at everybody's command, with a fretful patient waiting for him a mile beyond St Roque's; and all these dazzling moments, which had rapt the unfortunate young fellow into another world, were so much time lost to the prose figure that had to help Nettie down and let her go, and betake himself soberly about his own business. Perhaps Nettie felt it a little disenchanting too, when she was dropped upon the bare street, and went into the common shop, and saw the doctor's drag flash off in the red frosty sunshine with a darting movement of exasperation and impatience on the part of its aggravated driver. For once in her life Nettie felt disposed to be impatient with the children, who, unceremoniously ejected from their perch behind, were not in the most obedient frame of mind. The two young people possibly agreed in their mutual sentiment of disgust with other people's society just at that moment. However, there was no help for it. Dr Rider galloped his horse to his patient's door, and took it out of that unlucky individual, who was fortunately strong enough to be able to bear sharp practice. Nettie, when she had made her little purchases, walked home smartly to sing 'The fox jumped up on a moonlight night' to Freddy in his bedroom. This kind of interlude, however, as all young men and maidens ought to be aware, answers much better in the evening, when a natural interval of dreams interposes between it and the common work of existence. Nettie decided, thinking on it, that this would never do. She made up her mind not to have any more drives with the doctor. There was no telling what such proceedings might lead to. They were distinctly incompatible with the more serious business of her life.

CHAPTER VIII

SUCH a parting, however, is sadly apt to lead to future meetings. Notwithstanding his smouldering quarrel with Fred, which was always ready to burst out afresh, Dr Rider would not give up coming to St Roque's. He came to some clandestine arrangement with Mrs Smith, of which nobody ever was aware, and which he himself was rather ashamed of than otherwise; and he attended Freddy with the most dutiful exactness till the child was quite restored. But all this time Nettie put on a coat of armour, and looked so thoroughly unlike herself in her unusual reserve and propriety, that the doctor was heartily discouraged, and could go no further. Besides, it would not be positively correct to assert that— though he would gladly have carried her off in the drag anywhere, to the end of the world, in the enchantment of the moment—he was just as ready to propose setting up a new household, with Fred and his family hanging on to it as natural dependants. That was a step the doctor was not prepared for. Some people are compelled to take the prose concerns of life into full consideration even when they are in love, and Edward Rider was one of these unfortunate individuals. The boldness which puts everything to the touch to gain or lose* was not in this young man. He had been put to hard encounters enough in his day, and had learned to trust little to chance or good fortune. He did not possess the boldness which disarms an adverse fate, nor that confidence in his own powers which smooths down wounded pride, and accounts even for failure. He was, perhaps it is only right to say, not very capable of heroism: but he was capable of seeing the lack of the heroic in his own composition, and of feeling bitterly his own self-reproaches, and the remarks of the world, which is always so ready to taunt the very cowardice it creates. After that moment in which he could have dared anything for her and with her, it is sad to be obliged to admit that perhaps Dr Edward too, like Nettie, withdrew a little from that climax of feeling. Not that his heart grew colder or his sentiments changed; but only that, in sight of the inevitable result, the poor young fellow paused and pondered, obeying the necessity of his nature. People who jump at conclusions, if they have to bear the consequences of folly often enough, are at least spared these preliminary heartaches. Dr Rider, eager as love and youth could make him, was yet incapable of shutting his eyes to the precipice at his feet. That he despised himself for doing so, did not make the matter easier. These were the limits of his nature, and beyond them he could not pass.

Accordingly matters went on in this dangerous fashion for many weeks longer. The fire smouldered, strengthening its pent-up flames. Day by day malicious sprites of thought went out behind Dr Rider in his drag, leading him into the wildest calculations, the most painful complication of schemes. If Fred and his family could only be persuaded to return to Australia, his brother thought—if any bribe within Edward's means could tempt the ruined man to such a step; and when he was there, why there was Providence to take care of the helpless unlovely household, and necessity might compel the wretched father to work for his children. Such were the vain projects that revolved and fermented through the doctor's agitated brain as he went among his patients. Luckily he had a very favourable and well-disposed lot of sick people at that crisis—they all got well in spite of the doctor, and gave their own special cases and his anxiety all the credit for his grave looks; and all these half-finished streets and rough new roads in the east end of Carlingford were sown thick with the bootless suggestions of Dr Rider's love and fears. The crop did not show upon the vulgar soil, but gave lurking associations to every half-built street-corner which he passed in his rounds many a day after, and served at this present momentous era to confuse doubly the chaos of his thoughts.

At last one night the crisis came. Spring had begun to show faintly in the lengthening days—spring, that so often belies itself, and comes with a serpent's tooth. Dr Rider on that particular day had met Dr Marjoribanks at some meeting convened in the interests of Carlingford. The old physician had been very gracious and cordial to the young one—had spoken of his own declining health, of his possible retirement, of the excellent prospects which a rising young man in their profession had in Carlingford; and, finally, had asked Dr Rider to go with him next day to see an interesting patient, and advise as to the treatment of the case.

The young doctor was more pleased than he could or would have told any one; and, with a natural impulse, seized the earliest moment to direct his steps towards St Roque's.

It was twilight when Dr Edward went down the long and rather tiresome line of Grange Lane. These garden-walls, so delicious in their bowery retirements within, were not interesting outside to the pedestrian. But the doctor's attention was so speedily riveted on two figures eagerly talking near Mr Wodehouse's garden-door, that the long sweep of wall seemed but a single step to him as he hurried along. These two figures were unquestionably Nettie for one, and Mr Wentworth for another. Handsome young coxcomb, with all his Puseyitical pretences!* Was Lucy Wodehouse not enough for him, that he must have Nettie too? Dr Rider hurried forward to interrupt that meeting. He was actually turning with her, walking slowly back again the very way he had just come! Edward's blood boiled in his impatient veins. He swept along in a whirlwind of sudden wrath. When he came up to them Nettie was talking low, and the curate's lofty head was bent to hear her in a manner which, it is probable, Lucy Wodehouse would no more have admired than Edward Rider. They came to a sudden pause when he joined them, in that particular conversation. The doctor's dread civility did not improve matters. Without asking himself what cause he had, this amiable young man plunged into the wildest jealousy without pause or interval. He bestowed upon Nettie the most cutting looks, the most overwhelming politeness. When the three had marched solemnly abreast down the road for some few minutes, the curate, perhaps with an intuition of fellow-feeling, perceiving how the matter was, stopped short and said good-bye. 'I will make inquiries, and let you know next time I pass the cottage,' said Mr Wentworth; and he and the doctor took off their hats, not without deadly thoughts on one side at least. When the young clergyman left them, Nettie and her sulky cavalier went on in silence. That intrepid little woman was not in her usual spirits, it appeared. She had no talk for Dr Edward any more than he had for her. She carried a multiplicity of little parcels in her hands, and walked with a certain air of fatigue. The doctor walked on, stealing silent looks at her, till his heart melted. But the melting of his heart displayed itself characteristically. He would not come down from his elevation without suffering her to see how angry he was.

'I fear I interrupted an interesting conversation—I that have so little hope of equalling Mr Wentworth. Priests are always infallible with women,' said the doctor, betraying his ill-temper in vulgar sneers.

'I was asking him for some one to teach the boys,' said Nettie. 'Johnnie ought to have his education attended to now. Mr Wentworth is very good-tempered, Dr Edward. Though he was just going to knock at Miss Wodehouse's door when I met him, he offered, and would have done it if you had not come up, to walk home with me. Not that I wanted anybody to walk home with me; but it was very kind,' said Nettie, with rising spirit.

'I am afraid I am a very poor substitute for Mr Wentworth,' said the jealous doctor, 'and I don't pretend to be kind. But I am surprised to find Miss Underwood walking so late. This is not a road for a lady by herself.'

'You know I don't mind in the least for the road,' said Nettie, with a little indignation. 'How wonderfully cross you are sometimes! If you are going as far as the Cottage,' she added, with a little sigh of fatigue, 'will you please carry some of these things for me? I could not get out sooner, I have been so busy to-day. It is wonderful how much needlework it takes to keep three children going, and how many little jobs there are to do. If you take this parcel, carry it carefully, please: it is something for my bonnet. There! Don't be absurd. I am quite able to walk by myself, thank you—I'd rather, please!'

This remonstrance was called forth by the fact that the re-lenting doctor, much moved by having the parcels confided to his care, had drawn the little hand which gave them within his arm, a proceeding which Nettie distinctly disapproved of. She withdrew her hand quickly, and walked on with much dignity by his side.

'I can carry your parcels,' said Edward, after a little pause, 'but you will not let me help yourself. You take the heaviest burdens upon your shoulders, and then will have no assistance in bearing them. How long are these children of Fred's— detestable little imps!—to work you to death?'

'You are speaking of *my* children, sir!' cried Nettie, with a little blaze of resentment. 'But you don't mean it, Dr Edward,' she said, a moment after, in a slightly coaxing tone. 'You are tired and cross after your day's work. Perhaps it will be best, if you are very cross, not to come down all the way to the Cottage, thank you. I don't want you to quarrel with Fred.'

'Cross! Nettie, you are enough to drive twenty men distrac-ted!' cried the poor doctor. 'You know as well as I do what I have been dying to say to you these three months past; and to see you go on with these confounded children without so much as a glance for a fellow who——'

'Don't speak like that,' cried Nettie, with brilliant female instinct; 'you'll be sorry for it after; for you know, Dr Edward, you have *not* said anything particular to me these three months past.'

This touch gave the last exasperation to the agitated mind of the doctor. He burst forth into a passionate outbreak of love and anger, curiously mingled, but too warm and real to leave Nettie much coolness of observation under the circumstances. She took the advantage over him which a woman naturally does in such a case. She went on softly, trembling sufficiently to her own consciousness, but not to his, suffering him to pour out that torrent without interruption. She made no answer till the whole agitated self-disclosure was complete. In the interval she got a little command of herself, and was able to speak when it came to her turn.

'Dr Edward,' said Nettie, solemnly, 'you know it is impossible. If we cared for each other ever so much, what could we do? I am not free to—to make any change; and I know very well, and so do you, that you never could put up with Fred and Susan and the children, were things as you say ten times over. I don't mean I don't believe you. I don't mean I might not have been pleased had things been different. But you know it is just plainly impossible. You know your own temper and your own spirit—and perhaps you know mine as well. No, no—we cannot manage it anyhow, Dr Edward,' said Nettie, with a little sigh.

'Is this all you have to say to me?' cried the astonished lover.

'I am sure I do not know what else to say,' said Nettie, with matter-of-fact distinctness. 'I don't need to enter into all the business again, and tell you how things stand; you know as well as I do. One may be sorry, but one must do what one has to do all the same.'

A painful pause followed. Nettie, with all her feminine acuteness, could not divine that this calm way of treating a business which had wrought her companion into such a pitch of passion, was the most humiliating and mortifying possible to a man in whose bosom love and pride were so combined. He tried to speak more than once, but could not. Nettie said nothing more—she was uneasy, but secure in the necessity of her own position. What else could she do or say?

'Then, I presume, this is my answer,' said the doctor, at last, gulping an amount of shame and anger which Nettie could not conceive of, and which the darkness concealed from her sight.

'Oh, Dr Edward, what can I say?' cried the girl; 'you know it all as well as I do. I cannot change it with a word. I am very, very sorry,' said Nettie, faltering and startled, waking to a sudden perception of the case all at once, by reason of catching a sudden gleam of his eyes. They came to a dead stop opposite each other, she half frightened and confused, he desperate with love and rage and mortification. By this time they had almost reached the cottage door.

'Don't take the trouble to be sorry. I'll—oh, I'll get over it!' cried the doctor, with a sneer at himself and his passion, which came out of the bitterness of his heart. Then, after a pause—'Nettie!' cried the young man—'Nettie! do you see what you are doing?—do you choose Fred and those wretched imps instead of your own life and mine? You are not so indifferent as you think you are. We shall never get over it, neither you nor me. Nettie, once for all, is this all you have to say?'

'If I were to say all the words in the language,' said Nettie, after a pause, with a breathless indistinctness and haste, 'words will not change *things* if we should break our hearts.'

The open door, with the light shining out from it, shone upon them at that moment, and Mrs Smith waiting to let the young lady in. Neither of the two dared face that sudden gleam. The doctor laid down his parcels on the step, muttered something, which she could not distinguish, into Nettie's agitated ear, and vanished back again into the darkness. Only now was Nettie awaking to the sense of what had happened, and its real importance. Perhaps another minute, another word, might have made a difference—that other word and minute that are always wanting. She gazed out after him blankly, scarcely able to persuade herself that it was all over, and then went in with a kind of stupefied, stunned sensation, not to be described. Edward Rider heard the door shut in the calm silence, and swore fierce oaths in his heart over her composure and cold-heartedness. As usual, it was the woman who had to face the light and observation, and to veil her trouble. The man rushed back into the darkness, smarting with wounds which fell as severely upon his pride as upon his heart. Nettie went in, suddenly conscious that the world was changed, and that she had entered upon another life.

CHAPTER IX

ANOTHER life and a changed world! What small matters sometimes bring about that sullen disenchantment! Two or three words exchanged without much thought—one figure disappearing out of the landscape—and, lo! all the prismatic colours have faded from the horizon, and blank daylight glares upon startled eyes! Nettie had not, up to this time, entertained a suspicion of how distinct a place the doctor held in her limited firmament—she was totally unaware how much exhilaration and support there was in his troubled, exasperated, impatient admiration. Now, all at once, she found it out. It was the same life, yet it was different. Her occupations were unchanged, her surroundings just what they used to be. She had still to tolerate Fred, to manage Susan, to superintend with steady economy all the expenditure of the strange little household. The very rooms and aspect of everything was the same; yet had she been suddenly transported back again to the Antipodes, life could not have been more completely changed to Nettie. She recognised it at once with some surprise, but without any struggle. The fact was too clearly apparent to leave her in any doubt. Nobody but herself had the slightest insight into the great event which had happened—nobody could know of it, or offer Nettie any sympathy in that unforeseen personal trial. In her youth and buoyant freshness, half contemptuous of the outside troubles which were no match for her indomitable heart, Nettie had been fighting against hard external circumstances for a great part of her valorous little life, and had not hesitated to take upon herself the heaviest burdens of outside existence. Such struggles are not hard when one's heart is light and sound. With a certain splendid youthful scorn of all these labours and drudgeries, Nettie had gone on her triumphant way, wearing her bonds as if they were ornaments. Suddenly, without any premonition, the heart had died out of her existence. A personal blow, striking with subtle force into that unseen centre of courage and hope, had suddenly disabled Nettie. She said not a word on the subject to any living creature—if she shed any tears over it, they were dropped in the darkness, and left no witness behind; but she silently recognised and understood what had happened to her. It was not that she had lost her lover—it was not that the romance of youth had glimmered and disappeared from before her eyes. It was not that she had ever entered, even in thought, as Edward Rider had done, into that life, glorified out of common existence, which the two could have lived together. Such was not the form which this extraordinary loss took to Nettie. It was her personal happiness, wonderful wine of life, which had suddenly failed to the brave little girl. Ah, the difference it made! Labours, disgusts, endurances of all kinds: what cannot one undertake so long as one has that cordial at one's heart? When the endurance and the labour remain, and the cordial is gone, it is a changed world into which the surprised soul enters. This was what happened to Nettie. Nobody suspected the sudden change which had passed upon everything. The only individual in the world who could have divined it, had persuaded himself in a flush of anger and mortification that she did not care. He consoled himself by elaborate avoidance of that road which led past St Roque's— by bows of elaborate politeness when he encountered her anywhere in the streets of Carlingford—by taking a sudden plunge into such society as was open to him in the town, and devoting himself to Miss Marjoribanks, the old physician's daughter. Nettie was not moved by these demonstrations, which showed her sway still undiminished over the doctor's angry and jealous heart. She did not regard the petulant shows of pretended indifference by which a more experienced young woman might have consoled herself. She had enough to do, now that the unsuspected stimulus of her life was withdrawn for the moment, to go on steadily without making any outward show of it. She had come to the first real trial of her strength and worthiness. And Nettie did not know what a piece of heroism she was enacting, nor that the hardest lesson of youthful life—how to go on stoutly without the happiness which that absolute essence of existence demands and will not be refused—was being taught her now. She only knew it was dull work just for the moment—a tedious sort of routine, which one was glad to think could not last for ever; and so went on, the steadfast little soul, no one being any the wiser, upon that suddenly-clouded, laborious way.

It is sad to be obliged to confess that Dr Rider's conduct was nothing like so heroical. He, injured and indignant and angry, thought first of all of revenging himself upon Nettie—of proving to her that he would get over it, and that there were women in the world more reasonable than herself. Dr Marjoribanks, who had already made those advances to the doctor which that poor young fellow had gone to carry the news of, not without elation of heart, on that memorable night, to St Roque's, asked Edward to dinner a few days after; and Miss Marjoribanks made herself very agreeable, with just that degree of delicate regard and evident pleasure in his society which is so soothing when one has met with a recent discomfiture. Miss Marjoribanks, it is true, was over thirty, and by no means a Titania. Edward Rider, who had retired from the field in Bessie Christian's case, and whom Nettie had rejected, asked himself savagely why he should not make an advantageous marriage now, when the chance offered. Old Marjoribanks's practice and savings, with a not unagreeable, rather clever, middle-aged wife—why should he not take it into consideration? The young doctor thought of that possibility with a certain thrill of cruel pleasure. He said to himself that he would make his fortune, and be revenged on Nettie. Whenever there was a chance of Nettie hearing of it, he paid the most devoted attentions to Miss Marjoribanks. Ready gossips took it up and made the matter public. Everybody agreed it would be an admirable arrangement. 'The most sensible thing I've heard of for years— step into the old fellow's practice, and set himself up for life— eh, don't you think so?—that's my opinion,' said Mr Wodehouse. Mr Wodehouse's daughters talked over the matter, and settled exactly between themselves what was Miss Marjoribanks's age, and how much older she was than her supposed-suitor—a question always interesting to the female mind. And it was natural that in these circumstances Nettie should come to hear of it all, in its full details, with the various comments naturally suggesting themselves thereupon. What Nettie's opinion was, however, nobody could ever gather; perhaps she thought Dr Edward was justified in putting an immediate barrier between himself and her. At all events, she was perfectly clear upon the point that it could not have been otherwise, and that no other decision was possible to herself.

The spring lagged on, accordingly, under these circumstances. Those commonplace unalterable days, varied in nothing but the natural fluctuations of making and mending,—those evenings with Fred sulky by the fire—always sulky, because deprived by Nettie's presence of his usual indulgences; or if not so, then enjoying himself after his dismal fashion in his own room, with most likely Susan bearing him company, and the little maiden head of the house left all by herself in the solitary parlour,—passed on one by one, each more tedious than the other. It seemed impossible that such heavy hours could last, and prolong themselves into infinitude, as they did; but still one succeeded another in endless hard procession. And Nettie shed back her silky load of hair, and pressed her tiny fingers on her eyes, and went on again, always dauntless. She said to herself, with homely philosophy, that this could not last very long; not with any tragical meaning, but with a recognition of the ordinary laws of nature which young ladies under the pressure of a first disappointment are not apt to recur to. She tried, indeed, to calculate in herself, with forlorn heroism, how long it might be expected to last, and, though she could not fix the period, endeavoured to content herself with the thought that things must eventually fall into their natural condition. In the mean time it was slow and tedious work enough—but they did pass one after another, these inevitable days.

One night Nettie was sitting by herself in the parlour busy over her needlework. Fred and his wife, she thought, were upstairs. They had left her early in the evening,—Susan to lie down, being tired—Fred to his ordinary amusements. It was a matter of course, and cost Nettie no special thought. After the children went to bed, she sat all by herself, with her thread and scissors on the table, working on steadily and quietly at the little garment she was making. Her needle flew swift and nimbly; the sleeve of her dress rustled as she moved her arm; her soft breath went and came: but for that regular monotonous movement, and those faint steady sounds of life, it might have been a picture of domestic tranquillity and quiet, and not a living woman with aches in her heart. It did not matter what she was thinking. She was facing life and fortune—indomitable, not to be discouraged. In the silence of the house she sat late over her needlework, anxious to have some special task finished. She heard the mistress of the cottage locking up, but took no notice of that performance, and went on at her work, forgetting time. It got to be very silent in the house and without; not a sound in the rooms where everybody was asleep; not a sound outside, except an occasional rustle of the night wind through the bare willow-branches—deep night and not a creature awake but herself, sitting in the heart of that intense and throbbing silence. Somehow there was a kind of pleasure to Nettie in the isolation which was so impossible to her at other hours. She sat rapt in that laborious quiet as if her busy fingers were under some spell.

When suddenly she heard a startled motion up-stairs, as if some one had got up hastily; then a rustling about the room overhead, which was Susan's room. After a while, during which Nettie, restored by the sound to all her growing cares, rose instantly to consideration of the question, What had happened now? the door above was stealthily opened, and a footstep came softly down the stair. Nettie put down her work and listened breathlessly. Presently Susan's head peeped in at the parlour door. After all, then, it was only some restlessness of Susan's. Nettie took up her work, impatient, perhaps almost disappointed, with the dead calm in which nothing ever happened. Susan came in stealthy, pale, trembling with cold and fright. She came forward to the table in her white night-dress like a faded ghost. 'Fred has never come in,' said Susan, in a shivering whisper; 'is it very late? He promised he would only be gone an hour. Where *can* he have gone? Nettie, Nettie, don't sit so quiet and stare at me. I fell asleep, or I should have found it out sooner; all the house is locked up, and he has never come in.'

'If he comes we can unlock the house,' said Nettie. 'When did he go out, and why didn't you tell me? Of course I should have let Mrs Smith know, not to frighten her; but I told Fred pretty plainly last time that we could not do with such hours. It will make him ill if he does not mind. Go to bed, and I'll let him in.'

'Go to bed! it is very easy for you to say so; don't you know it's the middle of the night, and as dark as pitch, and my husband out all by himself?' cried Susan. 'Oh, Fred, Fred! after all the promises you made, to use me like this again! Do you think I can go up-stairs and lie shivering in the dark, and imagining all sorts of dreadful things happening to him? I shall stay here with you till he comes in.'

Nettie entered into no controversy. She got up quietly and fetched a shawl, and put it round her shivering sister; then sat down again and took up her needlework. But Susan's excited nerves could not bear the sight of that occupation. The rustle of Nettie's softly-moving hand distracted her. 'It sounds always like Fred's step on the way,' said the fretful anxious woman. 'Oh, Nettie, Nettie! do open the end window and look out; perhaps he is looking for the light in the windows to guide him straight! It is so dark! Open the shutters, Nettie, and, oh, do look out and see! Where do you suppose he can have gone to? I feel such a pang at my heart, I believe I shall die.'

'Oh, no, you will not die,' said Nettie. 'Take a book and read, or do something. We know what is about the worst that will happen to Fred. He will come home *like that* you know, as he did before. We can't mend it, but we need not break our hearts over it. Lie down on the sofa, and put up your feet and wrap the shawl round you if you won't go to bed. I can fancy all very well how it will be. It is nothing new, Susan, that you should break your heart.'

'It's you that have no feeling. Oh, Nettie, how hard you are! I don't believe you know what it is to love anybody,' said Susan. 'Hark! is that some one coming now?'

They thought some one was coming fifty times in the course of that dreadful lingering night. Nobody came; the silence closed in deeper and deeper around the two silent women. All the world—everything round about them, to the veriest atom—seemed asleep. The cricket had stopped his chirrup in the kitchen, and no mouse stirred in the slumbering house. By times Susan dozed on the sofa, shivering, notwithstanding her shawl, and Nettie took up her needlework for the moment to distract her thoughts. When Susan started from these snatches of slumber, she importuned her sister with ceaseless questions and entreaties. Where had he gone?—where did Nettie imagine he could have gone?—and oh! would she go to the window and look out to see if any one was coming, or put the candle to the window to guide him, if perhaps he might have lost the way? At last the terrible pale dawn came in and took the light out of Nettie's candle. The two looked at each other, and acknowledged with a mutual start that the night was over. They had watched these long hours through with sentiments very different; now a certain thrill of sympathy drew Nettie nearer to her sister. It was daylight again, remorseless and uncompromising, and where was Fred, who loved the darkness? He had little money and less credit in the limited place where himself and his story were known. What could have become of him? Nettie acknowledged that there was ground for anxiety. She folded up her work and put out her candle, and promptly took into consideration what she could do.

'If you will go to bed, Susan, I shall go out and look for him,' said Nettie. 'He might have stumbled in the field and fallen asleep. Men have done such things before now, and been none the worse for it. If you will go and lie down, I'll see after it, Susan. Now it's daylight, you know, no great harm can happen to him. Come and lie down, and leave me to look for Fred.'

'But you don't know where to go, and he won't like to have you going after him. Nettie, send to Edward,' said Susan; 'he ought to come and look after his brother: he ought to have done it all through, and not to have left us to manage everything; and he hasn't even been to see us for ever so long. But send to Edward, Nettie—it's his business. For Fred won't like to have you going after him, and you don't know where to go.'

'Fred must have me going after him whether he likes it or no,' said Nettie, sharply, 'and I shall not send to Dr Edward. You choose to insult him whenever you can, and then you think it is his business to look after his brother. Go to bed, and leave it to me. I can't leave you shivering here, to catch something, and be ill, and laid up for weeks. I want to get my bonnet on, and to see you in bed. Make haste, and come up-stairs with me.'

Susan obeyed with some mutterings of inarticulate discontent. The daylight, after the first shock of finding that the night was really over, brought some comfort to her foolish heart. She thought that as Nettie said 'no more harm' could come to him, he must be sleeping somewhere, the foolish fellow. She thought most likely Nettie was right, and that she had best go to bed to consume the weary time till there could be something heard of him; and Nettie, of course, would find it all out.

Such was the arrangement accordingly. Susan covered herself up warm, and lay thinking all she should say to him when he came home, and how she certainly never would again let him go out and keep it secret from Nettie. Nettie, for her part, bathed her hot eyes, put on her bonnet, and went out, quietly undoing all the bolts and bars, into the chill morning world, where nobody was yet awake. She was a little uncertain which way to turn, but noway uncertain of her business. Whether he had gone into the town, or towards the low quarter by the banks of the canal, she felt it difficult to conclude. But remembering her own suggestion that he might have stumbled in the field, and fallen asleep there, she took her way across the misty grass. It was still spring, and a little hoar-frost crisped the wintry sod. Everything lay forlorn and chill under the leaden morning skies—not even an early market-cart disturbed the echoes. When the cock crew somewhere, it startled Nettie. She went like a spectre across the misty fields, looking down into the ditches and all the inequalities of the way. On the other side lay the canal, not visible, except by the line of road that wound beside it, from the dead flat around. She bent her steps in that direction, thinking of a certain mean little tavern which, somehow, when she saw it, she had associated with Fred—a place where the men at the door looked slovenly and heated, like Fred himself, and lounged with their hands in their pockets at noon of working-days. Some instinct guided Nettie there.

But she had no need to go so far. Before she reached that place the first sounds of life that she had yet heard attracted Nettie's attention. They came from a boat which lay in the canal, in which the bargemen seemed preparing to start on their day's journey. Some men were leisurely leading forward the horses to the towing-path, while two in the boat were preparing for their start inside. All at once a strange cry rang into the still, chill air—such a cry as startles all who can hear it. The men with the horses hurried forward to the edge of the canal, the bargemen hung over the side of their boat; visible excitement rose among them about something there. Nettie, never afraid, was less timid than ever this morning. Without thinking of the risk of trusting herself with these rude fellows alone, she went straight forward into the midst of them with a curiosity for which she could scarcely account; not anxiety, only a certain wonder and impatience, possessed her to see what they had here.

What had they there?—not a man—a dreadful drowned image, all soiled and swollen—a squalid tragic form, immovable, never to move more. Nettie did not need to look at the dread, uncovered, upturned face. The moment she saw the vague shape of it rising against the side of the boat, a heap of dead limbs, recognisable only as something human, the terrible truth flashed upon Nettie. She had found not him, but It. She saw nothing more for one awful moment—heaven and earth reeling and circling around her, and a horror of darkness on her eyes. Then the cold light opened up again—the group of living creatures against the colourless skies, the dead creature staring and ghastly, with awful dead eyes gazing blank into the shuddering day. The girl steadied herself as she could on the brink of the sluggish current, and collected her thoughts. The conclusion to her search, and answer to all her questions, lay, not to be doubted or questioned, before her.

She dared not yield to her own horror, or grief, or dismay. Susan sleeping, unsuspicious, in full trust of his return—the slumbering house into which this dreadful figure must be carried—obliterated all personal impressions from Nettie's mind. She explained to the amazed group who and what the dead man was—where he must be brought to—instantly, silently, before the world was awake. She watched them lay the heavy form upon a board, and took off her own shawl to lay over it, to conceal it from the face of day. Then she went on before them, with her tiny figure in its girlish dress, like a child in the shadow of the rough but pitying group that followed. Nettie did not know why the wind went so chill to her heart after she had taken off her shawl. She did not see the unequal sod under her feet as she went back upon that dread and solemn road. Nothing in the world but what she had to do occupied the throbbing heroic heart. There was nobody else to do it. How could the girl help but execute the work put into her hand? Thinking neither of the hardship nor the horror of such dread work falling to her lot, but only this, that she must do it, Nettie took home to the unconscious sleeping cottage that thing which was Fred Rider; no heavier on his bearers' hands to-day than he had been already for years of his wasted life.*

CHAPTER X

WHEN Nettie opened the door of the sleeping house with the great key she had carried with her in her early dreadful expedition, there was still nobody stirring in the unconscious cottage. She paused at the door, with the four men behind her carrying shoulder-high that terrible motionless burden. Where was she to lay it? In her own room, where she had not slept that night, little Freddy was still sleeping. In another was the widow, overcome by watching and fretful anxiety. The other fatherless creatures lay in the little dressing-room. Nowhere but in the parlour, from which Fred not so very long ago had driven his disgusted brother—the only place she had where Nettie's own feminine niceties could find expression, and where the accessories of her own daily life and work were all accumulated. She lingered even at that dread moment with a pang of natural reluctance to associate that little sanctuary with the horror and misery of this bringing-home; but when every feeling gave way to the pressure of necessity, that superficial one was not like to resist it. Her companions were not aware that she had hesitated even for that moment. She seemed to them to glide softly, steadfastly, without any faltering, before them into the little silent womanly room, where her night's work was folded tidily upon the table, and her tiny thimble and scissors laid beside it. What a heartrending contrast lay between those domestic traces and that dreadful muffled figure, covered from the light of day with Nettie's shawl, which was now laid down there, Nettie did not pause to think of. She stood still for a moment, gazing at it with a sob of excitement and agitation swelling into her throat; scarcely grief—perhaps that was not possible—but the intensest remorseful pity over the lost life. The rude fellows beside her stood silent, not without a certain pang of tenderness and sympathy in their half-savage hearts. She took her little purse out and emptied it of its few silver coins among them. They trod softly, but their heavy footsteps were heard, notwithstanding, through all the little house. Nettie could already hear the alarmed stirring up-stairs of the master and mistress of the cottage; and, knowing what explanations she must give, and all the dreadful business before her, made haste to get her strange companions away before Mrs Smith came down-stairs. One of them, however, as he followed his comrades out of the room, from some confused instinct of help and pity, asked whether he should not fetch a doctor? The question struck the resolute little girl with a pang sharper than this morning's horror had yet given her. Had she perhaps neglected the first duty of all, the possibility of restoration? She went back, without answering him, to lift the shawl from that dreadful face, and satisfy herself whether she had done that last irremediable wrong to Fred. As she met the dreadful stare of those dead eyes, all the revulsion of feeling which comes to the hearts of the living in presence of the dead overpowered Nettie. She gave a little cry of inarticulate momentary anguish. The soul of that confused and tremulous outcry was Pardon! pardon! What love was ever so true, what tenderness so constant and unfailing, that did not instinctively utter that cry when the watched life had ended, and pardon could no longer come from those sealed lips? Nettie had not loved that shamed and ruined man—she had done him the offices of affection, and endured and sometimes scorned him. She stood remorseful by his side in that first dread hour, which had changed Fred's shabby presence into something awful; and her generous soul burst forth in that cry of penitence which every human creature owes its brother. The tender-hearted bargeman who had asked leave to fetch a doctor, drew near her with a kindred instinct—'Don't take on, miss—there's the crowner yet—and a deal to look to,' said the kind rough fellow, who knew Nettie. The words recalled her to herself—but with the softened feelings of the moment a certain longing for somebody to stand by her in this unlooked-for extremity came over the forlorn courageous creature, who never yet, amid all her labours, had encountered an emergency like this. She laid the shawl reverently back over that dead face, and sent a message to the doctor with lips that trembled in spite of herself. 'Tell him what has happened, and say he is to come as soon as he can,' said Nettie; 'for I do not understand all that has to be done. Tell him I sent you; and now go—please go before they all come down-stairs.'

But when Nettie turned in again, after closing the door, into that house so entirely changed in character by the solemn inmate who had entered it, she was confronted by the amazed and troubled apparition of Mrs Smith, half-dressed, and full of wonder and indignation. A gasping exclamation of 'Miss!' was all that good woman could utter. She had with her own eyes perceived some of the 'roughs' of Carlingford emerging from her respectable door under Nettie's grave supervision, and yet could not in her heart, notwithstanding appearances, think any harm of Nettie; while, at the same time, a hundred alarms for the safety of her household goods shook her soul.

Nettie turned towards her steadily, with her face pallid and her brilliant eyes heavy. 'Hush,' she said; 'Susan knows nothing yet. Let her have her rest while she can. We have been watching for him all night, and poor Susan is sleeping, and does not know.'

'Know what?—what has happened?—he's been and killed himself? Oh, miss, don't you go for to say so!' cried Mrs Smith, in natural dismay and terror.

'No,' cried Nettie, with a long sigh that relieved her breast, 'not so bad as that, thank Heaven; but hush, hush! I cannot go and tell Susan just yet—not just yet. Oh, give me a moment to get breath! For he is dead! I tell you, *hush!*' cried Nettie, seizing the woman's hand, and wringing it, in the extremity of her terror for alarming Susan. 'Don't you understand me? She is a widow, and she does not know—her husband is dead, and she does not know. Have you no pity for her in your own heart?'

'Lord ha' mercy! but wait till I call Smith,' cried the alarmed landlady, shrinking, yet eager to know the horribly interesting details of that tragedy. She ran breathless up-stairs on that errand, while Nettie went back to the door of the parlour, resolutely locked it, and took away the key. 'Nobody shall go gazing and talking over him, and making a wonder of poor Fred,' said Nettie to herself, shaking off from her long eyelashes the tear which came out of the compunction of her heart. 'Poor Fred!' She sat down on one of the chairs of the little hall beside that closed door. The children and their mother up-stairs still slept unsuspicious; and their young guardian, with a world of thoughts rising in her mind, sat still and pondered. The past was suddenly cut off from the future by this dreadful unthought-of event. She had come to a dead pause in that life, which to every spectator was so strangely out of accordance with her youth, but which was to herself such simple and plain necessity as to permit no questioning. She was brought suddenly to a standstill at this terrible moment, and sat turning her dauntless little face to the new trial before her, pale, but undismayed. Nettie did not deceive herself even in her thoughts. She saw, with the intuitive foresight of a keen observer, her sister's violent momentary grief, her indolent acceptance of the position after a while, the selfish reserve of repining and discontent which Susan would establish in the memory of poor Fred: she saw how, with fuller certainty than ever, because now more naturally, she herself, her mind, her laborious hands, her little fortune, would belong to the fatherless family. She did not sigh over the prospect, or falter; but she exercised no self-delusion on the subject. There was nobody but she to do it—nobody but she, in her tender maidenhood, to manage all the vulgar tragical business which must, this very day, confirm to the knowledge of the little surrounding world the event which had happened—nobody but herself to tell the tale to the widow, to bear all the burdens of the time. Nettie did not think over these particulars with self-pity, or wonder over her hard lot. She did not imagine herself to have chosen this lot at all. There was nobody else to do it—that was the simple secret of her strength.

But this interval of forlorn repose was a very brief one. Smith came down putting on his coat, and looking scared and bewildered; his wife, eager, curious, and excited, closely following. Nettie rose when they approached her to forestall their questions.

'My brother-in-law is dead,' she said. 'He fell into the canal last night and was drowned. I went out to look for him, and—and found him, poor fellow! Oh, don't cry out or make a noise: remember Susan does not know! Now, dear Mrs Smith, I know you are kind—I know you will not vex me just at this moment. I have had him laid *there* till his brother comes. Oh, don't say it's dreadful! Do you think I cannot see how dreadful it is? but we must not think about that, only what has to be done. When Dr Edward comes, I will wake my sister; but just for this moment, oh have patience! I had no place to put him except *there*.'

'But, Lord bless us, he mightn't be clean gone: he might be recovered, poor gentleman! Smith can run for Dr Marjoribanks; he is nearer nor Dr Rider,' cried the curious excited landlady, with her hand upon the locked door.

Nettie made no answer. She took them into the room in solemn silence, and showed them the stark and ghastly figure, for which all possibilities had been over in the dark midnight waters hours ago. The earliest gleam of sunshine came shining in at that moment through the window which last night Nettie had opened that Fred might see the light in it and be guided home. It seemed to strike like a reproach upon that quick-throbbing impatient heart, which felt as a sin against the dead its own lack of natural grief and affection. She went hurriedly to draw down the blinds and close out the unwelcome light. 'Now he is gone, nobody shall slight or scorn him,' said Nettie to herself, with hot tears; and she turned the wondering dismayed couple—already awakening out of their first horror, to think of the injury done to their house and 'lodgings,' and all the notoriety of an inquest—out of the room, and locked the door upon the unwilling owners, whom nothing but her resolute face prevented from bursting forth in selfish but natural lamentations over their own secondary share in so disastrous an event. Nettie sat down again, a silent little sentinel by the closed door, without her shawl, and with her tiny chilled feet on the cold tiles. Nettie sat silent, too much occupied even to ascertain the causes of her personal discomfort. She had indeed enough to think of; and while her little girlish figure, so dainty, so light, so unlike her fortunes, remained in that unusual stillness, her mind and heart were palpitating with thoughts—all kinds of thoughts; not only considerations worthy the solemnity and horror of the moment, but every kind of trivial and secondary necessity, passed through that restless soul, all throbbing with life and action, more self-conscious than usual from the fact of its outward stillness. A hundred rapid conclusions and calculations about the funeral, the mourning, the change of domestic habits involved, darted through Nettie's mind. It was a relief to her to leap forward into these after-matters. The immediate necessity before her— the dreadful errand on which she must presently go to her sister's bedside—the burst of wailing and reproachful grief which all alone Nettie would have to encounter and subdue, were not to be thought of. She bent down her little head into her hands, and once more shed back that hair which, never relieved out of its braids through all this long night, began to droop over her pale cheeks; and a quick sigh of impatience, of energy restrained, of such powerlessness as her courageous capable soul, in the very excess of its courage and capacity, felt in its approaching conflict with the feeble foolish creature, who never could be stimulated out of her own narrow possibilities, burst from Nettie's breast. But the sigh was as much physical as mental—the long-drawn breath of mingled weariness and restlessness—the instinct to be doing, and the exhaustion of long labour and emotion, blended together. Thus she waited while the cold spring morning brightened, and Mrs Smith went about her early domestic business, returning often into the little back-parlour with the mullioned window, of which domestic Gothic treatment had made a condemned cell, to re-express her anxieties and horrors. Nettie had an instinctive consciousness even of Mrs Smith's grievance. She knew this dismal association would ruin 'the lodgings,' and felt that here was another bond upon her to remain at St Roque's, however much she might long to escape and flee away.

All these crowding and breathless thoughts were a few minutes after reduced to absolute momentary stillness. It was by a step outside coming hastily with rapid purpose along the silent way. Nettie rose up to meet Edward Rider; not as the angry lover still fiercely resentful of that rejection, which was no rejection, but only a bare and simple statement of necessity; not as the suitor of Miss Marjoribanks; simply as the only creature in the world who could help her, or to whom she would delegate any portion of her own hard but inevitable work. She opened the door before he had time to knock, and held out her hand to him silently, quite unawares betraying her recognition of his step—her comfort in his presence. That meeting flushed the doctor's anxious face with a mingled shame and triumph not expressible in words, but left Nettie as pale, as preoccupied, as much absorbed in her thoughts and duties as before.

'Dr Edward, I should not have sent for you if I could have done it all myself,' said Nettie; 'but I knew you would think it right to be here now. And I have Susan and the children to look to. I commit this to you.'

'Do they know?' said the doctor, taking the key she gave him, and holding fast, with an instinct of compassion almost more strong than love, the little hand which never trembled.

'I will tell Susan, now that you have come—I could not before,' said Nettie, with another sigh. 'Poor Susan! I was glad to let her sleep.'

'But there is no one to think whether you sleep or not,' cried Edward Rider. 'And those eyes have watched all night. Nettie, Nettie, could not you have sent for me sooner? A word would have brought me at any moment.'

'You were not wanted till now,' said Nettie, not without a touch of womanly pride. 'I have always been able to do my own work, Dr Edward. But, now, don't let us quarrel any more,' she said, after a pause. 'You were angry once, and I don't wonder. Never mind all that, but let us be friends; and don't let all the people, and strangers, and men who don't belong to us,' cried Nettie once more, with hot tears in her eyes, 'be hard upon poor Fred!'

The next moment she had vanished up-stairs and left the doctor alone, standing in the little cold hall with the key in his hand, and Mrs Smith's troubled countenance beholding him from far. Edward Rider paused before he entered upon his dismal share of this morning's work. Death itself did not suffice to endear Fred Rider to his brother. But he stood still, with a certain self-reproach, to withdraw his thoughts, if he could, from Nettie, and to subdue the thrill—the most living touch of life—which this meeting had stirred within him, before he entered that miserable chamber of death.

CHAPTER XI

THAT dreadful day ebbed over slowly—tedious, yet so full of events and dismal business that it looked like a year rather than a day. The necessary investigations were got through without any special call upon Nettie. She spent the most of the day up-stairs with Susan, whose wild refusal to believe at first, and sullen stupor afterwards, were little different from the picture which Nettie's imagination had already made. The children received the news with wondering stares and questions. That they did not understand it was little, but that they scarcely were interested after the first movement of curiosity, disappointed and wounded the impatient heart, which unconsciously chafed at its own total inability to convey the feelings natural to such a terrible occasion, into any bosom but its own. Nettie's perpetual activity had hitherto saved her from this disgust and disappointment. She had been bitterly intolerant by moments of Fred's disgraceful content and satisfaction with his own indulgences, but had never paused to fret over what she could not help, nor contrast her own high youthful honour and sense of duty with the dull insensibility around her. But to-day had rapt the heroic little girl into a different atmosphere from that she had been breathing hitherto. To-day she was aware that her work had been so far taken out of her hands, and acknowledged in her heart that it was best it should be so. She heard the heavy feet of men coming and going, but was not obliged to descend into immediate conflict with all the circumstances of so horrible a crisis. It was a new sensation to Nettie. A year ago, perhaps, she would not have relinquished even that dreadful business to any one;—to-day, the thought of having some one else who did it for her, and took comfort in relieving her burdened hands, fell with singular soothing power upon the heart which had come to a knowledge of its own weakness in these last tedious months; and as Nettie sat up-stairs with all the remorseful thoughts of nature in her softened heart, the impossibility of impressing her own emotions upon those around her struck her with a deeper sense of impatience, disappointment, and disgust than ever before. When she went softly into the darkened room where Susan lay in her gloomy bed, divided between wailings over the injuries which poor Fred had suffered, the harshness that had driven him out of doors, and the want of his brother or somebody to take care of him, which had brought the poor fellow to such an end—and complaints of the wrong done to herself, the 'want of feeling' shown by her sister, the neglect with which she was treated, Nettie gazed at the sobbing creature with eyes unconsciously wondering, yet but half-surprised. She knew very well beforehand that this was how her dreadful tidings would be received; yet out of her own softened, awed, compunctious heart—her pity too deep for tears over that lost life—Nettie looked with the unbelief of nature at the widowed woman, the creature who had loved him, and been his wife—yet who could only think of somebody else to be blamed, and of herself injured, at that terrible moment when the companion of her life was violently withdrawn from her. And to go out of that obstinately darkened refuge of fretful sorrow, into the room where the blind had been drawn up the moment her back was turned, and where these three tearless children, totally unimpressed by the information which they had received as a piece of news with mingled curiosity and scepticism, occupied themselves with their usual sports, or listened keenly, with sharp remarks, to the sounds below, which only the utmost stretch of Nettie's authority could keep them from descending to investigate, afforded a wonderful reverse to the picture, which startled her in her momentary clear-sightedness. The contrast between her own feelings—she who had no bonds of natural affection to Fred, and to whom he had been, by times, a very irksome burden—and theirs, who were his very own, and belonged to him, appeared to Nettie as no such contrast had ever appeared before. *Her* heart alone was heavy with regret over the ruined man—the now for ever unredeemable life: she only, to whom his death was no loss, but even, if she could have permitted that cruel thought to intervene, a gain and relief, recognised with a pang of compassion almost as sharp as grief, that grievous, miserable fate. When, a few minutes after, the noise of the children's play rose to an outburst, Nettie flushed into a momentary effusion of temper, and silenced the heartless imps with a voice and look which they dared not venture to resist. Her rebuke was, however, interrupted by a sudden call from their mother. 'How can you have the heart!—Oh, Nettie, Nettie! I knew you had no feeling!—you never had any feeling since you were a baby—but how can you speak so to his poor children, now that he has left them on the cold world?' cried Susan, sobbing, from her bed. If Nettie sprang to her feet in sudden heat and disgust, and peremptorily closed the doors intervening between the children and their mother, nobody will much wonder at that movement of impatience. Perhaps Nettie's eyes had never been so entirely opened to the hopeless character of the charge she had taken upon her, as in the temporary seclusion of that day.

And meanwhile, down-stairs, Edward Rider was superintending all the arrangements of the time for Nettie's sake. Not because it was his brother who lay there, no longer a burden to any man; nor because natural duty pointed him out as the natural guardian of the orphaned family. The doctor, indeed, would have done his duty in such a hard case, however it had been required of him; but the circumstances were different now: the melancholy bustle, the shame, the consciousness that everybody knew what manner of existence this lost life had been, the exposure, the publicity—all that would have wrung with a hundred sharp wounds a spirit so susceptible to public comments—came with dulled force upon the doctor's mind to-day. When the people about saw the grave and seemly composure with which he went about this dismal business, without those starts and flushes of grievous irritation and shame which the very mention of his brother had once brought upon him, they believed, and honoured him in the belief, that death had awakened the ancient fraternal kindness in Edward Rider's heart. But it was not fraternal kindness that smoothed off the rude edges of that burden; it was the consciousness of doing Nettie's work for her, taking her place, sparing that creature, over whom his heart yearned, the hardest and painfulest business she had yet been involved in. We cannot take credit for the doctor which he did not deserve. He forgave Fred when he saw his motionless figure, never more to do evil or offend in this world, laid in pitiful solitude in that room, which still was Nettie's room, and which even in death he grudged to his brother. But Edward's distinct apprehension of right and wrong, and Fred's deserts in this world, were not altered by that diviner compunction which had moved Nettie. He forgave, but did not forget, nor defend with remorseful tenderness his brother's memory. Not for Fred's sake, but Nettie's, he held his place in the troubled cottage, and assumed the position of head of the family. Hard certainties of experience prevented the doctor's unimaginative mind from respecting here the ideal anguish of sudden widowhood and bereavement. This was a conclusion noways unnatural or surprising for such a life as Fred's—and Edward knew, with that contemptuous hardness into which incessant personal contact with the world drives most men, that neither the wife nor the children were capable of deep or permanent feeling. 'They will only hang upon *her* all the heavier,' he said to himself, bitterly; and for her, with repentant love, Edward Rider exerted himself. In all the house no heart, but Nettie's alone, acknowledged an ache of pity for Fred and his ruined life. 'Mrs Rider, to be sure, will feel at first—it's only natural,' said Mrs Smith; 'but there wasn't nothing else to be looked for; and if it were not hardhearted to say it, and him lying in his coffin, they'll be a deal better off without him nor with him. But Smith and me, we have ourselves to look to, and it's a terrible blow, is this, to a house, as was always as respectable as e'er a one in Carlingford. The lodgings is ruined! The very marks of the feet, if it was nothing else!' cried the afflicted landlady, contemplating the scratched tiles in the hall with actual tears of vexation and regret. But this was the true state of the case to every unconcerned spectator. Only Nettie, on whom the burden had fallen, and was yet to fall heaviest, felt the eyes, which were hot and heavy with watching, grow dim with tears of unspeakable compassion. From the fulness of her youth and strength—strength so burdened, youth so dauntless and dutiful—Nettie gazed with a pity too deep for words at the awful spectacle of that existence lost. That the lifeless thing in the room below could have been a man, and yet have come and gone so disastrously through the world, was terrible to think of, to that living labouring creature, in the depth of her own strange toils and responsibilities. Her heart ached over that wretched, miserable fate. Neither toil nor anguish was to

be compared to the dread loss of a life sustained by that
departed soul.

CHAPTER XII

IN a few days all this solemn crisis was over, and life went on
again in its ordinary tame current, closing over the dishon-
oured grave where Fred found his rest, henceforward name-
less in the world that had suffered his existence as a cumberer
of the ground for so many years. Had he been the prop of his
house and the light of their eyes, life would have gone on
again after that interruption, all the same, with a persistency
which nothing can impair. As it was, the diminished household resumed its ordinary course of existence, after a very few
days, with little more than outward marks of what had
befallen them. It is true that Nettie sat down with a repug-
nance which she scarcely could either overcome or conceal, to
dispense the domestic provisions at the table which shortly
before had borne so dread a burden. But nobody thought of
that except Nettie; and but for the black dresses and Susan's
cap,* Fred was as if he had never been.

About a week after the funeral, the doctor went solemnly to
visit them in one of those lengthening spring afternoons. Dr
Rider was undeniably nervous and excited about this
interview. He had been at home under pretence of having
luncheon, but in reality to make a solemn toilette, and wind
himself up to the courage necessary for a settlement of affairs.
As he dashed with agitated haste down Grange Lane, he saw
Miss Wodehouse and her sister Lucy coming from St
Roque's, where very probably they too had been making a
visit of condolence to Nettie; and a little nearer that scene of
all his cogitations and troubles appeared, a much less welcome
sight, Miss Marjoribanks, whom all Carlingford, a month ago,
had declared Dr Rider to be 'paying his addresses' to. The
guilty doctor took off his hat to that stout and sensible
wayfarer, with a pang of self-disgust which avenged Nettie.
Along the very road where that little Titania, eager and rapid,

had gone upon her dauntless way so often, to see that comely well-dressed figure, handsome, sprightly, clever—but with such a world of bright youth, tenderness, loveliness, everything that touches the heart of man, between the two! No harm to Miss Marjoribanks; only shame to the doctor, who, out of angry love, pique, and mortification, to vex Nettie, had pretended to transfer the homage due to the fairy princess to that handsome and judicious woman. The experiment had failed as entirely as it deserved to do; and here was Edward Rider, coming back wiser and humbler, content to put that question over again, and stand once more his chance of what his pride had called a rejection, perhaps content to make still greater sacrifices, if the truth were known, and to do anything Nettie asked him, if Nettie would but condescend to ask or enter into terms at all.

He drew up before St Roque's with a dash, which was much more of agitation than display, and, throwing the reins at the head of his little groom, leaped out like a man who did not see where he was going. He saw Mr Wentworth, however, coming out of the church, and turning round amazed to look what vehicle had come to so sudden a standstill there. All the world seemed to be on the road to St Roque's Cottage that spring afternoon. The doctor made a surly gesture of recognition as he passed the curate, who gazed at him in calm astonishment from the church porch. No other intruder appeared between him and the Cottage. He hurried along past the willow-trees with their drooping tassels, surrounded by a certain maze of excitement and agitation. As he went up to the door, it occurred to him suddenly how Nettie had recognised his step that dread morning of Fred's death. The thought came like a stimulus and encouragement to the doctor. He went in with a brighter look, a heart more hopeful. She had opened the door to him before he could knock, held out to him that tiny morsel of a hand which laboured so hard and constantly, said—what did Nettie say? how many times had the doctor conned it over as he went between his patients?— 'You were angry once, and, indeed, I don't wonder.' The doctor went boldly in under the cordial of these simple words.

If she did not wonder that he was angry once, could she think of saying over again that same conclusion which had cast him into such wrathful despair? He went in to try his fortune a second time, secure of his temper at least. *That* could never fail, nor sin against Nettie again.

Edward Rider went in, expectant somehow, even against his reason, to find an altered world in that house from which Fred had gone. He knew better, to be sure, but nature beguiled the young man out of his wisdom. When he went in to the parlour his eyes were opened. Upon the sofa—that same sofa where Fred had lain, all slovenly and mean in his idleness, with his pipe, polluting Nettie's sole retirement—Mrs Fred lay now in her sombre black dress, with the white cap circling her faded face. She had her white handkerchief in her hand, and was carefully arranged upon the sofa, with a chair placed near for sympathisers. At the table, working rapidly as usual, sat Nettie. Sometimes she turned a momentary glance of mingled curiosity and wonder upon her sister. Evidently she did not interfere with this development of sorrow. Nettie had enough to do, besides, with her needlework, and to enjoin a moderate amount of quietness upon Freddy and his little sister, who were building wooden bricks into houses and castles on the floor by her side. When the doctor entered the room he saw how it was with instantaneous insight. Mrs Fred was sitting in state, in the pomp of woe, to receive all the compassionate people who might come to condole with her. Nettie, half impatient, half glad that her sister could amuse herself so, sat in busy toleration, putting up with it, carrying on her own work through it all—and still, as always, those bonds of her own making closed hard and tenacious upon the prop of the house. Even the chance of speaking with her by herself died off into extreme distance. Young Rider, who came in with the full conviction that anger could never more rise in his heart against Nettie, grew pale with passion, resentment, and impatience before he had been a minute in the room. Always the same! Not relieved out of her bondage—closer bound and prisoned than ever! He took, with an impatient involuntary commotion, the chair placed beside the sofa, and sat down in it abruptly with the briefest salutations. His hopes and anticipations all went bitterly back upon his heart. The rustle of Nettie's arm as she spread out that little black frock upon the table, and put on its melancholy trimmings, exasperated afresh the man who five minutes ago did not believe it possible that he ever could feel an impulse of displeasure against her again.

'I cannot say that I expected to see you, Mr Edward,' said Mrs Fred, lifting her handkerchief to her eyes; 'indeed, when I remember the last time you were here, I wonder you could think of coming near us. But now my poor dear Fred is gone, we have nobody to protect us—and of course you don't mind how you hurt my feelings. If you had done your duty by my poor fellow when he was living, he might never—never—'

Here Mrs Fred paused, choked by spiteful tears.

'Dr Edward, don't mind what Susan says,' said Nettie. 'It is very kind of you to come, after everything— If you would only tell the people not to take any notice, but just to let us go on as usual. They all want to be kind, you know—they keep coming, and asking what they can do; and you understand very well there is nothing to do,' said Nettie, with a little pride. 'We are just as we were before—nothing is changed: one does not like to be unkind, but nobody needs to do anything. We shall get along all the same.'

'So it seems, indeed,' said Dr Rider, with irrepressible bitterness; 'all the same! But, indeed, I came specially to ask what my sister-in-law meant to do,' continued the doctor, bent on one last appeal. 'Now that you are left to yourself, Mrs Rider, what do you think of doing? Of course you must have some plans about the children and your future life?'

Mrs Fred looked up at him with momentary alarm and dismay. She did not know what the question meant, but a certain vague terror seized her. It seemed to imply somehow that she was now to be left to her own resources. She gave a certain gasp of appeal to 'Nettie!' and took refuge once more in her handkerchief. The doctor was desperate—he had no mercy in him.

'Nettie! always Nettie!' cried the young man. 'And is it true,

Nettie—is it all the same? Are you always to go on toiling for the miserable comforts of other people? What is to become of us? Have you sold yourself to this fate?'

Nettie laid down the little black frock out of her laborious hands. 'You have been up all night, Dr Edward,' she said, with a certain tenderness, looking at his agitated face; 'you are tired out and sick at the heart. I know it makes you say things you would not say; but after all, you know, except poor Fred, whom none of you think of, everything is the very same. I cannot make it different—nothing can make it different. There is Susan plain enough to be seen—and there are the children. Sometimes it has come into my mind,' said Nettie, 'that as I shall never be able to afford a *very* good education for the children, it would be better to take them out to the colony again, where they might get on better than here. But it is a dreadful long voyage; and we have no near friends there, or anywhere else: and,' concluded the steadfast creature, who had dropped these last words from her lips sentence by sentence, as if eager to impress upon her own mind the arguments against that proceeding—'and,' said Nettie, with wistful pathetic honesty, not able to deny the real cause of the reluctance altogether, 'I don't seem to have the heart for it now.'

Dr Rider started up from his chair. He went to Nettie's side with a sudden thrill of agitation and passion. He clasped the hand with which Nettie was smoothing out that little frock, and crushed the delicate fingers in his inconsiderate grasp. 'Nettie! if you must carry them always upon your shoulders, cannot we do it together, at least?' cried the doctor, carried away beyond every boundary of sense or prudence. He got down on his knees beside the table, not kneeling to her, but only compelling her attention—demanding to see the answer of her eyes, the quiver of her mouth. For that moment Nettie's defences too fell before this unlooked-for outburst of a love that had forgotten prudence. Her mouth quivered, her eyes filled. If it were possible—if it were only possible!—— They had both forgotten the spectators who gazed with curious eyes, all unaware how deeply their own fate was involved; and that fate was still trembling in the breathless interval, when a vulgar finger touched those delicate balances of possibility, and the crisis was over, perhaps never to return.

'Nettie!' cried Mrs Fred, 'if Edward Rider has no respect for me, nor for my poor Fred—my poor, dear, injured husband, that helped to bring him up, and gave up his practice to him, and died, as I might say, by his neglect—Nettie! how can you be so cruel to your sister? How can you go taking his hand, and looking as if he were your lover? You never had any feeling for me, though everybody thinks so much of you. And now I know what I have to expect. The moment my poor dear Fred's head is laid in the grave—as soon as ever you have me in your own hands, and nobody to protect me!—oh, my Fred! my Fred!—as soon as you are gone, this is how they are using your poor helpless family!—and soon, soon I shall die too, and you will not be encumbered with *me!*'

Long before this sobbing speech was concluded, Dr Rider had risen to his feet, and was pacing through the little room with hasty steps of disgust and rage, and an agitation which overwhelmed all his attempts to master it; while Nettie sat supporting her head in her hands, pressing her fingers upon her hot eyes, beholding that fair impossible vision break and disappear from before her. Nettie's heart groaned within her, and beat against the delicate bosom which, in its tender weakness, was mighty as a giant's. She made no answer to her sister's outcry, nor attempted to comfort the hysterical sobbing into which Susan fell. Nettie gave up the hopeless business without being deceived by those selfish demonstrations. She was not even fortunate enough to be able to persuade herself into admiring love and enthusiasm for those to whom necessity obliged her to give up her own life. She said nothing; she knew the sobs would subside, the end would be gained, the insignificant soul lapse into comfort, and with a sigh of compulsory resignation Nettie yielded once more to her fate.

'Dr Edward, do not think of me any more,' she said, resolutely, rising and going out to the door with him, in her simplicity and courage. 'You see very well it is impossible. I know you see it as well as I do. If we could be friends as we once were, I should be very, very glad, but I don't think it is possible just now. Don't say anything. We both know how it is, and neither of us can help it. If we could get not to think of each other, that would be best,' said Nettie, with another sigh; 'but in the mean time let us say good-bye, and speak of it no more.'

If the doctor did not take his dismissal exactly so—if Nettie's identification of her own sentiments with his did lead to a warmer tenderness in that farewell, which could not be final while such a bond united them, it was at least with an absolute conviction of the impossibility of any closer union that they parted. The doctor sprang into his drag and dashed away to his patients, plunging into the work which he had somewhat neglected during that exciting day. He was not without some comfort as he went about his business with Care behind him, but that very comfort embittered the pang of the compulsory submission. To think he must leave her there with those burdens upon her delicate shoulders—to believe her his, yet not his, the victim of an unnatural bondage—drove Edward Rider desperate as he devoured the way. A hundred times in an hour he made up his mind to hasten back again and snatch her forcibly out of that thraldom, and yet a hundred times had to fall back consuming his heart with fiery irritation, and chafing at all that seemed duty and necessity to Nettie. As he was proceeding on his troubled way it occurred to him to meet—surely everybody in Carlingford was out of doors this particular afternoon!—that prosperous wife, Mrs John Brown, who had once been Bessie Christian. She was a very pale apparition now to the doctor, engrossed as he was with an influence much more imperious and enthralling than hers had ever been; but the sight of her, on this day of all others, was not without its effect upon Edward Rider. Had not she too been burdened with responsibilities which the doctor would not venture to take upon his shoulders, but which another man, more daring, *had* taken, and rendered bearable? As the thought of that possibility occurred to him, a sudden vision of Mrs Fred's faded figure flashed across his eyes. In the excitement of the moment he touched too sharply with his whip that horse which had suffered the penalty of most of his vagaries of temper and imagination for some time past. The long-suffering beast was aggravated out of patience by that unexpected irritation. It was all the doctor could do for the next ten minutes to keep his seat and his command over the exasperated animal, whose sudden frenzy terrified Mrs Brown, and drove her to take refuge in the nearest shop. How little the Carlingford public, who paused at a respectful distance to look on, guessed those emotions which moved the doctor as they watched him subduing his rebellious horse with vigorous arm and passionate looks! Bessie, with a little palpitation at her heart, could not refrain from a passing wonder whether the sight of herself had anything to do with that sudden conflict. Mrs Brown knew little about St Roque's Cottage, but had heard of Miss Marjoribanks, who it was not to be supposed could hold a very absolute sway over the doctor. Meanwhile Dr Rider struggled with his horse with all the intensity of determination with which he would have struggled against his fate had that been practicable. With set teeth and eyes that blazed with sudden rage and resolution, he subdued the unruly brute, and forced it to acknowledge his mastery. When he drove the vanquished animal, all quivering with pain and passion, on its further course, the struggle had refreshed his mind a little. Ah, if life and adverse fortune could but be vanquished so!—but all Edward Rider's resolution and courage died into hopeless disgust before the recollection of Mrs Fred upon that sofa. Even with Nettie at one hand, that peevish phantom on the other, those heartless imps in insolent possession of the wonderful little guardian who would not forsake them, made up a picture which made the doctor's heart sick. No! Nettie was right. It was impossible. Love, patience, charity, after all, are but human qualities, when they have to be held against daily disgusts, irritations, and miseries. The doctor knew as well as Nettie did that he could not bear it. He knew even, as perhaps Nettie did not know, that her own image would suffer from the association; and that a man so faulty and imperfect as himself could not long refrain from resenting upon his wife the dismal restraints of such a burden. With a self-disgust which was most cutting of all, Edward Rider felt that he should descend to that injustice; and that not even Nettie herself would be safe against the effusions of his impatience and indignation. All through the course of this exciting episode in his life, his own foresight and knowledge of himself had been torture to the doctor, and had brought him, in addition to all other trials, silent agonies of self-contempt which nobody could guess. But he could not alter his nature. He went through his day's work very wretched and dejected, yet with an ineffable touch of secret comfort behind all, which sometimes would look him in the face for a moment like a passing sunbeam, yet sometimes seemed to exasperate beyond bearing the tantalising misery of his fate. A more agitated, disturbed, passionate, and self-consuming man than the doctor was not in Carlingford, nor within a hundred miles; yet it was not perfect wretchedness after all.

Nettie, on her part, went back to Mrs Fred in the parlour, after she had parted from Edward Rider, with feelings somewhat different from the doctor's. Perhaps she too had indulged a certain pang of expectation as to what might follow after Fred was gone, in the new world that should be after that change; for Nettie, with all her wisdom of experience, was still too young not to believe that circumstances did change everything now and then, even dispositions and hearts. But before Dr Rider knew it—before he had even wound up his courage to the pitch of asking what was now to happen to them—the little Australian had made up her mind to that which was inevitable. The same Susan whose ceaseless discontents and selfish love had driven Nettie across the seas to look for Fred, was now reposing on that sofa in her widow's cap, altogether unchanged, as helpless and unabandonable, as dependent, as much a fool as ever. The superior wretchedness of Fred's presence and life had partially veiled Susan's character since they came to Carlingford. Now she had the field to herself again, and Nettie recognised at once the familiar picture. From the moment when Susan in her mourning came down-stairs, Nettie acknowledged the weakness of circumstances, the pertinacity of nature. What could she do?—she gave up the scarcely-formed germ of hope that had begun to appear in her breast. She made up her mind silently to what must be. No agonies of martyrdom could have made Nettie desert her post and abandon these helpless souls. They could do nothing for themselves, old or young of them; and who was there to do it all? she asked herself, with that perpetual reference to necessity which was Nettie's sole process of reasoning on the subject. Thus considered, the arguments were short and telling, the conclusion unmistakable. Here was this visible piece of business— four helpless creatures to be supported and provided and thrust through life somehow—with nobody in the world but Nettie to do it; to bring them daily bread and hourly tendance, to keep them alive, and shelter their helplessness with refuge and protection. She drew up her tiny Titania figure, and put back her silken flood of hair, and stood upright to the full extent of her little stature, when she recognised the truth. Nobody could share with her that warfare which was hard to flesh and blood. There was nothing to be said on the subject— no possibility of help. She was almost glad when that interview, which she foresaw, was over, and when Edward had recognised as well as herself the necessities of the matter. She went back again out of the little hall where, for one moment and no more, the lights of youth and love had flushed over Nettie, suffusing her paleness with rose-blushes. Now it was all over. The romance was ended, the hero gone, and life had begun anew.

'I can't say I ever liked this place,' sighed Mrs Fred, when the lamp was lit that evening, and Nettie had come downstairs again after seeing the children in bed. 'It was always dull and dreary to me. If we hadn't been so far out of Carlingford, things might have been very different. My poor Fred! instead of taking care of him, all the dangers that ever could be were put in his way.'

This sentence was concluded by some weeping, of which, however, Nettie did not take any notice. Making mourning by lamp-light is hard work, as all poor seamstresses know. Nettie had no tears in the eyes that were fixed intently upon the little coat which was to complete Freddy's outfit; and she did not even look up from that urgent occupation to deprecate Susan's tears.

'I tell you, Nettie, I never could bear this place,' said Mrs Fred; 'and now, whenever I move, the dreadful thoughts that come into my mind are enough to kill me. You always were strong from a baby, and of course it is not to be expected that you can understand what my feelings are. And Mrs Smith is anything but kind, or indeed civil, sometimes; and I don't think I could live through another of these cold English winters. I am sure I never could keep alive through another winter, now my poor Fred's gone.'

'Well?' asked Nettie, with involuntary harshness in her voice.

'I don't care for myself,' sobbed Mrs Fred, 'but it's dreadful to see you so unfeeling, and to think what would become of his poor children if anything were to happen to me. I do believe you would marry Edward Rider if it were not for me, and go and wrong the poor children, and leave them destitute. Nobody has the feeling for them that a mother has; but if I live another winter in England, I know I shall die.'

'You have thought of dying a great many times,' said Nettie, 'but it has never come to anything. Never mind that just now. What do you want? Do you want me to take you back to the colony all these thousands of miles, after so many expenses as there have been already?—or what is it you want me to do?'

'You always speak of expenses, Nettie: you are very poor-spirited, though people think so much of you,' said Susan; 'and don't you think it is natural I should wish to go home, now my poor Fred has been taken away from me? And you confessed it would be best for the children. We know scarcely anybody here, and the very sight of *that* Edward that was so cruel to my poor Fred——'

'Susan, don't be a fool,' said Nettie; 'you know better in your heart. If you will tell me plainly what you want, I shall listen to you; but if not, I will go up-stairs and put away Freddy's things. Only one thing I may tell you at once; you may leave Carlingford if you please, but I shall not. I cannot take you back again to have you ill all the way, and the children threatening to fall overboard twenty times in a day. I did it once, but I will not do it again.'

'You *will* not?' cried Susan. 'Ah, I know what you mean: I know very well what you mean. You think Edward Rider——'

Nettie rose up and faced her sister with a little gasp of resolution which frightened Mrs Fred. 'I don't intend to have anything said about Edward Rider,' said Nettie; 'he has nothing to do with it one way or another. I tell you what I told him, that I have not the heart to carry you all back again; and I cannot afford it either; and if you want anything more, Susan,' added the peremptory creature, flashing forth into something of her old spirit, 'I shan't go—and that is surely enough.'

With which words Nettie went off like a little sprite to put away Freddy's coat, newly completed, along with the other articles of his wardrobe, at which she had been working all day. In that momentary impulse of decision and self-will, a few notes of a song came unawares from Nettie's lip, as she glanced, light and rapid as a fairy, up-stairs. She stopped a minute after with a sigh. Were Nettie's singing days over? She had at least come at last to find her life hard, and to acknowledge that this necessity which was laid upon her was grievous by times to flesh and blood; but not the less for that did she arrange Freddy's little garments daintily in the drawers, and pause, before she went down-stairs again, to cover him up in his little bed.

Susan still sat pondering and crying over the fire. Her tears were a great resource to Mrs Fred. They occupied her when she had nothing else to occupy herself with; and when she cast a weeping glance up from her handkerchief to see Nettie draw her chair again to the table, and lay down a little pile of pinafores and tuckers which required supervision, Susan wept still more, and said it was well to be Nettie, who never was overcome by her feelings. Thus the evening passed dully enough. Just then, perhaps, Nettie was not a very conversable companion. Such interviews as that of this day linger in the heads of the interlocutors, and perhaps produce more notable effects afterwards than at the moment. Nettie was not thinking about it. She was simply going over it again, finding out the tones and meanings which, in the haste and excitement of their occurrence, did not have their full force. The fulness of detail that lingers about such pictures, which are not half apprehended till they have been gone over again and again, is marvellous. The pinafores went unconsciously through Nettie's fingers. She was scarcely aware of Susan crying by the fire. Though it had been in some degree a final and almost hopeless parting, there was comfort behind the cloud to Nettie as well as to the doctor. She had forgotten all about the discussion with which the evening began before Susan spoke again.

'Richard Chatham came home with the last mail,' said Susan, making a feeble effort to renew the fight. 'He sent me a letter last week, you know. I daresay he will come to see us. Richard Chatham from Melbourne, Nettie. I daresay he will not stay out of the colony long.'

Nettie, who was lost in her own thoughts, made no reply.

'I daresay,' repeated Mrs Fred, 'he will be going out again in a month or two. I do not believe he could bear this dreadful English winter any more than I could. I daresay he'd be glad to take care of us out—if you should change your mind about going, Nettie.'

Nettie gave her sister a glance of resolution and impatience —a swift glance upward from her work, enough to show she marked and understood—but still did not speak.

'Richard Chatham was always very good-natured: it would be such a good thing for us to go in the same ship—if you should happen to change your mind about going, Nettie,' said Mrs Fred, rising to retire to her room. 'I am going to bed to try to get a little sleep. Such wretched nights as I have would kill anybody. I should not wonder if Richard Chatham came some of these days to see us. Poor fellow! he had always a great fancy for *our* family; and it would be *such* a thing for us, Nettie, if you should change your mind about going, to go in the same ship!'

With which Parthian shot Mrs Fred made her way up-stairs and retired from the field. Nettie woke with a startled consciousness out of her dreams, to perceive that here was the process of iteration begun which drives the wisest to do the will of fools. She woke up to it for a moment, and, raising her drooping head, watched her sister make her way, with her handkerchief in her hand, and the broad white bands of her cap streaming over her shoulders, to the door. Susan stole a glance round before she disappeared, to catch the startled glance of that resolute little face, only half woke up, but wholly determined. Though Mrs Fred dared not say another word at that moment, she disappeared full of the conviction that her arrow had told, and that the endless persistence with which she herself, a woman and a fool, was gifted, need only be duly exercised to win the day. When Susan was gone, that parting arrow did quiver for a moment in Nettie's heart; but the brave little girl had, for that one night, a protection which her sister wist* not of. After the door closed, Nettie fell back once more into that hour of existence which expanded and opened out the more for every new approach which memory made to it. Sweet nature, gentle youth, and the Magician greater than either, came round her in a potent circle and defended Nettie. The woman was better off than the man in this hour of their separation, yet union. He chafed at the consolation which was but visionary; she, perhaps, in that visionary, ineffable solacement found a happiness greater than any reality could ever give.

CHAPTER XIII

IT was some months after the time of this conversation when a man, unlike the usual aspect of man in Carlingford, appeared at the inn with a carpet-bag, and asked his way to St Roque's Cottage. Beards were not common in those days: nobody grew one in Carlingford except Mr Lake,* who, in his joint capacity of portrait-painter and drawing-master, represented the erratic and lawless followers of Art to the imagination of the respectable town. But the stranger who made his sudden appearance at the Blue Boar wore such a forest of hair on the lower part of his burly countenance as obliterated all ordinary landmarks in that region, and by comparison made Mr Lake's dainty little moustache and *etceteras* sink into utter propriety and respectableness. The rest of the figure corresponded with this luxuriant feature; the man was large and burly, a trifle too stout for a perfect athlete, but powerful and vigorous almost beyond anything then known in Carlingford. It was now summer, and warm weather, and the dress of the new-comer was as unusual as the other particulars of his appearance. In his broad straw-hat and linen coat he stood cool and large in the shady hall of the Blue Boar, with glimpses of white English linen appearing under his forest of beard, and round his brown sun-scorched wrists. A very small stretch of imagination was necessary to thrust pistols into his belt and a cutlass into his hand, and reveal him as the settler-adventurer of a half-savage disturbed country, equally ready to work or to fight, and more at home in the shifts and expedients of the wilderness than among the bonds of civilisation; yet always retaining, as English adventurers will, certain dainty personal particulars—such, for instance, as that prejudice in favour of clean linen, which only the highest civilisation can cultivate into perfection. He went off down Grange Lane with the swing and poise of a Hercules when the admiring waiters directed him to the Cottage. Miss Wodehouse, who was standing at the door with Lucy, in the long grey cloak and close bonnet lately adopted by the sisterhood of mercy, which had timidly, under the auspices of the perpetual curate, set itself a-going at St Roque's, looked after the savage man with an instinct of gentle curiosity, wondering where he was going and where he came from. To tell the truth, that tender-hearted soul could with more comfort to herself have stepped down a little on the road to St Roque's, and watched whether that extraordinary figure was in search of Nettie—a suspicion which immediately occurred to her—than she could set out upon the district-visiting, to which Lucy now led her forth. But Miss Wodehouse had tremulously taken example by the late rector, whose abrupt retirement from the duties for which he did not feel himself qualified, the good people in Carlingford had scarcely stopped discussing. Miss Wodehouse, deeply impressed in her gentle mind by the incidents of that time, had considered it her duty to reclaim if possible—she who had no circle of college dons to retire into—her own life from its habits of quiet indolence. She consented to go with Lucy into all the charitable affairs of Carlingford. She stood silent with a pitying face, and believed in all the pretences of beggary which Lucy saw through by natural insight. But it was no more her natural element than the long grey cloak was a natural garment for that spotless, dove-coloured woman. Her eyes turned wistfully after the stranger with suppressed impulses of gentle curiosity and gossip. She knew very well he did not belong to Carlingford. She knew nobody in Grange Lane or the neighbourhood to whom he could belong. She wanted very much to stop and inquire at the stable-boy of the Blue Boar, their own gardener's son, who and what this new-comer was, and turned back to look after him before she turned out of George Street following Lucy, with lively anxiety to know whether he was going to St Roque's. Perhaps the labours of a sisterhood of mercy require a special organisation even of the kind female soul. Miss Wodehouse, the most tender-hearted of human creatures, did not rise to that development; and, with a little pang of unsatisfied wonder, saw the unaccustomed Hercules disappear in the distance without being able to make out whither he was bound.

Nobody, however, who had been privileged to share the advantages of Mrs Fred Rider's conversation for some time back, could be at a loss to guess who this messenger from the wilderness was. It was Richard Chatham come at last—he with whose name Nettie had been bored and punctured through and through from the first day of his introduction into Susan's talk till now. Mrs Fred had used largely in the interval that all-potent torture of the 'continual dropping;'—used it so perpetually as, though without producing any visible effect upon Nettie's resolution, to introduce often a certain sickness and disgust with everything into that steadfast soul. Nor did she content herself with her own exertions, but skilfully managed to introduce the idea into the minds of the children—ready, as all children are, for change and novelty. Nettie had led a hard enough life for these three months. She could not meet Edward Rider, nor he her, with a calm pretence of friendship; and Susan, always insolent and spiteful, and now mistress of the position, filled the doctor with an amount of angry irritation which his longings for Nettie's society could not quite subdue. That perpetual barrier between them dismayed both. Meetings which always ended in pain were best avoided, except at those intervals when longing love could not, even under that penalty, refuse itself the gratification; but the dismal life which was lighted up only by those unfrequent, agitating, exasperating encounters, and which flowed on through a hundred petty toilsome duties to the fretful accompaniment of Susan's iterations and the novel persecution now carried on by the children, was naturally irksome to the high-spirited and impatient nature which, now no longer heart-whole or fancy-free, did not find it so easy to carry its own way triumphantly through those heavy clogs of helplessness and folly. In the days when Miss Wodehouse pitied and wondered, Nettie had required no sympathy; she had carried on her course victorious, more entirely conscious of the supreme gratification of having her own way than of the utter self-sacrifice which she made to Fred and his family. But now the time predicted by Miss Wodehouse had arrived. Nettie's own personal happiness had come to be at stake, and had been unhesitatingly given up. But the knowledge of that renunciation dwelt with Nettie. Not all the natural generosity of her mind—not that still stronger argument which she used so often, the mere necessity and inevitableness of the case—could blind her eyes to the fact that she *had* given up her own happiness; and bitter flashes of thought would intervene, notwithstanding even the self-contempt and reproach with which she became aware of them. That doubtful complicated matter, most hard and difficult of mortal problems, pressed hard upon Nettie's mind and heart. In former days, when she scornfully denied it to be self-sacrifice, and laboured on, always indomitable, unconscious that what she did was any-thing more than the simplest duty and necessity, all was well with the dauntless, all-enterprising soul; but growing know-ledge of her own heart, of other hearts, cast dark and perplexing shades upon Nettie, as upon all other wayfarers, in these com-plex paths. The effect upon her mind was different from the effect to be expected according to modern sentimental ethics. Nettie had never doubted of the true duty, the true necessity, of her position, till she became conscious of her vast sacrifice. Then a hundred doubts appalled her. Was she so entirely *right* as she had supposed? Was it best to relieve the helpless hands of Fred and Susan of their natural duties, and bear these burdens for them, and disable herself, when her time came, from the nobler natural yoke in which her full womanly influence might have told to an extent impossible to it now? These questions made Nettie's head, which knew no fanciful pangs, ache with painful thought, and confused her heart and dimmed her lights when she most needed them to burn brightly. While, at the very time when these doubts assailed her, her sister's repetitions and the rising discontent and agitations of the children, came in to overcloud the whole business in a mist of sick impatience and disgust. Return to Australia was never out of Susan's mind, never absent from her pertinacious foolish lips. Little Freddy harped upon it all day long, and so did his brother and sister. Nettie said nothing, but retired with exasperated weariness upon her own thoughts—sometimes thinking, tired of the con-flict, why not give in to them? why not complete the offering, and remove once for all into the region of impossibility that contradictory longing for another life that still stirred by times in her heart? She had never given expression to this weary inclination to make an end of it, which sometimes assailed her fatigued soul; but this was the condition in which Richard Chatham's visit found her, when that Bushman, breathing of the wilds and the winds, came down the quiet suburban road to St Roque's, and, filling the whole little parlour with his beard and his presence, came stumbling into the confined room, where Mrs Fred still lay on the sofa, and Nettie pursued her endless work.

'Sorry to hear of the poor doctor's accident,' said the Australian, to whom Fred bore that title. 'But he always was a bit of a rover; though it's sad when it comes to that. And so you are thinking of a return to the old colony? Can't do better, *I* should say—there ain't room in this blessed old country for anything but tax-gatherers and gossips. I can't find enough air to breathe, for my part—and what there is, is taxed—leastways the light is,* which is all the same. Well, Mrs Rider! say the word, ma'am, and I'm at your disposal. I'm not particular for a month or two, so as I get home before next summer; and if you'll only tell me your time, I'll make mine suit, and do the best I can for you all. Miss Nettie's afraid of the voyage, is she? That's a new line for her, I believe. Something taken her fancy in this horrid old box of a place, eh? Ha! ha! but I'll be head-nurse and courier to the party, Miss Nettie, if you trust yourselves to me.'

'We don't mean to go back, thank you,' said Nettie. 'It is only a fancy of Susan's. Nobody ever dreamt of going back. It is much too expensive and troublesome to be done so easily. Now we are here, we mean to stay.'

The Bushman looked a little startled, and his lips formed into a whistle of astonishment, which Nettie's resolute little face kept inaudible. 'Taken your fancy very much, eh, Miss Nettie?' said the jocular savage, who fancied raillery of one kind or other the proper style of conversation to address to a young lady. Nettie gave that big hero a flashing sudden glance which silenced him. Mr Chatham once more formed an inaudible whew! with his lips, and looked at Mrs Fred.

'But *your* heart inclines to the old colony, Miss Susan?—I beg your pardon—didn't remember what I was saying at that moment. Somehow you look so much as you used to do, barring the cap,' said the Australian, 'that one forgets all that has happened. You incline to cross the seas again, Mrs Rider, without thinking of the expense?—and very sensible too. There never was a place like this blessed old country for swallowing up a man's money. You'll save as much in a year in the colony as will take you across.'

'That is what I always say;—but of course my wishes are

little thought of,' said Mrs Fred, with a sigh; 'of course it's Nettie we have to look to now. If she does not choose, to be sure, it does not matter what I wish. Ah! if I don't look different, I feel different—things are changed *now*.'

The Bushman gave a puzzled glance, first at one sister and then at the other. It occurred to him that Fred had not been so much of a strength and protection to his family as this speech implied, and that Nettie had been the person whom Mrs Rider had to 'look to' even before they left that colony for which she now sighed. But Mrs Fred, in her sorrow and her white cap, was an interesting figure to the eyes which were not much accustomed to look upon womankind. He had no doubt hers was a hard case. Nettie sat opposite, very busy, silent, and resolute, flashing dangerous sudden glances occasionally at her languid sister and their big visitor. It was confusing to meet those brilliant, impatient, wrathful eyes; though they were wonderfully bright, they put out the wild man of the woods, and made him feel uncomfortable. He turned with relief to those milder orbs which Mrs Fred buried in her handkerchief. Poor little oppressed woman, dependent upon that little arbitrary sister! The sincerest pity awoke in the Bushman's heart.

'Well!' he said, good-humouredly, 'I hope you'll come to be of one mind when Miss Nettie thinks it over again; and you have only to drop me a line to let me know when your plans are formed; and it will go hard with me, but I'll make mine suit them one way or another. All that I can do for you in the way of outfit or securing your passages—or even, if you would allow me——'

Here the good fellow paused, afraid to venture any further. Nettie looked up in a sudden blaze, and transfixed him with her eye.

'We have enough for everything we want, thank you,' said Nettie, looking through and through his guilty benevolent intentions, and bringing a flush of confusion to his honest cheeks. 'When I say I cannot afford anything, I don't mean to aśk anybody's assistance, Mr Chatham. We can do very well by ourselves. If it came to be best for the children—or if Susan keeps on wishing it, and gets her own way, as she generally does,' said Nettie, with heightened colour, dropping her eyes, and going on at double speed with her work, 'I daresay we shall manage it as we did before. But that is my concern. Nobody in the world has anything to do with it but me.'

'Oh, Nettie, dear, you're giving in at last!—do say you'll go! and Mr Chatham promises he'll take care of us on the way,' cried Mrs Fred, clasping her hands. They were thin hands, and looked delicate in contrast with her black dress. She was very interesting, pathetic, and tender to the rough eyes of the Bushranger. He thought that imperative little creature opposite, with her brilliant glances, her small head drooping under those heavy braids of hair, her tiny figure and rapid fingers, looked like a little cruel sprite oppressing the melancholy soul. When Nettie rose from the table, goaded into sudden intolerance by that appeal, the climax of the 'continual dropping,' and threw her work indignantly on the table, and called Freddy to come directly, and get dressed for his walk, the impression made by her supposed arbitrary and imperious behaviour was not diminished. She went out disdainful, making no reply, and left those two to a private conference. Then Mrs Fred unbosomed her bereaved heart to that sympathetic stranger. She told him how different everything was now—how hard it was to be dependent even on one's sister—how far otherwise things might have been, if poor dear Fred had been more prudent: one way or other, all her life through, Susan had been an injured woman. All her desire was to take the children back to the colony before she died. 'If Nettie would but yield!' sighed Mrs Fred, clasping her hands.

'Nettie must yield!' cried the Bushranger, full of emotion; and Susan cried a little, and told him how much the poor dear children wished it; and knew in her fool's heart that she had driven Nettie to the extremest bounds of patience, and that a little more persistence and iteration would gain the day.

In the mean time Nettie went out with Freddy—the other two being at school—and took him across the fields for his afternoon walk. The little fellow talked of Australia all the way, with a childish treachery and betrayal of her cause which went to Nettie's heart. She walked by his side, hearing without listening, throbbing all over with secret disgust, impatience, and despair. She too perceived well enough the approaching crisis. She saw that once more all her own resolution—the purpose of her heart—would be overborne by the hopeless pertinacity of the unconvinceable, unreasoning fool. She did not call her sister hard names—she recognised the quality without giving it its appropriate title—and recognised also, with a bitterness of resistance, yet a sense of the inevitable, not to be described, the certain issue of the unequal contest. What chance had the generous little heart, the hasty temper, the quick and vivacious spirit, against that unwearying, unreasoning pertinacity? Once more she must arise, and go forth to the end of the world; and the sacrifice must be final now.

CHAPTER XIV

'WELL, it's to be hoped she's going to do well for herself—that's all we've got to do with it, eh? I suppose so,' said Mr Wodehouse; 'she's nothing to you, is she, but a little girl you've taken a deal of notice of?—more notice than was wanted, if I am any judge. If she does go and marry this fellow from Australia, and he's willing to take the whole bundle back to where they came from, it is the best thing that could happen, in *my* opinion. Sly young dog, that doctor, though, I must say—don't you think so? Well, that's how it appears to me. Let's see; there was Bessie——; hum! perhaps it's as well, in present circumstances, to name no names. There was *her*, in the first instance, you know; and the way he got out of that was beautiful; it was what I call instructive, was that. And then—why then, there was Miss Marjoribanks, you know—capital match that—just the thing for young Rider—set him up for life.'

'Papa, pray—*pray* don't talk nonsense,' said Miss Wodehouse, with gentle indignation. 'Miss Marjoribanks is at least ten years——'*

'Oh, stuff!—keep your old-maidish memory to yourself, Molly; who cares for a dozen years or so? Hasn't she all the old Scotchman's practice and his savings?—and a fine woman yet—a fine woman, eh? Well, yes, I think so; and then here's this little wretch of a sister-in-law. Why, the doctor's taken your *rôle*, Wentworth, eh? Well, I suppose what ought to be your *rôle*, you know, though I *have* seen you casting glances at the strange little creature yourself.'

'Indeed, I assure you, you are entirely mistaken,' said Mr Wentworth, hastily, with a sudden flush of either indignation or guilt. The curate glanced at Lucy Wodehouse, who was walking demurely by his side, but who certainly did prick up her ears at this little bit of news. She saw very well that he had looked at her, but would take no notice of his glance. But Lucy's curiosity was notably quickened, notwithstanding; St Roque's Cottage was wonderfully handy, if the perpetual curate of the pretty suburban church saw anything worth visiting there. Lucy drew up her pretty shoulders in her grey sister-of-mercy cloak, and opened her blue eyes a little wider. She was still in circumstances to defy her reverend lover, if his eyes had declined upon lower attractions than her own. She looked very straight before her with unpitying precision down the road, on which St Roque's Church and Cottage were becoming already visible. The whole party were walking briskly over a path hard with frost, which made their footsteps ring. The air was still with a winterly touch, benumbed with cold, yet every sound rang sharply through that clear cloudless atmosphere, reddened without being warmed by the sun as it approached the west. It was Christmas again, and they were wending their way towards St Roque's to assist at the holiday decorations, for which cartloads of laurel and holly had been already deposited within the church. Lucy Wodehouse was chief directress of these important operations. Her sister had accompanied her, partly to admire Lucy's work, and partly to call at the cottage and see how Nettie was going on. Mr Wodehouse himself had come merely for the pride and pleasure of seeing how much they were indebted to his little girl; and the attendance of the curate was most easily explainable. It was, indeed, astonishing how many extremely necessary and natural 'calls of duty' should bring Mr Wentworth's path parallel to that of the Wodehouses. This is why they were all proceeding together on this particular afternoon in the week before Christmas towards St Roque's.

In the church, when the party arrived, a little group of workers were busy. The chancel arch was already bristling with glossy holly-leaves. At a little distance from the active group occupied with this pleasant work, and full of chatter and consultation, as was natural, stood one little figure pointing out to two children the wonders of that decorative art. Every one of the new-comers, except Mr Wodehouse, recognised Nettie before she was aware of their presence. She stood with her bonnet fallen a little back, as it generally was, either by encounter of the wind, or by the quantity and luxuriance of her beautiful hair, looking upwards to the point where she had directed the children's eyes. She looked a little forlorn and solitary, as was natural, all by herself, so near that group of busy girls in the chancel—so little separated from them by age, so entirely divided by circumstances. If a certain softening of half-tender pity shone in the curate's eye, could Lucy Wodehouse blame him? But the fact was, Lucy swept past the little Australian with a very brief salutation, and burst into sudden criticism of the work that had been done in her absence which startled her collaborateurs, while Mr Wentworth followed her into the chancel with a meekness quite unusual to that young priest. Nettie noted both circumstances with a little surprise; but, not connecting them in the most distant degree with herself, turned round with a little twitch of Freddy's arm to go away, and in doing so almost walked into the arms of her older and more faithful friend. Miss Wodehouse kissed her quite suddenly, touching with her soft old cheek that rounder, fairer, youthful face, which turned, half wondering, half pleased, with the look of a child, to receive her caress. Nettie was as unconscious that Miss Wodehouse's unusual warmth was meant to make up for Lucy's careless greeting, as that Lucy had passed her with a positive flutter of resentment and indignation, and that she had been the subject of the conversation and thoughts of all the party. Miss Wodehouse turned with her, taking Freddy's other hand —a proceeding to which that hero rather demurred. They went out together to the frosty road, where the bare willow-branches rustled between the church and the cottage. When they reached the porch of St Roque's, Nettie instinctively held her breath, and stood still for a moment. Along the footpath in front of them a big figure was passing, and beyond that bearded shadow the doctor's drag flew past with all the separate tones of the horse's feet, the wheels, the jingle of the harness, ringing clear through the sharp unsoftened medium of that frosty atmosphere. The doctor himself had all his attention concentrated upon the windows of the cottage, in which the sun was blazing red. He did not see Nettie in the church porch. He was looking for her too intently in the crimsoned windows, to which he turned his head back as he dashed on. Unawares Nettie clasped the fingers of her little companion tighter in her hand as she watched that unexpected homage. The drag was out of sight in another moment; and in a few seconds more the bell of the cottage pealed audibly, and the door was heard to open, admitting the Bushman, who had come upon one of his frequent visits. That last sound disturbed Nettie's composure, and at the same time brought her back to herself.

'I cannot ask you to go in, for Mr Chatham is there, and Susan of course talking to him,' said Nettie, with a quiet breath of restrained impatience, 'but I should like to talk to you, please. Let me take the children home, and then I will walk up with you. Mrs Smith is very kind; she will take off their things for them: they behave better now, when I am out for a few minutes—though, to be sure, I never am out much to try them. Come, children; be good, and do not make a great noise till I come back.'

'What do you want to talk to *her* for?' asked the little girl, gazing coldly in Miss Wodehouse's face.

'When Nettie went out to tea, we made as much noise as we liked,' said Freddy, 'but there was papa there. Now there's only mamma, and she's so cross. I hate Chatham—mamma is always crossest when Chatham's there. What do you want to talk to people for, Nettie? Come in, and say there's to be toast, and let us have tea.'

'We never have any tea till Nettie comes back,' added his sister, looking full once more into Miss Wodehouse's face. The calm childish impertinence disconcerted that gentle woman. She gazed at the wonderful creatures with dumb amazement. Her eyes fell before their steady stare. 'I should be sorry to bring you out again, dear, if it's a trouble,' began Miss Wodehouse, turning her face with a sense of relief from the hard inspection of the children to their little guardian.

Nettie made no reply, but carried off her children to the cottage door, turned them peremptorily in, and issued her last orders. 'If you make a noise, you shall not go,' said Nettie; and then came back alert, with her rapid fairy steps, to Miss Wodehouse's side.

'Does not their mother take any charge of them?' faltered the gentle inquisitor. 'I never can understand you young people, Nettie. Things were different in my days. Do you think it's quite the best thing to do other people's duties for them, dear? and now I'm so sorry—oh, so sorry—to hear what you are going to do now.'

'Susan is delicate,' said Nettie. 'She never had any health to speak of—I mean, she always got better, you know, but never had any pleasure in it. There must be a great deal in that,' continued Nettie, reflectively; 'it never comes into my head to think whether I am ill or well; but poor Susan has always had to be thinking of it. Yes, I shall have to take them away,' she added again, after a pause. 'I am sorry, very sorry too, Miss Wodehouse. I did not think at one time that I had the heart to do it. But on the whole, you know, it seems so much better for them. Susan will be stronger out there, and I have not money enough to give the children a very good education. They will just have to push their way like the others; and in the colony, you know, things are so different. I have no doubt in my own mind now that it will be best for them all.'

'But, Nettie, Nettie, what of yourself? will it be best for you?' cried Miss Wodehouse, looking earnestly in her face.

'What is best for them will be best for me,' said Nettie, with a little impatient movement of her head. She said so with unfaltering spirit and promptitude. She had come to be impatient of the dreary maze in which she was involved. 'If one must break one's heart, it is best to do it at once and have done with it,' said Nettie, under her breath.

'What was that you said about your heart?' said Miss Wodehouse. 'Ah, my dear, that is what I wanted to speak of. You are going to be married, Nettie, and I wanted to suggest to you, if you won't be angry. Don't you think you could make some arrangement about your sister and her family, dear?— not to say a word against the Australian gentleman, Nettie, whom, of course, I don't know. A man may be the best of husbands, and yet not be able to put up with a whole family. I have no doubt the children are very nice clever children, but their manner is odd, you know, for such young creatures. You have been sacrificing yourself for them all this time; but remember what I say—if you want to live happily, my dear, you'll have to sacrifice them to your husband. I could not be content without saying as much to you, Nettie. I never was half the good in this world that you are, but I am nearly twice as old—and one does pick up some little hints on the way. That is what you must do, Nettie. Make some arrangement, dear. If he has promised to take them out with you, that is all right enough; but when you come to settle down in your new home, make some arrangement, dear.'

When Miss Wodehouse arrived breathless at the conclusion of a speech so unusually long for her, she met Nettie's eyes flashing upon her with the utmost surprise and curiosity. 'I shall never marry anybody,' said Nettie. 'What do you mean?'

'Don't say anything so foolish,' said Miss Wodehouse, a little nettled. 'Do you suppose I don't know and see *that* Mr Chatham coming and going? How often has he been seen since the first time, Nettie? and do you suppose it's all been benevolence? My dear, I know better.'

Nettie looked up with a startled glance. She did not blush, nor betray any pleasant consciousness. She cast one dismayed look back towards the cottage, and another at Miss Wodehouse.

'Can *that* be why he comes?' said Nettie, with quiet horror. 'Indeed, I never thought of it before—but all the same, I shall never marry anybody. Do you imagine,' cried the brilliant creature, flashing round upon poor Miss Wodehouse, so as to dazzle and confuse that gentlewoman, 'that a man has only to intend such a thing and it's all settled? I think differently. Twenty thousand Chathams would not move me. I shall never marry anybody, if I live to be as old as—as you, or Methuselah, or anybody. It is not my lot. I shall take the children out to Australia, and do the best I can for them. Three children want a great deal of looking after—and after a while in Carlingford, you will all forget that there ever was such a creature as Nettie. No, I am not crying. I never cry. I should scorn to cry about it. It is simply *my business.* That is what it is. One is sorry, of course, and now and then it feels hard, and all that. But what did one come into the world for, I should like to know? Does anybody suppose it was just to be comfortable, and have one's way? I have had my own way a great deal—more than most people. If I get crossed in some things, I have to bear it. That is all I am going to say. I have got other things to do, Miss Wodehouse. I shall never marry anybody all my life.'

'My dear, if you are thrown upon this Mr Chatham for society all the time of the voyage, and have nobody else to talk to—' said the prudent interlocutor.

'Then we'll go in another ship,' cried Nettie, promptly; 'that is easily managed. I know what it is, a long voyage with three children—they fall up the cabin stairs, and they fall down the forecastle; and they give you twenty frights in a day that they will drop overboard. One does not have much leisure for anything—not even for thinking, which is a comfort some- times,' added Nettie, confidentially, to herself.

'It depends upon what you think of, whether thinking is a comfort or not,' said good Miss Wodehouse. 'When I think of you young people, and all the perplexities you get into! There is Lucy now, vexed with Mr Wentworth about something— oh, nothing worth mentioning; and there was poor Dr Rider! How he did look behind him, to be sure, as he went past St

Roque's! I daresay it was you he was looking for, Nettie. I wish you and he could have fancied each other, and come to some arrangement about poor Mr Fred's family—to give them so much to live on, or something. I assure you, when I begin to think over such things, and how perverse both people and circumstances are, thinking is very little comfort to me.'

Miss Wodehouse drew a long sigh, and was by no means disinclined to cry over her little companion. Though she was the taller of the two, she leant upon Nettie's firm little fairy arm as they went up the quiet road. Already the rapid winter twilight had fallen, and before them, in the distance, glimmered the lights of Carlingford—foremost among which shone conspicuous the large placid white lamp (for professional reds and blues were beneath his dignity) which mounted guard at Dr Marjoribanks's garden-gate. Those lights, beginning to shine through the evening darkness, gave a wonderful look of home to the place. Instinctively there occurred to Nettie's mind a vision of how it would be on the sea, with a wide dark ocean heaving around the solitary speck on its breast. It did not matter! If a silent sob arose in her heart, it found no utterance. Might not Edward Rider have made that suggestion which had occurred only to Miss Wodehouse? Why did it never come into his head that Susan and her family might have a provision supplied for them, which would relieve Nettie? He had not thought of it, that was all. Instead of that, he had accepted the impossibility. Nettie's heart had grown impatient in the maze of might-be's. She turned her back upon the lights, and clasped Miss Wodehouse's hand and said good-night hastily. She went on by herself very rapidly along the hard gleaming road. She did not pay any attention to her friend's protestation that she too was coming back again to St Roque's to join Lucy—on the contrary, Nettie peremptorily left Miss Wodehouse, shaking hands with her in so resolute a manner that her gentle adviser felt somehow a kind of necessity upon her to pursue her way home; and, only when Nettie was nearly out of sight, turned again with hesitation to retrace her steps towards St Roque's. Nettie, meanwhile, went on at a pace which Miss Wodehouse

could not possibly have kept up with, clasping her tiny hands
together with a swell of scorn and disdain unusual to it in her
heart. Yes! Why did not Edward Rider propose the 'arrangement' which appeared feasible enough to Miss Wodehouse?
Supposing even Nettie had refused to consent to it, as she
might very probably have done with indignation—still, why
did it not occur to Dr Edward? She asked herself the question
with a heat and passion which she found it difficult to account
for. She half despised her lover, as woman will, for obeying
her—almost scorned him, as woman will, for the mere constancy which took no violent measures, but only suffered and
accepted the inevitable. To submit to what cannot be helped
is a woman's part. Nettie, hastening along that familiar path,
blazed into a sudden burst of rage against Edward because he
submitted. What he could do else she was as ignorant of as any
unreasonable creature could be. But that mattered little. With
indignation she saw herself standing on the verge of that
domestic precipice, and the doctor looking on, seeing her glide
out of his reach, yet putting forth no violent sudden hand to
detain her. All the impatience of her fiery nature boiled in her
veins as she hasted to the cottage, where Susan was discussing their journey with her Australian visitor. No remnant
of pathos or love-sickening remained about Nettie, as she
flashed in upon them in all her old haste and self-reliance—
resolute to precipitate the catastrophe which nobody took any
measures to prevent.

CHAPTER XV

IT was not long before the doctor was made aware of the
ghost in his troubled path. Nobody in Carlingford could meet
the big Bushman in those streets, which always looked too
narrow for him, without a certain curiosity about that savage
man. Dr Rider had observed him with jealous interest on his
very first appearance, but had hitherto connected no idea but
that of a return to Australia, which he felt sure Nettie would
never consent to, with the big stranger. With such a thought

he had seen him making his way towards the cottage that very evening when he himself turned back, as long as those crimsoned windows were visible, to look for Nettie, who did not show herself. The doctor was bound to see a distant patient, miles on the other side of Carlingford. As he dashed along over the echoing road he had time to imagine to himself how Nettie might at that very moment be badgered and persecuted; and when he had seen his patient and done his duty, and with the lamps lighted in the drag, and the frosty wind blowing keen on his face, and the lights of Carlingford cheering him on in the distance, was once more returning, an impatience, somewhat akin to Nettie's, suddenly came upon the doctor. Akin, yet different; for in his case it was an impulse of sensation, an inspiration of the exhilarating speed and energy of motion with which he flew through the bracing air, master of himself, his horse, and the long sweep of solitary road before him. Again it occurred to Dr Rider to dash forward to St Roque's and carry off Nettie, oppose it who would. The idea pleased him as he swept along in the darkness, its very impossibility making the vision sweeter. To carry her off at a stroke, in glorious defiance of circumstances, and win happiness and love, whatever might ensue. In the flush of the moment the doctor suddenly asked himself whether this, after all, were not the wisest course? whether, whatever might come of it, happiness was not worth the encounter of the dark array of troubles behind? and whether to precipitate everything by a sudden conclusion might not be the best way of solving all the intricacies of the matter? He was still in this mood when he arrived at his own house, where dinner, as usual, was not improved by having been ready for an hour. The lamp was not lighted when he came in, and only the cold reflection of the street lights outside, with a particoloured gleam at the corner window from his own red and blue professional ensign at the surgery door, lighted the solitary little room, where he looked in vain even for so much as a note or letter to bring some shadow of human fellowship to his home; the fire smouldering dully, the big chair turned with a sullen back against the wall, as if nobody ever sat there—though Nettie had once and for ever appropriated it to her use—everything in such inhuman trim and good order disgusted the doctor. He rang his bell violently for the lights and refreshments which were so slow of coming, and, throwing himself into that chair, bit his nails and stared out at the lamplight in the rapid access of thought that came upon him. The first thing that disturbed him in this was the apparition of a figure outside peering in with some anxiety at the blank windows—somebody who was evidently curious to know whether the doctor had yet come home. The unhappy doctor started, and rang his bell once more with furious iteration. He knew what was coming. Somebody else, no doubt, had taken ill, without any consideration for young Rider's dinner, which, however, a man must manage to swallow even when tormented with importunate patients, and in love. But the knock of the untimely visitor sounded at the much-assailed door before Mary, sulky and resistant, had been able to arrange before the hungry doctor the half-warm half-cold viands which his impatience would not permit to be duly 'heated-up;' and he had just seated himself to dispose of the unsatisfactory meal when the little groom, who was as tired as his master, opened the door for Mrs Smith from St Roque's. Mrs Smith was a familiar periodical visitor at Dr Rider's. She had not ceased to hold to that hasty and unwise financial arrangement into which the doctor was persuaded to enter when Fred's pipe had exasperated the landlady into rebellion. He had supplemented the rent at that exciting moment rather than have Nettie disturbed; and now that poor Fred's pipe was extinguished for ever, the doctor still paid the imposition demanded from him—half because he had no time to contest it, half because it was, however improper and unnecessary, a kind of pleasure to do something for Nettie, little as she knew and deeply as she would have resented it. Dr Rider's brows cleared up at sight of Nettie's landlady. He expected some little private anecdotes of her and her ways, such as no one else could give him. He gave Mrs Smith a chair with a benignity to which she had no personal claim. Her arrival made Dr Rider's beefsteak palatable, though the cookery and condition of the same were, to say the least, far from perfect. Mrs Smith evidently was a little embarrassed with the gracious reception she received. She twisted the corner of her shawl in her fingers as if it had been that apron with which women of her class habitually relieve their feelings. She was in a false position. She came with the worst of news to the melancholy lover, and he treated her as if she brought some special message or favour from the lady of his thoughts.

'Well, Mrs Smith, and how are you all at the cottage?' said the doctor, applying himself leisurely to his beefsteak.

'Well, doctor, nothing to brag of,' said Mrs Smith, fixing her eyes upon the fringe of her shawl. 'I haven't nothing to say that's pleasant, more the pity. I don' know, sir, how you'll take it when you come to hear; but it's come very hard upon me. Not for the sake of the lodgings, as'll let again fast enough, now the poor gentleman's sad fate is partly forgotten; but you know, doctor, a body gets attached-like when one set of people stays long enough to feel at home; and there ain't many young ladies like Miss if you were to search the country through. But, now she's really give in to it herself, there ain't no more to be said. I never could bring myself to think Miss would give in till to-night when she told me; though Smith he always said, when the stranger gentleman took to coming so constant, as he knew how it would be.'

'For heaven's sake, what do you mean?' cried Dr Rider, pushing away his plate, and rising hurriedly from that dinner which was fated never to be eaten. Mrs Smith shook her head and drew out her handkerchief.

'I know nothing more, doctor, but just they're going off to Australia,' said the landlady, mournfully; 'and Miss has started packing the big boxes as have been in the hattic since ever they come: they're going off back where they come from —that's all as I know.'

'Impossible!' cried the doctor.

'I'd have said so myself this morning,' said Mrs Smith; 'but there ain't nothing impossible, doctor, as Miss takes in her head. Don't you go and rush out after her, Dr Rider. I beg of you upon my knees, if it was my last word! I said to Smith

I'd come up and tell the doctor, that he mightn't hear from nobody promiscuous as couldn't explain, and mightn't come rushing down to the cottage to know the rights of it and find the gentleman there unexpected. If there's one thing I'm afeard of, it's a quarrel between gentlemen in my house. So, doctor, for the love of peace, don't you go anear the cottage. I'll tell you everything if you listen to me.'

The doctor, who had snatched up his hat and made a rapid step towards the door, came back and seized hold of his visitor's shoulder, all his benignity having been put to flight by her unlooked-for revelation. 'Look here! I want the truth, and no gossip! What do you mean—what gentleman? What is it all about?' cried Dr Rider, hoarse with sudden passion.

'Oh, bless you, doctor, don't blame it upon me, sir,' cried Mrs Smith. 'It ain't neither my fault nor my business, but that you've always been kind, and my heart warms to Miss. It's the gentleman from Australia as has come and come again; and being an unmarried gentleman, and Miss—you know what she is, sir—and, I ask you, candid, Dr Rider, what was anybody to suppose?'

The doctor grew wildly red up to his hair. He bit his lips over some furious words which Carlingford would have been horrified to hear, and grasped Mrs Smith's shoulder with a closer pressure. 'What did she tell you?' said the doctor. 'Let me have it word for word. Did she say she was going away?—did she speak of this—this—fellow?' exclaimed the doctor, with an adjective over which charity drops a tear. 'Can't you tell me, without any supposes, what did she say?'

'I'm not the woman to stand being shook—let me go this minute, sir,' cried Mrs Smith. 'The Australian gentleman is a very nice-spoken civil man, as was always very respectful to me. She came into my back-parlour, doctor, if you will know so particular—all shining and flashing, like as she does when something's happened. I don't make no doubt they had been settling matters, them two, and so I told Smith. "Mrs Smith," said Miss, in her hasty way, enough to catch your breath coming all of a sudden, "I can't stand this no longer—I shall have to go away—it ain't no good resisting." Them were her

very words, Dr Rider. "Get me out the big boxes, please,"
said Miss. "It's best done quietly. You must take your week's
notice, Mrs Smith, from this day;" and with that she kept
moving about the room all in a flutter like, not able to rest.
"Do go and get me out those boxes; there's always a ship on
the 24th," she says, taking up my knitting and falling to work
at it to keep her hands steady. "The day afore Christmas!"
says I; "and oh, Miss, it's running in the face of Providence
to sail at this time of the year. You'll have dreadful weather,
as sure as life." You should have seen her, doctor! She gave
a sort of smile up at me, all flashing as if those eyes of her were
the sides of a lantern, and the light bursting out both there and
all over. "All the better," she says, as if she'd have liked to
fight the very wind and sea, and have her own way even there.
Bless you, she's dreadful for having her own way. A good easy
gentleman now, as didn't mind much—Dr Rider—Doctor!—
you're not agoing, after all I've told you? Doctor, doctor, I
say——'

But what Mrs Smith said was inaudible to Edward Rider.
The door rang in her ears as he dashed it after him, leaving
her mistress of the field. There, where he had once left Nettie,
he now, all-forgetful of his usual fastidious dislike of gossip,
left Mrs Smith sole occupant of his most private territories.
At this unlooked-for crisis the doctor had neither a word nor
a moment to spend on any one. He rushed out of the house,
oblivious of all those professional necessities which limit the
comings and goings of a doctor in great practice; he did not
even know what he was going to do. Perhaps it was an anxious
husband or father whom he all but upset as he came out, with
sudden impetuosity, into the unfrequented street; but he did
not stop to see. Pale and desperate, he faced the cold wind
which rushed up between the blank garden-walls of Grange
Lane. At Mr Wodehouse's door he stumbled against young
Wentworth coming out, and passed him with a muttered exclamation which startled the curate. All the floating momentary jealousies of the past rushed back upon the doctor's mind
as he passed that tall figure in the wintry road: how he had
snatched Nettie from the vague kindnesses of the young

clergyman—the words he had addressed to her on this very road—the answer she had given him once, which had driven him wild with passion and resentment. Impossible! the Australian, it appeared, had found nothing impossible in those circumstances in which Nettie had intrenched herself. Had the doctor's wisdom been monstrous folly, and his prudence the blindest shortsightedness? He asked himself the question as he rushed on towards that lighted window shining far along the dark road—the same window which he had seen Nettie's shadow cross, which had been opened to light poor Fred upon the way he never could tread again. Within that jealous blind, shining in that softened domestic light, what drama, murderous to the doctor's peace, might be going on now?

CHAPTER XVI

NETTIE had taken her resolution all at once. Breathless in sudden conviction, angry, heated, yet seeing in the midst of her excitement no help but in immediate action, the hasty little woman had darted into the heart of the difficulty at once. Every moment she lingered wore her out and disgusted her more with the life and fate which, nevertheless, it was impossible to abandon or shrink from. Nothing was so safe as to make matters irrevocable—to plunge over the verge at once. All gleaming with resolve and animation—with the frosty, chill, exhilarating air which had kindled the colour in her cheeks and the light in her eyes—with haste, resentment, every feeling that can quicken the heart and make the pulses leap—Nettie had flashed into the little parlour, where all was so quiet and leisurely. There Susan sat in close confabulation with the Bushman. The children had been banished out of the room, because their mother's head was not equal to their noise and restlessness. When they came in with Nettie, as was inevitable, Mrs Fred sustained the invasion with fretful looks and a certain peevish abstraction. She was evidently interrupted by the rapid entrance, which was as unwelcome as it was hasty. Cold though the night was, Mrs Fred, leaning back upon her sofa, fanned her pink cheeks with her handkerchief, and looked annoyed as well as disturbed when her children came trooping into the room clamorous for tea behind the little impetuous figure which at once hushed and protected them. Susan became silent all at once, sank back on the sofa, and concealed the faded flush upon her cheeks and the embarrassed conscious air she wore behind the handkerchief which she used so assiduously. Neither she nor her visitor took much share in the conversation that rose round the domestic table. Nettie, too, was sufficiently absorbed in her own concerns to say little, and nobody there was sufficiently observant to remark what a sudden breath of haste and nervous decision inspired the little household ruler as she dispensed the family bread-and-butter. When tea was over, Nettie sent her children out of the way with peremptory distinctness, and stayed behind them to make her communication. If she noticed vaguely a certain confused impatience and desire to get rid of her in the looks of her sister and the Australian, she attached no distinct meaning to it, but spoke out with all the simplicity of an independent power, knowing all authority and executive force to lie in her own hands alone.

'When do you think you can be ready to start? My mind is made up. I shall set to work immediately to prepare,' said Nettie. 'Now, look here, Susan: you have been thinking of it for months, so it is not like taking you by surprise. There is a ship that sails on the 24th. If everything is packed and ready, will you consent to go on that day?'

Mrs Fred started with unfeigned surprise, and, not without a little consternation, turned her eyes towards her friend before answering her sister. 'It is just Nettie's way,' cried Susan—'just how she always does—holds out against you to the very last, and then turns round and darts off before you can draw your breath. The 24th! and this is the 19th! Of course we can't do it, Nettie. I shall want quantities of things, and Mr Chatham, you know, is not used to your ways, and can't be whisked off in a moment whenever you please.'

'I daresay it's very kind of Mr Chatham,' said Nettie; 'but I can take you out very well by myself—just as well as I brought you here. And I can't afford to get you quantities of things, Susan. So please to understand I am going off to pack up, and on the 24th we shall go.'

Once more, under Nettie's impatient eyes, a look and a smile passed between her sister and the Australian. Never very patient at any time, the girl was entirely aggravated out of all toleration now.

'I can't tell what you may have to smile to each other about,' said Nettie. 'It is no very smiling business to me. But since I am driven to it, I shall go at once or not at all. And so that you understand me, that is all I want to say.'

With which words she disappeared suddenly to the multi-tudinous work that lay before her, thinking as little of Susan's opposition as of the clamour raised by the children, when the hard sentence of going half an hour earlier to bed was pronounced upon them. Nettie's haste and peremptoriness were mixed, if it must be told, with a little resentment against the world in general. She had ceased being sad—she was roused and indignant. By the time she had subdued the refractory children, and disposed of them for the night, those vast Australian boxes, which they had brought with them across the seas, were placed in the little hall, under the pale light of the lamp, ready for the process of packing, into which Nettie plunged without a moment's interval. While Mrs Smith told Edward Rider her story, Nettie was flying up and down the stairs with armfuls of things to be packed, and pressing Smith himself into her service. Ere long the hall was piled with heaps of personal property, ready to be transferred to those big receptacles. In the excitement of the work her spirit rose. The headlong haste with which she carried on her operations kept her mind in balance. Once or twice Susan peeped out from the parlour door, and something like an echo of laughter rang out into the hall after one of those inspec-tions. Nettie took no notice either of the look or the laugh. She built in those piles of baggage with the rapidest symmetrical arrangement, to the admiration of Smith, who stood wonder-ing by, and did what he could to help her, with troubled good-nature. She did not stop to make any sentimental reflections,

or to think of the thankless office in which she was about to
confirm herself beyond remedy by this sudden and precipitate
step. Thinking had done Nettie little good hitherto. She felt
herself on her true ground again, when she took to doing
instead. The lamp burned dimly overhead, throwing down a
light confused with frost upon the hall, all encumbered with
the goods of the wandering family. Perhaps it was with a
certain unconscious symbolism that Nettie buried her own
personal wardrobe deep in the lowest depths, making that the
foundation for all the after superstructure. Smith stood by,
ready to hand her anything she might want, gazing at her with
doubtful amazement. The idea of setting off to Australia at a
few days' notice filled him with respect and admiration.

'A matter of a three months' voyage,' said Smith; 'and if I
might make bold to ask, Miss, if the weather ain't too bad for
anything, how will you pass away the time on board ship
when there ain't nobody to speak to?—but, to be sure, the
gentleman——'

'The gentleman is not going with us,' said Nettie,
peremptorily—'and there are the children to pass away
the time. My time passes too quick, whatever other people's
may do. Where is Mrs Smith, that I see nothing of her to-
night? Gone out!—how very odd she should go out now, of all
times in the world. Where has she gone, do you suppose? Not
to be ungrateful to you, who are very kind, a woman is, of
course, twenty times the use a man is, in most things. Thank
you—not that; those coloured frocks now—there! that bundle
with the pink and the blue. One would suppose that even a
man might know coloured frocks when he saw them,' said
Nettie, with despairing resignation, springing up from her
knees to seize what she wanted. 'Thank you—I think, perhaps,
if you would just go and make yourself comfortable, and read
your paper, I should get on better. I am not used to having
anybody to help me. I get on quite as well, thank you, by
myself.'

Smith withdrew, not without some confusion and discomfort, to his condemned cell, and Nettie went on silent and
swift with her labours. 'Quite as well! better!' said Nettie to

herself. 'Other people never will understand. Now, I know better than to try anybody.' If that hasty breath was a sigh, there was little sound of sorrow in it. It was a little gust of impatience, indignation, intolerance even, and hasty self-assertion. She alone knew what she could do, and must do. Not one other soul in the world beside could enter into her inevitable work and way.

Nettie did not hear the footstep which she might have recognised ringing rapidly down the frosty road. She was too busy rustling about with perpetual motion, folding and refolding, and smoothing into miraculous compactness all the heterogeneous elements of that mass. When a sudden knock came to the door she started, struck with alarm, then paused a moment, looking round her, and perceiving at one hasty glance that nobody could possibly enter without seeing both herself and her occupation, made one prompt step to the door, which nobody appeared to open. It was Mrs Smith, no doubt; but the sudden breathless flutter which came upon Nettie cast doubts upon that rapid conclusion. She opened it quickly, with a certain breathless, sudden promptitude, and looked out pale and dauntless, understanding by instinct that some new trial to her fortitude was there. On the other hand, Edward Rider pressed in suddenly, almost without perceiving it was Nettie. They were both standing in the hall together, before they fully recognised each other. Then the doctor, gazing round him at the unusual confusion, gave an involuntary groan out of the depths of his heart. 'Then it is true!' said Dr Rider. He stood among the chaos, and saw all his own dreams broken up and shattered in pieces. Even passion failed him in that first bitterness of conviction. Nettie stood opposite, with the sleeves of her black dress turned up from her little white nimble wrists, her hair pushed back from her cheeks, pushed quite behind one delicate ear, her eyes shining with all those lights of energy and purpose which came to them as soon as she took up her own character again. She met his eye with a little air of defiance, involuntary, and almost unconscious. 'It is quite true,' said Nettie, bursting forth in sudden self-justification; 'I have my work to do, and must do it as best I can. I cannot keep considering you all, and losing my life. I must do what God has given me to do, or I must die.'

Never had Nettie been so near breaking down, and falling into sudden womanish tears and despair. She would not yield to the overpowering momentary passion. She clutched at the bundle of frocks again, and made room for them spasmodically in the box which she had already packed. Edward Rider stood silent, gazing at her as in her sudden anguish Nettie pulled down and reconstructed that curious honeycomb. But he had not come here merely to gaze, while the catastrophe was preparing. He went up and seized her busy hands, raised her up in spite of her resistance, and thrust away, with an exclamation of disgust, that great box in which all his hopes were being packed away. 'There is first a question to settle between you and me,' cried the doctor: 'you shall not do it. No! I forbid it, Nettie. Because you are wilful,' cried Edward Rider, hoarse and violent, grasping the hands tighter, with a strain in which other passions than love mingled, 'am I to give up all the rights of a man? You are going away without even giving me just warning—without a word, without a sign; and you think I will permit it, Nettie? Never—by heaven!'

'Dr Edward,' said Nettie, trembling, half with terror, half with resolution, 'you have no authority over me. We are two people—we are not one. I should not have gone away without a word or a sign. I should have said good-bye to you, whatever had happened; but that is different from permitting or forbidding. Let us say good-bye now, and get it over, if that will please you better,' she cried, drawing her hands from his grasp; 'but I do not interfere with your business, and I must do mine my own way.'

The doctor was in no mood to argue. He thrust the big box she had packed away into a corner, and closed it with a vindictive clang. It gave him a little room to move in that little commonplace hall, with its dim lamp, which had witnessed so many of the memorable scenes of his life. 'Look here,' cried Dr Rider; 'authority has little to do with it. If you had been my wife, Nettie, to be sure you could not have deserted me. It is as great a cruelty—it is as hard upon me, this you are trying to do. I have submitted hitherto, and heaven knows it has been bitter enough; and you scorn me for my submission,' said the doctor, making the discovery by instinct. 'When a fellow obeys you, it is only contempt you feel for him; but I tell you, Nettie, I will bear it no longer. You shall not go away. This is not to be. I will neither say good-bye, nor think of it. What is your business is my business; and I declare to you, you shall not go unless I go too. Ah—I forgot. They tell me there is a fellow, an Australian, who ventures to pretend—I don't mean to say I believe it. You think *he* will not object to your burdens! Nettie! Don't let us kill each other. Let us take all the world on our shoulders,' cried the doctor, drawing near again, with passionate looks, 'rather than part!'

There was a pause—neither of them could speak at that moment. Nettie, who felt her resolution going, her heart melting, yet knew she dared not give way, clasped her hands tight in each other and stood trembling, yet refusing to tremble; collecting her voice and thoughts. The doctor occupied that moment of suspense in a way which might have looked ludicrous in other circumstances, but was a relief to the passion that possessed him. He dragged the other vast Australian box to the same corner where he had set the first, and piled them one above the other. Then he collected with awkward care all the heaps of garments which lay about, and carried them off in the other direction to the stairs, where he laid them carefully with a clumsy tenderness. When he had swept away all these encumbrances, as by a sudden gust of wind, he came back to Nettie, and once more clasped the firm hands which held each other fast. She broke away from him with a sudden cry—

'You acknowledged it was impossible!' cried Nettie. 'It is not my doing, or anybody's; no one shall take the world on his shoulders for my sake—I ask nobody to bear my burdens. Thank you for not believing it—that is a comfort at least. Never, surely, any one else—and not you, not you! Dr Edward, let us make an end of it. I will never consent to put my yoke upon your shoulders, but I—I will never forget you or blame you—any more. It is all hard, but we cannot help it.

Good-bye—don't make it harder, you, who are the only one that—; good-bye,—no more—don't say any more.'

At this moment the parlour door opened suddenly; Nettie's trembling mouth and frame, and the wild protest and contradiction which were bursting from the lips of the doctor, were lost upon the spectator absorbed in her own affairs, and full of excitement on her own account, who looked out. 'Perhaps Mr Edward will walk in,' said Mrs Fred. 'Now he is here to witness what I mean, I should like to speak to you, please, Nettie. I did not think I should ever appeal to you, Mr Edward, against Nettie's wilfulness—but, really now, we, none of us, can put up with it any longer. Please to walk in and hear what I've got to say.'

The big Bushman stood before the little fire in the parlour, extinguishing its tiny glow with his vast shadow. The lamp burned dimly upon the table. A certain air of confusion was in the room. Perhaps it was because Nettie had already swept her own particular belongings out of that apartment, which once, to the doctor's eyes, had breathed of her presence in every corner—but it did not look like Nettie's parlour to-night. Mrs Fred, with the broad white bands of her cap streaming over her black dress, had just assumed her place on the sofa, which was her domestic throne. Nettie, much startled and taken by surprise, stood by the table, waiting with a certain air of wondering impatience what was to be said to her—with still the sleeves turned up from her tiny wrists, and her fingers unconsciously busy expressing her restless intolerance of this delay by a hundred involuntary tricks and movements. The doctor stood close by her, looking only at Nettie, watching her with eyes intent as if she might suddenly disappear from under his very gaze. As for the Australian, he stood uneasy under Nettie's rapid investigating glance, and the slower survey which Dr Rider made on entering. He plucked at his big beard, and spread out his large person with a confusion and embarrassment rather more than merely belonged to the stranger in a family party; while Mrs Fred, upon her sofa, took up her handkerchief and once more began to fan her pink cheeks. What was coming? After a moment's pause, upon which Nettie could scarcely keep herself from breaking, Susan spoke.

'Nettie has always had the upper hand so much that she thinks I am always to do exactly as she pleases,' burst forth Mrs Fred; 'and I don't doubt poor Fred encouraged her in it, because he felt he was obliged to my family, and always gave in to her; but now I have somebody to stand by me,' added Susan, fanning still more violently, and with a sound in her voice which betrayed a possibility of tears—'now I have somebody to stand by me—I tell you once for all, Nettie, I will not go on the 24th.'

Nettie gazed at her sister in silence without attempting to say anything. Then she lifted her eyes inquiringly to the Australian, in his uneasy spectator position before the fire. She was not much discomposed, evidently, by that sudden assertion of will—possibly Nettie was used to it—but she looked curious and roused, and rather eager to know what was it now?

'I will not go on the 24th,' cried Mrs Fred, with a hysterical toss of her head. 'I will not be treated like a child, and told to get ready whenever Nettie pleases. She pretends it is all for our sake, but it is for the sake of having her own will, and because she has taken a sudden disgust at something. I asked you in, Mr Edward, because you are her friend, and because you are the children's uncle, and ought to know how they are provided for. Mr Chatham and I,' said Susan, overcome by her feelings, and agitating the handkerchief violently, 'have settled—to be—married first before we set out.'

If a shell had fallen in the peaceful apartment, the effect could not have been more startling. The two who had been called in to receive that intimation, and who up to this moment had been standing together listening languidly enough, too much absorbed in the matter between themselves to be very deeply concerned about anything Mrs Fred could say or do, fell suddenly apart with the wildest amazement in their looks. 'Susan, you are mad!' cried Nettie, gazing aghast at her sister, with an air of mingled astonishment and incredulity. The doctor, too much excited to receive with ordinary decorum information so important, made a sudden step up to the big embarrassed Australian, who stood before the fire gazing into vacancy, and looking the very embodiment of conscious awkwardness. Dr Rider stretched out both his hands and grasped the gigantic fist of the Bushman with an effusion which took that worthy altogether by surprise. 'My dear fellow, I wish you joy—I wish you joy. Anything I can be of use to you in, command me!' cried the doctor, with a suppressed shout of half-incredulous triumph. Then he returned restlessly towards Nettie—they all turned to her with instinctive curiosity. Never in all her troubles had Nettie been so pale; she looked in her sister's face with a kind of despair. 'Is this *true*, Susan?' she said, with a sorrowful wonder as different as possible from the doctor's joyful surprise—'not something said to vex us—really true? And this has been going on, and I knew nothing of it; and all this time you have been urging me to go back to the colony—*me*—as if you had no other thoughts. If you had made up your mind to this, what was the use of driving me desperate?' cried Nettie, in a sudden outburst of that incomprehension which aches in generous hearts. Then she stopped suddenly and looked from her sister, uttering suppressed sobs, and hiding her face in her handkerchief on the sofa, to the Australian before the fire. 'What is the good of talking?' said Nettie, with a certain indignant impatient indulgence, coming to an abrupt conclusion. Nobody knew so well as she did how utterly useless it was to remonstrate or complain. She dropt into the nearest chair, and began with hasty tremulous hands to smooth down the cuffs of her black sleeves. In the bitterness of the moment it was not the sudden deliverance, but the heartlessness and domestic treachery that struck Nettie. She, the champion and defender of this helpless family for years—who had given them bread, and served it to them with her own cheerful unwearied hands—who had protected as well as provided for them in her dauntless innocence and youth. When she was thus cast off on the brink of the costliest sacrifice of all, it was not the delightful sensation of freedom which occurred to Nettie. She fell back with a silent pang of injury swelling in her heart, and, all tremulous and hasty, gave her agitated attention to the simple act of smoothing down her sleeves—a simple but symbolical act, which conveyed a world of meaning to the mind of the doctor as he stood watching her. The work she had meant to do was over. Nettie's occupation was gone. With the next act of the domestic drama she had nothing to do. For the first time in her life utterly vanquished, with silent promptitude she abdicated on the instant. She seemed unable to strike a blow for the leadership thus snatched from her hands. With proud surprise and magnanimity she withdrew, forbearing even the useless reproaches of which she had impatiently asked, 'What was the good?' Never abdicated emperor laid aside his robes with more ominous significance, than Nettie, with fingers trembling between haste and agitation, smoothed down round her shapely wrists those turned-up sleeves.

The doctor's better genius saved him from driving the indignant Titania desperate at that critical moment by any ill-advised rejoicings; and the sight of Nettie's agitation so far calmed Dr Rider that he made the most sober and decorous congratulations to the sister-in-law, whom for the first time he felt grateful to. Perhaps, had he been less absorbed in his own affairs, he could scarcely have failed to remember how, not yet a year ago, the shabby form of Fred lay on that same sofa from which Susan had announced her new prospects; but in this unexampled revolution of affairs no thought of Fred disturbed his brother, whose mind was thoroughly occupied with the sudden tumult of his own hopes. 'Oh yes, I hope I shall be happy at last. After all my troubles I have to look to myself, Mr Edward; and your poor brother would have been the last to blame me,' sobbed Mrs Fred, with involuntary self-vindication. Then followed a pause. The change was too sudden and extraordinary, and involved results too deeply important to every individual present, to make words possible. Mrs Fred, with her face buried in her handkerchief, and Nettie, her whole frame thrilling with mortification and failure, tremulously trying to button her sleeves, and bestowing her whole mind upon that operation, were discouraging interlocutors; and after the doctor and the Bushman had shaken hands, their powers of communication were exhausted. The silence was at length broken by the Australian, who, clearing his voice between every three words, delivered his embarrassed sentiments as follows:—

'I trust, Miss Nettie, you'll not think you've been unfairly dealt by, or that any change is necessary so far as you are concerned. Of course,' said Mr Chatham, growing red, and plucking at his beard, 'neither your sister nor I—found out— till quite lately—how things were going to be; and as for you making any change in consequence, or thinking we could be anything but glad to have you with us——'

Here the alarming countenance of Nettie, who had left off buttoning her sleeves, brought her new relation to a sudden stop. Under the blaze of her inquiring eyes the Bushman could go no farther. He looked at Susan for assistance, but Susan was still absorbed in her handkerchief; and while he paused for expression, the little abdicated monarch took up the broken thread.

'Thank you,' said Nettie, rising suddenly; 'I knew you were honest. It is very good of you, too, to be glad to have me with you. You don't know any better. I'm abdicated, Mr Chatham; but because it's rather startling to have one's business taken out of one's hands like this, it will be very kind of everybody not to say anything more to-night. I don't understand it all just at this moment. Good-night, Dr Edward. We can talk to-morrow, please; not to-night. You surely understand me, don't you? When one's life is changed all in a moment, one does not exactly see where one is standing just at once. Good-night. I mean what I say,' she continued, holding her head high with restrained excitement, and trying to conceal the nervous agitation which possessed her as the doctor hastened before her to open the door. 'Don't come after me, please; don't say anything; I cannot bear any more to-night.'

'But to-morrow,' said the doctor, holding fast the trembling hand. Nettie was too much overstrained and excited to speak more. A single sudden sob burst from her as she drew her hand out of his, and disappeared like a flying sprite. The doctor saw the heaving of her breast, the height of

self-restraint which could go no further. He went back into the
parlour like a true lover, and spied no more upon Nettie's
hour of weakness. Without her, it looked a vulgar scene
enough in that little sitting-room, from which the smoke of
Fred's pipe had never fairly disappeared, and where Fred
himself had lain in dismal state. Dr Rider said a hasty good-
night to Fred's successor, and went off hurriedly into the
changed world which surrounded that unconscious cottage.
Though the frost had not relaxed, and the air breathed no
balm, no sudden leap from December to June could have
changed the atmosphere so entirely to the excited wayfarer
who traced back the joyful path towards the lights of Carlingford twinkling brilliant through the Christmas frost. As he
paused to look back upon that house which now contained all
his hopes, a sudden shadow appeared at a lighted window,
looking out. Nettie could not see the owner of the footsteps
which moved her to that sudden involuntary expression of
what was in her thoughts, but he could see her standing full
in the light, and the sight went to the doctor's heart. He took
off his hat insanely in the darkness and waved his hand to her,
though she could not see him; and, after the shadow had
disappeared, continued to stand watching with tender folly if
perhaps some indication of Nettie's presence might again
reveal itself. He walked upon air as he went back, at last, cold
but joyful, through the blank solitude of Grange Lane. Nothing could have come amiss to the doctor in that dawn of
happiness. He could have found it in his heart to mount his
drag again and drive ten miles in celestial patience at the call
of any capricious invalid. He was half-disappointed to find no
summons awaiting him when he went home—no outlet for the
universal charity and loving-kindness that possessed him.
Instead, he set his easy-chair tenderly by the side of the
blazing fire, and, drawing another chair opposite, gazed with
secret smiles at the visionary Nettie, who once had taken up
her position there. Was it by prophetic instinct that the little
colonial girl, whose first appearance so discomposed the
doctor, had assumed that place? Dr Rider contemplated the
empty chair with smiles that would have compromised his

character for sanity with any uninstructed observer. When the mournful Mary disturbed his reverie by her noiseless and penitent entrance with the little supper which she meant at once for a peace-offering and compensation for the dinner lost, she carried down-stairs with her a vivid impression that somebody had left her master a fortune. Under such beatific circumstances closed the evening that had opened amid such clouds. Henceforth, so far as the doctor could read the future, no difficulties but those common to all wooers beset the course of his true love.

CHAPTER XVII

WHEN the red gleams of the early sunshine shone into that window from which Nettie had looked out last night, the wintry light came in with agitating revelations not simply upon another morning, but upon a new world. As usual, Nettie's thoughts were expressed in things tangible. She had risen from her sleepless bed while it was still almost dark, and to look at her now, a stranger might have supposed her to be proceeding with her last night's work with the constancy of a monomaniac. Little Freddy sat up in his crib rubbing his eyes and marvelling what Nettie could be about, as indeed anybody might have marvelled. With all those boxes and drawers about, and heaps of personal belongings, what was she going to do? She could not have answered the question without pain; but had you waited long enough, Nettie's object would have been apparent. Not entirely free of that air of agitated haste—not recovered from the excitement of this discovery, she was relieving her restless activity by a significant rearrangement of all the possessions of the family. She was separating with rapid fingers those stores which had hitherto lain lovingly together common property. For the first time for years Nettie had set herself to discriminate what belonged to herself from the general store; and, perhaps by way of softening that disjunction, was separating into harmonious order the little wardrobes which were no longer to be under her charge. Freddy opened his eyes to see all his own special belongings, articles which he recognised with all the tenacious proprietorship of childhood, going into one little box by themselves in dreadful isolation. The child did not know what horrible sentence might have been passed upon him while he slept. He gazed at those swift inexorable fingers with the gradual sob rising in his poor little breast. That silent tempest heaved and rose as he saw all the well-known items following each other; and when his last new acquisition, the latest addition to his wardrobe, lay solemnly smoothed down upon the top, Freddy's patience could bear no more. Bursting into a long howl of affliction, he called aloud upon Nettie to explain that mystery. Was he going to be sent away? Was some mysterious executioner, black man, or other horrid vision of fate, coming for the victim? Freddy's appeal roused from her work the abdicated family sovereign. 'If I'm to be sent away, I shan't go!' cried Freddy. 'I'll run off and come back again. I shan't go anywhere unless you go, Nettie. I'll hold on so fast, you can't put me away; and, oh, I'll be good!—I'll be so good!' Nettie, who was not much given to caresses, came up and put sudden arms round her special nursling. She laid her cheek to his, with a little outbreak of natural emotion. 'It is I who am to be sent away!' cried Nettie, yielding for a moment to the natural bitterness. Then she bethought herself of certain thoughts of comfort which had not failed to interject themselves into her heart, and withdrew with a little precipitation, alarmed by the inconsistency—the insincerity of her feelings. 'Get up, Freddy; you are not going away, except home to the colony, where you want to go,' she said. 'Be good, all the same; for you know you must not trouble mamma. And make haste, and don't be always calling for Nettie. Don't you know you must do without Nettie some time? Jump up, and be a man.'

'When I am a man, I shan't want you,' said Freddy, getting up with reluctance; 'but I can't be a man now. And what am I to do with the buttons if you won't help me? I shall not have buttons like those when I am a man.'

It was not in human nature to refrain from giving the little savage an admonitory shake. 'That is all I am good for— nothing but buttons!' said Nettie, with whimsical mortification. When they went down to breakfast, she sent the child before her, and came last instead of first, waiting till they were all assembled. Mrs Fred watched her advent with apprehensive eyes. Thinking it over after her first triumph, it occurred to Mrs Fred that the loss of Nettie would make a serious difference to her own comfort. Who was to take charge of the children, and conduct those vulgar affairs for which Susan's feelings disqualified her? She did her best to decipher the pale face which appeared over the breakfast cups and saucers opposite. What did Nettie mean to do? Susan revolved the question in considerable panic, seeing but too clearly that the firm little hand no longer trembled, and that Nettie was absorbed by her own thoughts—thoughts with which her present companions had but little to do. Mrs Fred essayed another stroke.

'Perhaps I was hasty, Nettie, last night; but Richard, you know, poor fellow,' said Susan, 'was not to be put off. It won't make any difference between you and me, Nettie dear? We have always been so united, whatever has happened; and the children are so fond of you; and as for me,' said Mrs Fred, putting back the strings of her cap, and pressing her handkerchief upon her eyes, 'with my health, and after all I have gone through, how I could ever exist without you, I can't tell; and Richard will be so pleased——'

'I don't want to hear anything about Richard, please,' said Nettie—'not, so far as I am concerned. I should have taken you out, and taken care of you, had you chosen me; but you can't have two people, you know. One is enough for anybody. Never mind what we are talking about, Freddy. It is only your buttons—nothing else. As long as you were my business, I should have scorned to complain,' said Nettie, with a little quiver of her lip. 'Nothing would have made me forsake you, or leave you to yourself; but now you are somebody else's business; and to speak of it making no difference, and Richard being pleased, and so forth, as if I had nothing else to do in the world, and wanted to go back to the colony! It is simply not my business any longer,' cried Nettie, rising impatiently from her chair—'that is all that can be said. But I shan't desert you till I deliver you over to my successor, Susan—don't fear.'

'Then you don't feel any love for us, Nettie! It was only because you could not help it. Children, Nettie is going to leave us,' said Mrs Fred, in a lamentable voice.

'Then who is to be instead of Nettie? Oh, look here—I know—it's Chatham,' said the little girl.

'I hate Chatham,' said Freddy, with a little shriek. 'I shall go where Nettie goes—all my things are in my box. Nettie is going to take me; she loves me best of you all. I'll kick Chatham if he touches me.'

'Why can't some one tell Nettie she's to go too?' said the eldest boy. 'She's most good of all. What does Nettie want to go away for? But I don't mind; for we have to do what Nettie tells us, and nobody cares for Chatham,' cried the sweet child, making a triumphant somersault out of his chair. Nettie stood looking on, without attempting to stop the tumult which arose. She left them with their mother, after a few minutes, and went out to breathe the outside air, where at least there was quiet and freedom. To think as she went out into the red morning sunshine that her old life was over, made Nettie's head swim with bewildering giddiness. She went up softly, like a creature in a dream, past St Roque's, where already the Christmas decorators had begun their pretty work—that work which, several ages ago, being yesterday, Nettie had taken the children in to see. Of all things that had happened between that moment and this, perhaps the impulse of escaping out into the open air without anything to do, was one of the most miraculous. Insensibly Nettie's footsteps quickened as she became aware of that extraordinary fact. The hour, the temperature, the customs of her life, were equally against such an indulgence. It was a comfort to recollect that, though everything else in the universe was altered, the family must still have some dinner, and that it was as easy to think while walking to the butcher's as while idling and doing nothing. She went up, accordingly, towards Grange Lane, in a kind of wistful solitude, drifted apart from her former life, and not yet definitely attached to any other, feeling as though the few passengers she met must perceive in her face that her whole fortune was changed. It was hard for Nettie to realise that she could do absolutely nothing at this moment, and still harder for her to think that her fate lay undecided in Edward Rider's hands. Though she had not a doubt of him, yet the mere fact that it was he who must take the first step was somewhat galling to the pride and temper of the little autocrat. Before she had reached the butcher, or even come near enough to recognise Lucy Wodehouse, where she stood at the garden gate, setting out for St Roque's, Nettie heard the headlong wheels of something approaching which had not yet come in sight. She wound herself up in a kind of nervous desperation for the encounter that was coming. No need to warn her who it was. Nobody but the doctor flying upon wings of haste and love could drive in that break-neck fashion down the respectable streets of Carlingford. Here he came sweeping round that corner at the Blue Boar, where Nettie herself had once mounted the drag, and plunged down Grange Lane in a maze of speed which confused horse, vehicle, and driver in one indistinct gleaming circle to the excited eyes of the spectator, who forced herself to go on, facing them with an exertion of all her powers, and strenuous resistance of the impulse to turn and escape. Why should Nettie escape?—it must be decided one way or other. She held on dimly with rapid trembling steps. To her own agitated mind, Nettie, herself, left adrift and companionless, seemed the suitor. The only remnants of her natural force that remained to her united in the one resolution not to run away.

It was well for the doctor that his little groom had the eyes and activity of a monkey, and knew the exact moment at which to dart forward and catch the reins which his master flung at him, almost without pausing in his perilous career. The doctor made a leap out of the drag, which was more like that of a mad adventurer than a man whose business it was to keep other people's limbs in due repair. Before Nettie was aware that he had stopped, he was by her side.

'Dr Edward,' she exclaimed, breathlessly, 'hear me first! Now I am left unrestrained, but I am not without resources.

Don't think you are bound in honour to say anything over again. What may have gone before I forget now. I will not hold you to your word. You are not to have pity upon me!' cried Nettie, not well aware what she was saying. The doctor drew her arm into his; found out, sorely against her will, that she was trembling, and held her fast, not without a sympathetic tremor in the arm on which she was constrained to lean.

'But I hold you to yours!' said the doctor; 'there has not been any obstacle between us for months but this; and now it is gone, do you think I will forget what you have said, Nettie? You told me it was impossible once——'

'And you did not contradict me, Dr Edward,' said the wilful creature, withdrawing her hand from his arm. 'I can walk very well by myself, thank you. You did not contradict me! You were content to submit to what could not be helped. And so am I. An obstacle which is only removed by Richard Chatham,' said Nettie, with female cruelty, turning her eyes full and suddenly upon her unhappy lover, 'does not count for much. I do not hold you to anything. We are both free.'

What dismayed answer the doctor might have made to this heartless speech can never be known. He was so entirely taken aback that he paused, clearing his throat with but one amazed exclamation of her name; but before his astonishment and indignation had shaped itself into words, their interview was interrupted. An irregular patter of hasty little steps, and outcries of a childish voice behind, had not caught the attention of either in that moment of excitement; but just as Nettie delivered this cruel outbreak of feminine pride and self-assertion, the little pursuing figure made up to them, and plunged at her dress. Freddy, in primitive unconcern for anybody but himself, rushed head-foremost between these two at the critical instant. He made a clutch at Nettie with one hand, and with all the force of the other thrust away the astonished doctor. Freddy's errand was of life or death.

'I shan't go with any one but Nettie,' cried the child, clinging to her dress. 'I hate Chatham and everybody. I will jump into the sea and swim back again. I will never, never leave go of her, if you should cut my hands off. Nettie! Nettie!

—take me with you. Let me go where you are going! I will never be naughty any more! I will never, never go away till Nettie goes! I love Nettie best! Go away, all of you!' cried Freddy, in desperation, pushing off the doctor with hand and feet alike. 'I will stay with Nettie. Nobody loves Nettie but me.'

Nettie had no power left to resist this new assault. She dropped down on one knee beside the child, and clasped him to her in a passion of restrained tears and sobbing. The emotion which her pride would not permit her to show before, the gathering agitation of the whole morning, broke forth at this irresistible touch. She held Freddy close and supported herself by him, leaning all her troubled heart and trembling frame upon the little figure which clung to her bewildered, suddenly growing silent and afraid in that passionate grasp. Freddy spoke no more, but turned his frightened eyes upon the doctor, trembling with the great throbs of Nettie's breast. In the early wintry sunshine, on the quiet rural highroad, that climax of the gathering emotion of years befell Nettie. She could exercise no further self-control. She could only hide her face, that no one might see, and close her quivering lips tight that no one might hear the bursting forth of her heart. No one was there either to hear or see—nobody but Edward Rider, who stood bending with sorrowful tenderness over the wilful fairy creature, whose words of defiance had scarcely died from her lips. It was Freddy, and not the doctor, who had van-quished Nettie; but the insulted lover came in for his revenge. Dr Rider raised her up quietly, asking no leave, and lifted her into the drag, where Nettie had been before, and where Freddy, elated and joyful, took his place beside the groom, convinced that he was to go now with the only true guardian his little life had known. The doctor drove down that familiar road as slowly as he had dashed furiously up to it. He took quiet possession of the agitated trembling creature who had carried her empire over herself too far. At last Nettie had broken down; and now he had it all his own way.

When they came to the cottage, Mrs Fred, whom excite-ment had raised to a troublesome activity, came eagerly out to the door to see what had happened; and the two children, who, emancipated from all control, were sliding down the banisters of the stair, one after the other, in wild glee and recklessness, paused in their dangerous amusement to watch the new arrival. 'Oh! look here; Nettie's crying!' said one to the other, with calm observation. The words brought Nettie to herself.

'I am not crying now,' she said, waking into sudden strength. 'Do you want them to get killed before they go away, all you people? Susan, go in, and never mind. I was not—not quite well out of doors; but I don't mean to suffer this, you know, as long as I am beside them. Dr Edward, come in. I have something to say to you. We have nowhere to speak to each other but here,' said Nettie, pausing in the little hall, from which that childish tumult had died away in sudden awe of her presence; 'but we have spoken to each other here before now. I did not mean to vex you then—at least, I did mean to vex you, but nothing more.' Here she paused with a sob, the echo of her past trouble breaking upon her words, as happened from time to time, like the passion of a child; then burst forth again a moment after in a sudden question. 'Will you let me have Freddy?' she cried, surrendering at discretion, and looking eagerly up in the doctor's face; 'if they will leave him, may I keep him with me?'

It is unnecessary to record the doctor's answer. He would have swallowed not Freddy only, but Mrs Fred and the entire family, had that gulp been needful to satisfy Nettie, but was not suffiently blinded to his own interests to grant this except under certain conditions satisfactory to himself. When the doctor mounted the drag again he drove away into Elysium, with a smiling Cupid behind him, instead of the little groom who had been his unconscious master's confidant so long, and had watched the fluctuations of his wooing with such lively curiosity. Those patients who had paid for Dr Rider's disappointments in many a violent prescription, got compensation to-day in honeyed draughts and hopeful prognostications. Wherever the doctor went he saw a vision of that little drooping head, reposing, after all the agitation of the morning, in the silence and rest he had enjoined, with brilliant eyes half-veiled, shining with thoughts in which he had the greatest share; and, with that picture before his eyes, went flashing along the wintry road with secret smiles, and carried hope wherever he went. Of course it was the merest fallacy, so far as Nettie's immediate occupation was concerned. That restless little woman had twenty times too much to do to think of rest—more to do than ever in all the suddenly-changed preparations which fell upon her busy hands. But the doctor kept his imagination all the same, and pleased himself with thoughts of her reposing in a visionary tranquillity, which, wherever it was to be found, certainly did not exist in St Roque's Cottage, in that sudden tumult of new events and hopes.

CHAPTER XVIII

'I ALWAYS thought there was good in him by his looks,' said Miss Wodehouse, standing in the porch of St Roque's, after the wedding-party had gone away. 'To think he should have come in such a sweet way and married Mrs Fred! just what we all were wishing for, if we could have ventured to think it possible. Indeed, I should have liked to have given Mr Chatham a little present, just to mark my sense of his goodness. Poor man! I wonder if he repents——'

'It is to be hoped not yet,' said Lucy, hurrying her sister away before Mr Wentworth could come out and join them; for affairs were seriously compromised between the perpetual curate and the object of his affections; and Lucy exhibited a certain acerbity under the circumstances which somewhat amazed the tender-hearted old maid.

'When people do repent, my belief is that they do it directly,' said Miss Wodehouse. 'I daresay he can see what she is already, poor man; and I hope, Lucy, it won't drive him into bad ways. As for Nettie, I am not at all afraid about her. Even if they should happen to quarrel, you know, things will always come right. I am glad they were not married both at the same time. Nettie has such sense! and of course, though it was the very best thing that could happen, and a great relief to everybody concerned, to be sure, one could not help being disgusted with that woman. And it is such a comfort they're going away. Nettie says——'

'Don't you think you could walk a little quicker? there is somebody in Grove Street that I have to see,' said Lucy, not so much interested as her sister; 'and papa will be home at one to lunch.'

'Then I shall go on, dear, if you have no objection, and ask when the doctor and Nettie are coming home,' said Miss Wodehouse, 'and take poor little Freddy the cakes I promised him. Poor child! to have his mother go off and marry and leave him. Never mind me, Lucy, dear; I do not walk so quickly as you do, and besides I have to go home first for the cakes.'

So saying the sisters separated; and Miss Wodehouse took her gentle way to the doctor's house, where everything had been brightened up, and where Freddy waited the return of his chosen guardians. It was still the new quarter of Carlingford, a region of half-built streets, vulgar new roads, and heaps of desolate brick and mortar. If the doctor had ever hoped to succeed Dr Marjoribanks in his bowery retirement in Grange Lane, that hope nowadays had receded into the darkest distance. The little surgery round the corner still shed twinkles of red and blue light across that desolate triangle of unbuilt ground upon the other corner houses where dwelt people unknown to society in Carlingford, and still Dr Rider consented to call himself M.R.C.S., and cultivate the patients who were afraid of a physician. Miss Wodehouse went in at the invitation of Mary to see the little drawing-room which the master of the house had provided for his wife. It had been only an unfurnished room in Dr Rider's bachelor days, and looked out upon nothing better than these same new streets—the vulgar suburb which Carlingford disowned. Miss Wodehouse lingered at the window with a little sigh over the perversity of circumstances. If Miss Marjoribanks had only been Nettie, or Nettie Miss Marjoribanks ! If not only love and happiness, but the old doctor's practice and savings, could but have been brought to heap up the measure of the young doctor's good-fortune! What a pity that one cannot have everything! The friendly visitor said so with a real sigh as she went down-stairs after her inspection. If the young people had but been settling in Grange Lane, in good society, and with Dr Marjoribanks's practice, this marriage would have been perfection indeed!

But when the doctor brought Nettie home, and set her in that easy-chair which her image had possessed so long, he saw few drawbacks at that moment to the felicity of his lot. If there was one particular in which his sky threatened clouds, it was not the want of Dr Marjoribanks's practice, but the presence of that little interloper, whom the doctor in his heart was apt to call by uncomplimentary names, and did not regard with unmixed favour. But when Susan and her Australian were fairly gone, and all fear of any invasion of the other imps—which Dr Rider inly dreaded up to the last moment—was over, Freddy grew more and more tolerable. Where Fred once lay and dozed, and filled the doctor's house with heavy fumes and discreditable gossip, a burden on his brother's reluctant hospitality, little Freddy now obliterated that dismal memory with prayers and slumbers of childhood; and where the discontented doctor had grumbled many a night and day over that bare habitation of his, which was a house, and not a home, Nettie diffused herself till the familiar happiness became so much a part of his belongings that the doctor learned to grumble once more at the womanish accessories which he had once missed so bitterly. And the little wayward heroine who, by dint of hard labour and sacrifice, had triumphantly had her own way in St Roque's Cottage, loved her own way still in the new house, and had it as often as was good for her. But so far as this narrator knows, nothing calling for special record has since appeared in the history of the doctor's family, thus reorganised under happier auspices, and discharging its duties, social and otherwise, though not exactly in society, to the satisfaction and approval of the observant population of Carlingford.

THE END

EXPLANATORY NOTES

THE EXECUTOR

Published in *Blackwood's Magazine*, May 1861.

9 *Grove Street*: this is where the humbler residents of Carlingford tend to live. The local aristocracy are in Grange Lane.

11 *primitive island which has preserved her name*: the Isle of Man.

13 *a region of half-built streets*: the new district of Carlingford was probably inspired by Birkenhead, where the author lived from 1850–2, when it was a fast-growing town.

21 *the year 'eight*: this dates the story in 1843, although this need not be taken too seriously.

26 *drag*: a small horse-drawn carriage.

27 *the three kingdoms*: England, Scotland, and Ireland.

28 *'Scholastic Agency'*: agency finding work for governesses.

THE RECTOR

Published in *Blackwood's Magazine*, September 1861. Reprinted in *Chronicles of Carlingford: The Rector and The Doctor's Family* (1863).

35 *Evangelicalism*: the late Rector, Mr Bury (who appears in a later Carlingford novel, *Miss Marjoribanks*) had been an Evangelical or Low Churchman. Evangelicals believed that those who wanted to be saved must undergo a personal conversion to Christianity. They were hostile to Rome, did not decorate their churches, and laid a great emphasis on preaching the gospel.

Salem Chapel: Dissenters—who are usually greengrocers or milkmen—worship at Salem Chapel. They had a good relationship with the Evangelical wing of the Church of England, and would have gone to Mr Bury's sermons because his views were not very different from theirs.

perpetual curate: an ordinary curate acted as an assistant to the parish priest, whereas a perpetual curate had his own church, but did not draw the full income as a rector did.

36 *topmost pinnacle of Anglicanism*: Mr Wentworth, the perpetual curate, is one of the new breed of clergymen who had been

influenced by the Anglo-Catholic or Oxford Movement. He fills his church with 'lovely upholstery', values the sacraments highly, and is sometimes accused of being sympathetic to Rome.

High, or Low, or Broad, muscular or sentimental: Mr Wentworth is High, Mr Bury was Low, and a Broad Churchman was one who interpreted the Bible in a liberal and undogmatic way. 'Muscular' Christians, associated with Charles Kingsley, laid a great stress on healthy physical activity.

does not himself appreciate the boon he conveys!: High Churchmen believed that children could not be saved if they were not christened. The Evangelicals laid far less stress on the ceremony.

37 *Frank Wentworth*: Cecil Wentworth in the original version.

Leghorn hat: hat of fine plaited straw.

38 *preferment to bestow*: promotion. Wentworth cannot afford to get married unless he becomes a Rector.

39 *tidy*: substantial, as in 'a tidy sum'.

morning service: High Churchmen were noted for holding services on weekdays.

40 *Thursday*: Mr Wodehouse reminds Wentworth that it is only Thursday, on the assumption that he fasts on Fridays.

flannels: woollen clothing.

42 *false quantity*: mispronunciation of Greek or Latin word; Miss Wodehouse knows the classics.

43 *establishment*: staff of servants.

the Rector's mother: Mrs Proctor is based on Mrs Janet Wilson, Margaret's cousin by marriage, who was seventy-five when she knew her in Edinburgh in 1861. 'Although deaf, she was an amusing and good talker', she wrote in her *Autobiography*. She was a great reader and encouraged her children, many of whom died before her, to take an interest in science. One of her sons, Professor George Wilson (1818–59), was the founder of the Royal Scottish Museum. She died in 1864.

45 *Evangelical ways*: Evangelicals did a great deal of preaching.

52 *dove-coloured*: warm grey.

54 *wonderful*: the author generally uses this word in the sense of 'extraordinary'.

59 *wanted to marry,'*: modern readers may need reminding that Oxford dons had to postpone marriage until they got a living. Mr Morgan and his new wife are important characters in *The Perpetual Curate*.

66 *our primeval mother*: Eve.

THE DOCTOR'S FAMILY

Published in *Blackwood's Magazine*, October 1861–January 1862. Reprinted in *Chronicles of Carlingford: The Rector and The Doctor's Family* (1863).

67 *M.R.C.S.*: Member of the Royal College of Surgeons.

   Dr Marjoribanks . . . Grange Lane: Dr Marjoribanks (pronounced Marchbanks) and his daughter, who are leading figures in the Carlingford series, live in the 'best' street in the town, Grange Lane.

69 *skeleton in young Rider's house*: compare this passage with the author's account of Willie, quoted on page viii.

71 *Croesus*: rich man.

82 *Titania*: the fairy queen.

95 *Gilbert Scott's churches*: Sir Gilbert Scott (1811–78) was one of the leading architects of the time. He renovated several old churches and designed new ones in the 'Gothic' (medieval) style which the Victorians favoured.

109 *hodman*: labourer.

118 *flags*: flagstones.

119 *to the touch to gain or lose*: reference to a well-known verse by the Marquis of Montrose:

> He either fears his fate too much
> Or his desert is small
> Who will not put it to the touch
> To gain or lose it all.

121 *Puseyitical pretences!*: Wentworth is a Puseyite or High Churchman. Edward Bouverie Pusey (1800–82) was a leader of the Oxford Movement.

135 *wasted life*: the manner of Fred's death may have been suggested by the drowning of the drunk Thias in *Adam Bede*.

147 *Susan's cap*: widow's cap.

160　*wist*: knew.

160　*Beards . . . Mr Lake*: most Englishmen did not wear beards until
　　　about 1860. Mr Lake and his family appear in *Miss Marjori-
　　　banks*.

165　*taxed—leastways the light is*: Chatham is referring to the window-
　　　tax, a primitive form of income tax which was not abolished until
　　　the mid-nineteenth century. In *Kirsteen*, the author described
　　　people blocking off their spare windows to avoid paying it.

168　*at least ten years—'*: the author tells us, in a later novel, that Miss
　　　Marjoribanks is twenty-nine, and that the public 'naturally added
　　　on seven or eight years to her age, and concluded her to be a great
　　　deal older than the young doctor' (*Miss Marjoribanks*, chapter 37).

THE WORLD'S CLASSICS

A Select List

HENRY JAMES: The Ambassadors
Edited by Christopher Butler

The Aspern Papers and Other Stories
Edited by Adrian Poole

The Awkward Age
Edited by Vivien Jones

The Bostonians
Edited with an introduction by R. D. Gooder

Daisy Miller and Other Stories
Edited by Jean Gooder

The Europeans
Edited with an introduction by Ian Campbell Ross

The Golden Bowl
Edited by Virginia Llewellyn Smith

The Portrait of a Lady
Edited by Nicola Bradbury
With an introduction by Graham Greene

Roderick Hudson
With an introduction by Tony Tanner

The Spoils of Poynton
Edited by Bernard Richards

Washington Square
Edited by Mark Le Fanu

What Maisie Knew
Edited by Douglas Jefferson

The Wings of the Dove
Edited by Peter Brooks

RICHARD JEFFERIES: After London *or* Wild England
With an introduction by John Fowles

CHARLES KINGSLEY: Alton Locke
Edited by Elizabeth Cripps

J. SHERIDAN LE FANU: Uncle Silas
Edited by W. J. McCormack

KATHERINE MANSFIELD: Selected Stories
Edited by D. M. Davin

The Raid and Other Stories
Translated by Louise and Aylmer Maude
With an introduction by P. N. Furbank

War and Peace (in two volumes)
Translated by Louise and Aylmer Maude
Edited by Henry Gifford